MW01622163

Amy Sherald

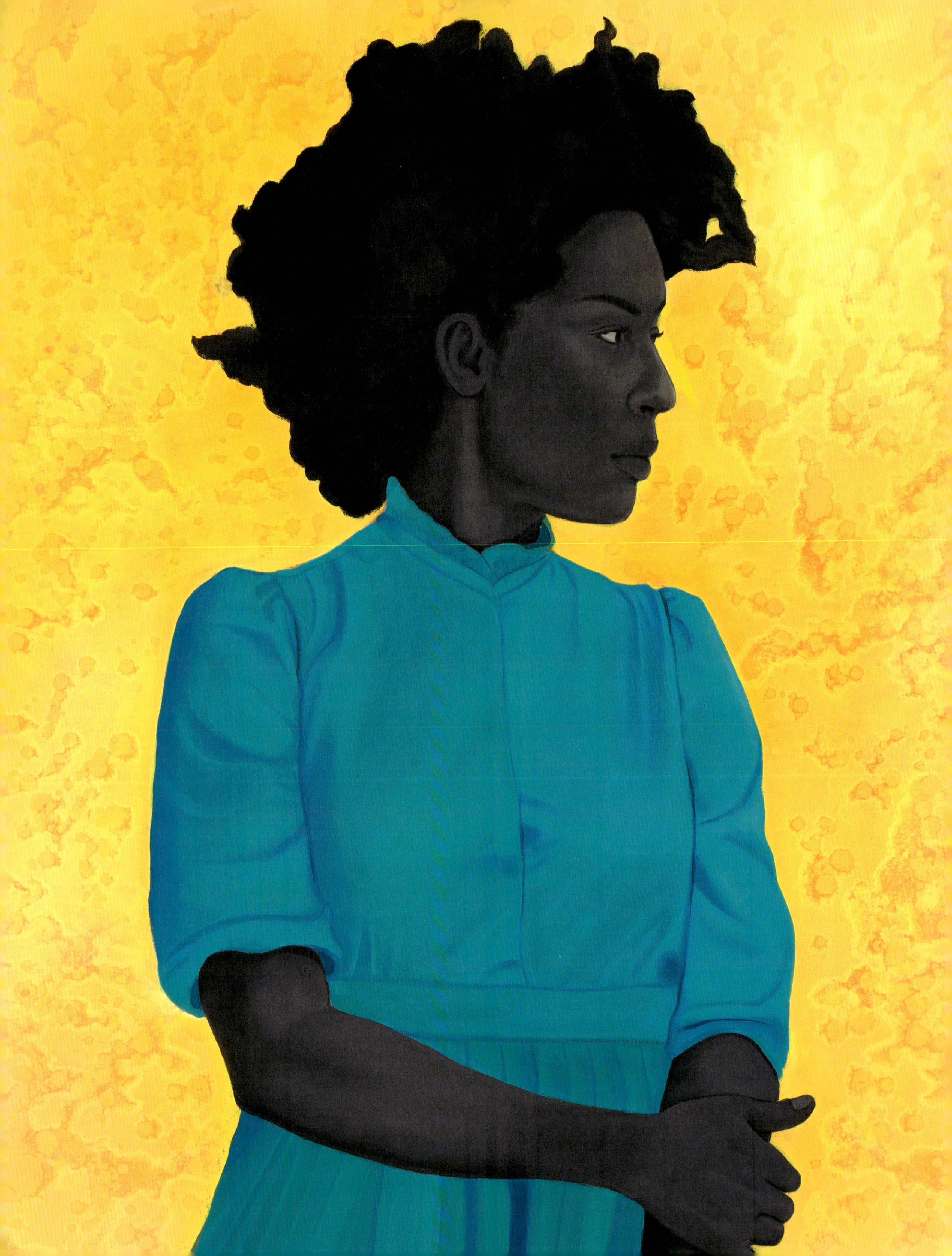

Amy Sherald

AMERICAN SUBLIME

EDITED BY SARAH ROBERTS

San Francisco Museum of Modern Art
in association with Yale University Press, New Haven and London

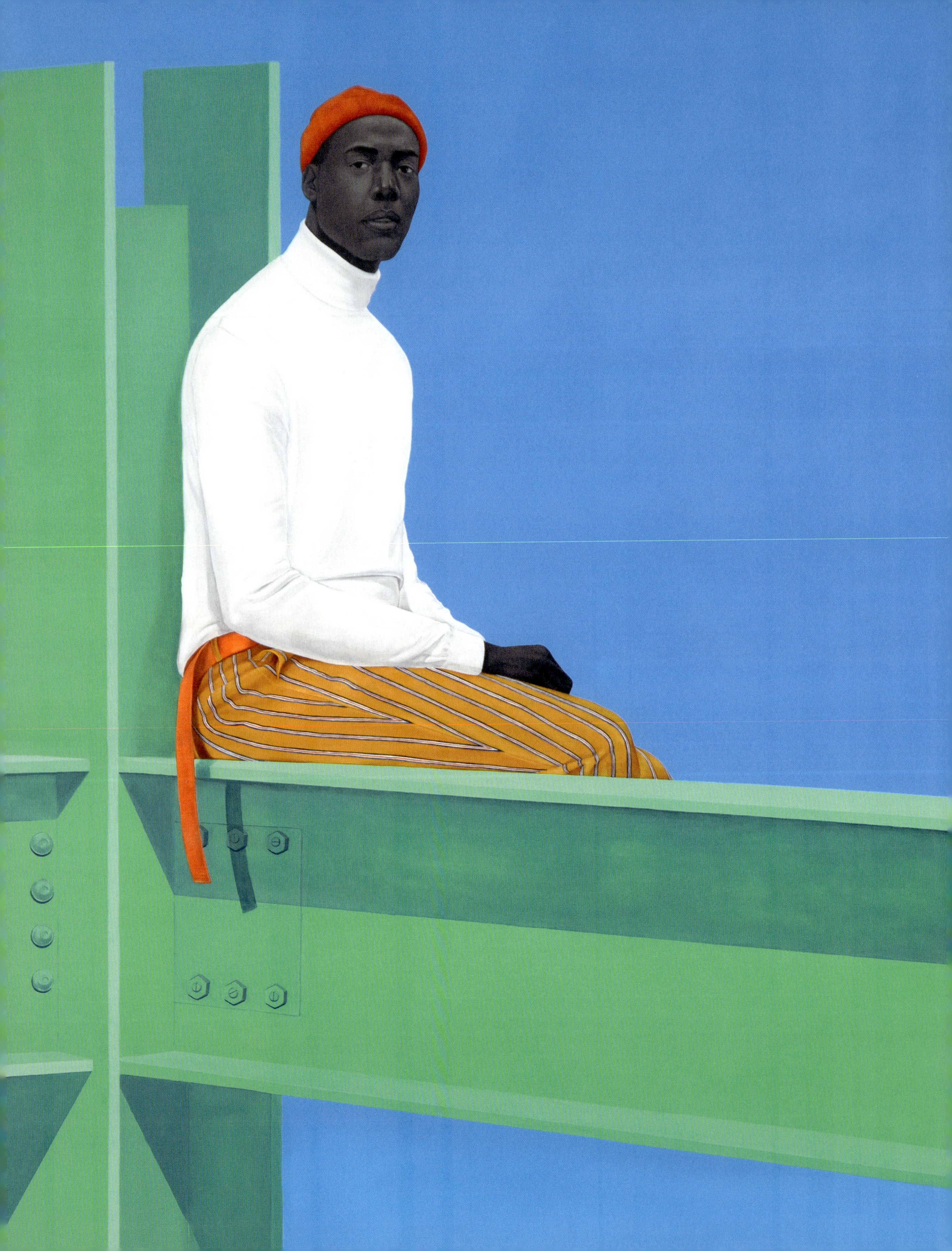

CONTENTS

Foreword

It is undeniable that an overwhelming share of the most relevant, timely, rich, and complex contemporary art being made today is being made by Black American artists and artists of the African diaspora. Front and center among this golden generation of transformational creatives is Amy Sherald, a painter who in reinventing portraiture also powerfully reenvisions American life and history. In this era of heightened consciousness of the incomplete histories and biases that have shaped museum collections and exhibition programming, institutions nationwide have taken steps to broaden the stories we tell in our galleries. A crucial aspect of this ongoing reparative work is a commitment to better representing and welcoming communities of people traditionally unrepresented within our walls. Sherald's profoundly affecting portrayals of Black Americans resonate deeply with these impulses, and SFMOMA could not be more honored to share this landmark survey of her art with audiences in San Francisco and beyond.

I first became aware of Sherald's work in 2016, when her studio was based in Baltimore and I, then the incoming Dorothy Wagner Wallis Director at the Baltimore Museum of Art, was beginning to acquaint myself with the local artist community. This was a momentous time for Sherald, as it was also the year she became the first woman and the first African American to receive the grand prize in the National Portrait Gallery's Outwin Boochever Portrait Competition for her painting *Miss Everything (Unsuppressed Deliverance)* (2014, p. 69). That honor led to the commission of one of her best-known works: the official portrait of former first lady Michelle LaVaughn Robinson Obama (2018, p. 101) for the Portrait Gallery's permanent collection. Sherald's exquisite renderings of her subjects, such as these and the many other stunning examples assembled within this book, encourage close looking and curiosity. She has described herself as a "conceptual portraitist," in the sense that her figurative paintings are not mere likenesses of her subjects. Instead Sherald creates fully imagined narratives, with real sitters at their core. There are histories and art historical referents behind her compositions, and she intends for every painting she makes to add to that visual record of American life. She challenges the concept of color-as-race by favoring grayscale for skin tones and creates finely rendered backgrounds that provide few context clues and ask viewers to focus instead on the inner lives of the individuals depicted. These works are not about display of surface realities or the projection of a persona. They instead distill, stripping away our preconceptions and staging eye-to-eye encounters between subject and viewer, asking us to engage with the figures on the canvas as they actually are. Individually they are striking and expansive. Collectively they hit with even greater force, asserting a corrective reimagining of a world that is and could be.

Kevin Quashie has written movingly of the effects of Sherald's work, noting its insistence on "*mere beauty*, a quiet, pulsing, just-there beauty." He explains that this assessment is not only an acknowledgment of Sherald's painterly skill but also a

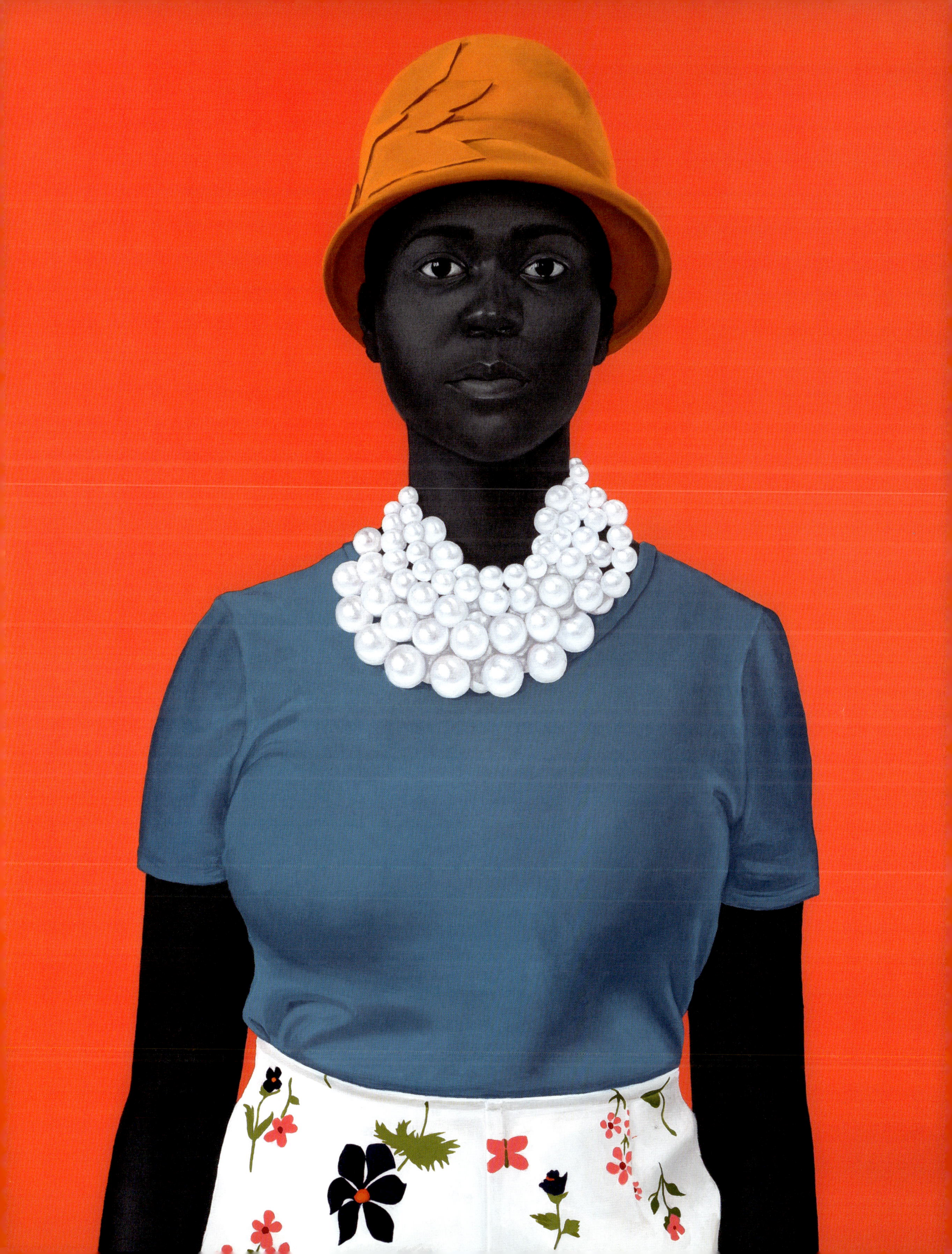

"gesture toward the sheer impact of encountering frame after frame of blackness: *mere beauty* as a proxy toward mere being, which has its own politic. Indeed, the very idea of *mere beauty* as idiom for viewing blackness responds to the world's incapacity to appreciate blackness exactly that way." *Amy Sherald: American Sublime*, the largest survey of her work to date, offers audiences an unprecedented opportunity to immerse themselves in Sherald's skill and the impact of her art. It also, crucially, holds significant space for a collective grappling with the quintessentially American histories, dreams, and possibilities her work engages and refigures.

Since becoming the Helen and Charles Schwab Director of SFMOMA in 2022, I have pushed for a program that moves away from telling a stylistic history of art in favor of creating a social history that is centered on people and resonates with the broadest possible audience. The idea is to take on the conventional art history that this institution has told very well, and to leverage the resources of the museum's board, the sheer space of the building, the existing collection, and the expertise of the staff to tell new stories. This is an ambitious shift, and in many cases—including mounting this project as a major fall 2024 exhibition—it has required great flexibility, effort, and collaboration on behalf of all those involved. I am tremendously grateful to Sarah Roberts, former Andrew W. Mellon Curator and Head of Painting and Sculpture at SFMOMA, for so swiftly and thoughtfully bringing together this landmark survey and publication. And I echo Sarah's thanks to the museum staff members named on pages 154–56 for the hard work and skill they have brought to bear on every aspect of this endeavor. I am also grateful to Marc Payot, Madeline Warren, and Johanna Rietveld at Hauser & Wirth for their partnership on this project, and to Scott Rothkopf, Rujeko Hockley, and their colleagues at the Whitney Museum of American Art for joining forces with us to present the exhibition in New York after its San Francisco run. The show will then travel to the National Portrait Gallery in Washington, DC, thanks to the enthusiastic efforts of Kim Sajet, Rhea L. Combs, and Marlene Harrison.

Immense gratitude is due to the project's many funders: Lead support for *Amy Sherald: American Sublime* is provided by the Mimi and Peter Haas Fund and Diana Nelson and John Atwater. Major support is provided by Sir Deryck and Lady Va Maughan, Katie and Matt Paige, and Shelagh Rohlen in memory of Tom Rohlen. Significant support is provided by Maria Manetti Shrem and Jan Shrem, Jessica Moment, Deborah and Kenneth Novack, and Sonja Hoel Perkins and Jonathan Perkins. Meaningful support is provided by Alka and Ravin Agrawal, Dolly and George Chammas, Jessica and Matt Farron, Maryellen and Frank Herringer, Alison Pincus, Komal Shah and Gaurav Garg, Gary Steele and Steven Rice, and Barbara and Stephan Vermut.

Amy has said that she paints the paintings she wants to see in museums. I offer my greatest thanks to her—for her art and her vision, and for collaborating with us on this pathbreaking exhibition, which will bring that vision to ever-wider audiences.

Christopher Bedford
Helen and Charles Schwab Director
San Francisco Museum of Modern Art

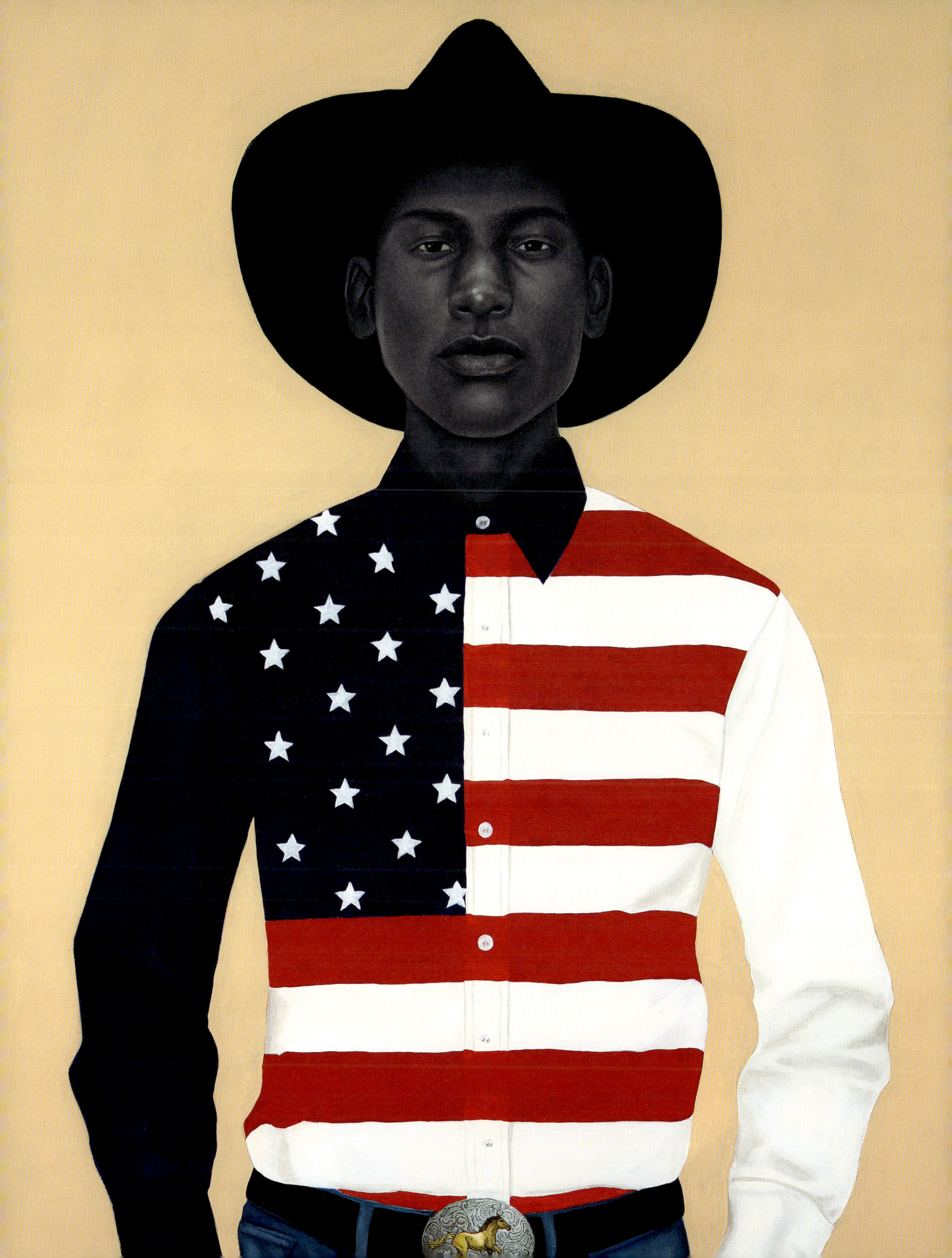

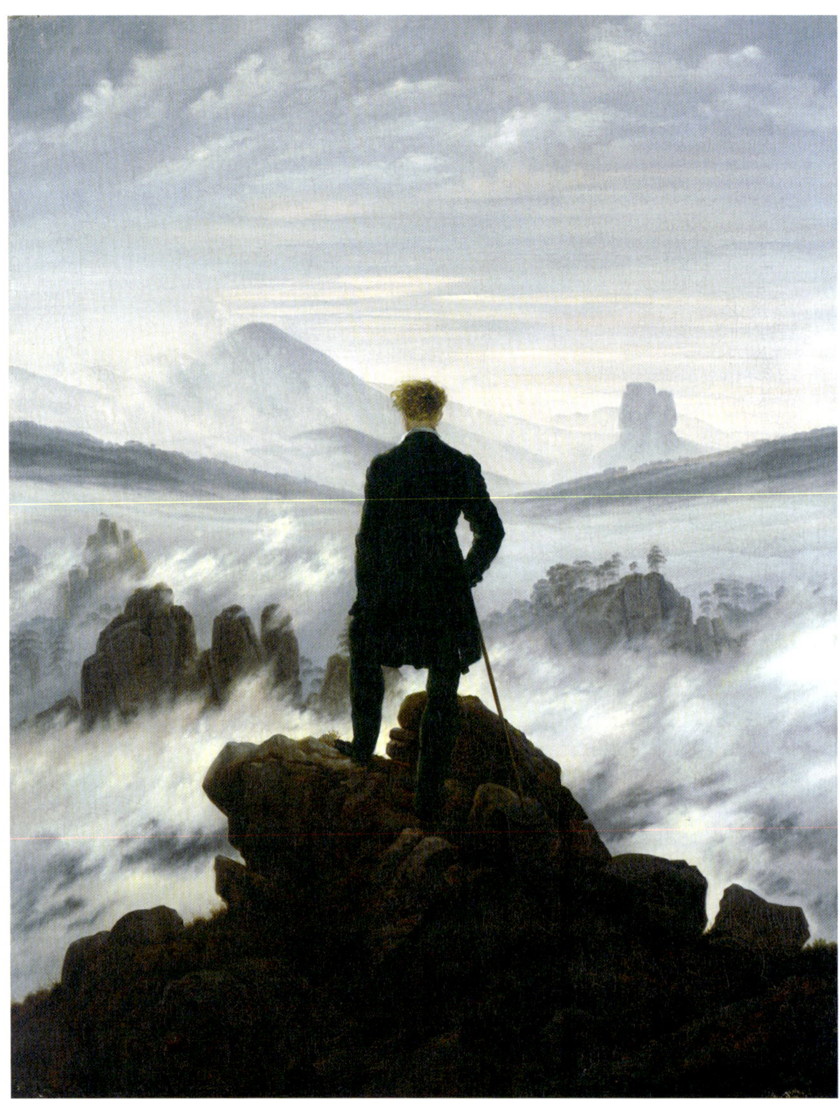

Fig. 1. Caspar David Friedrich, *Wanderer Above the Sea of Fog*, ca. 1817. Oil on canvas, 37¼ × 29¾ in. (94.8 × 74.8 cm). Hamburger Kunsthalle, on permanent loan from the Hamburg Art Collections Foundation, acquired in 1970

Amy Sherald's American Sublime

SARAH ROBERTS

Amy Sherald's paintings speak of the American present. Her works herald and exalt the complexity of each person she summons in paint, creating a world of each one and inviting us in. While these depictions must be understood within the context of centuries of violence against and negation of Black people in the United States, Sherald offers them as a counter-representation of Black life, one that speculates, What if? What if we hold all this history and conjure an entirely different vision of the present, one that is not circumscribed by historical narratives around race? What if the abundant humanity of every individual is a given, honored without qualification or preconception? The resulting paintings present a vision of Black Americans just *being* in this world, not in contention, not racialized, but simply living lives of richness, rightness, and greatness in their ordinariness. Both deeply rooted in and critical of American myths and ideals of freedom, beauty, ambition, and expansiveness, Sherald's body of work stems from her certainty about the power of art to induce emotion, create human connection, and spur personal and social change. She paints a better world by bringing our attention to the fact that it already exists in the tilt of a head, the air of a gaze, the fold of a hand. Such details convey the multitudes held within each of her subjects—these depictions grow out of individual experience and reach outward to engage with Black American culture, the American collective imagination, and history writ large. In this, Sherald's paintings offer nothing short of a new, transcendent vision of contemporary American life. An American sublime.

Sherald had the title of this book and the exhibition it accompanies in mind for some ten years before the project became concrete. The idea of the sublime has traveled in and out of Western art history since the mid-eighteenth century, and it offers a thought-provoking frame for considering Sherald's work. A sinuous concept essentially referring to an experiential state, it emerged as a Romantic notion describing instances of great emotional magnitude, ranging from terror and awe to boundlessness and spiritual elation, particularly in response to the natural world. The experience of feeling transported by or at one with nature while standing in a magnificent landscape or while looking at a painting that captures such splendor typifies the Romantic sublime.[1] In the nineteenth century, painters including Thomas Cole and Thomas Moran in the US, J. M. W. Turner in England, and Caspar David Friedrich in Germany (fig. 1) created works that trumpeted vast, glorious landscapes and underscored the insignificance and vulnerability of humans by comparison. Their Romantic sublime might be described as a sense of feeling overwhelmed and losing oneself in the face of nature, a recognition of the incommensurability of the individual with the broader world. In the US, this genre of painting helped to establish a shared national awe at the immense scale of the American landscape, perpetuate the problematic politics of westward expansion, and promote the mythologization of American individualism.[2]

Jump forward to the 1940s in the US, the period when American painters began creating enormous abstract canvases and drawing connections between their work and experiences of the vast national geography. Barnett Newman defined the sublime as the feeling of revelation inspired in viewers by his own abstract painting and that of some of his peers, including Mark Rothko, Jackson Pollock, and Clyfford Still.[3] For Newman, this sublime could only have arisen in this country, in response to its physical expanse and in contrast to European painters (he did not look beyond western Europe and the US), whom he saw as blinded by histories of beauty and representation in art. He argued that the American style of abstract painting he espoused met a universal desire for exalted emotional experience by offering self-evident, absorbing images free of references to beauty, history, religion, myth, and the traditions of art. Freed from such conventions, his abstraction centered instead on individualism—the painter's own mind and sensations. In his 1948 statement "The Sublime Is Now," he wrote, "Instead of making *cathedrals* out of Christ, man, or 'life,' we are making it [*sic*] out of ourselves, out of our own feelings."[4] Newman's American sublime encompasses paintings that capture an individual artist's emotions and ideas with such directness and authenticity that anyone open enough might feel moved or even identify with the subjective experience they convey. Rather than being cast as insignificant, Newman centers and exalts the individual. He heroizes the painter as the source of the sublime event and assumes the experience of it to be personal rather than collective or communal.

In the early 2000s, critic and curator Okwui Enwezor identified what he termed the "racial sublime" operating in American culture.[5] For Enwezor, the racial sublime takes the form of varying combinations of repression, violence, aestheticization, and desire in representations of Black Americans in much of the literature, music, film, mass media, and popular culture produced across US history and into the present. As with other formations of the sublime, both awe and, particularly, terror circulate in Enwezor's conception. Such representations continually generate an iconography of racial violence and embed knowledge of this violence against Black Americans deep in the social consciousness. The racial sublime he describes is thus uniquely American, pervasive, and a fundamental structure of US culture. In Enwezor's words, "It is never said enough that nothing escapes the racial sublime and the epistemic violence that surrounds it in American civilization."[6] He argues that artists Glenn Ligon, Kara Walker, Fred Wilson, and Lorna Simpson take up scrutiny of the racial sublime as a central strategy in their work, plumbing images and language that have perpetuated it to critique and unravel its functions. Thus, a work like Simpson's *Waterbearer* (fig. 2), with its text "SHE SAW HIM DISAPPEAR BY THE RIVER, / THEY ASKED HER TO TELL WHAT HAPPENED, / ONLY TO DISCOUNT HER MEMORY.," can only be understood after first acknowledging the histories of violence that necessarily structure any such attempt. Simpson's incisive works peel apart the cumulative layers of representation and signification to lay bare suppressed facets of American culture.

Sherald's paintings also critique this racial sublime, strategically activating imagery associated with ideas of Americanness and American history in order to define a

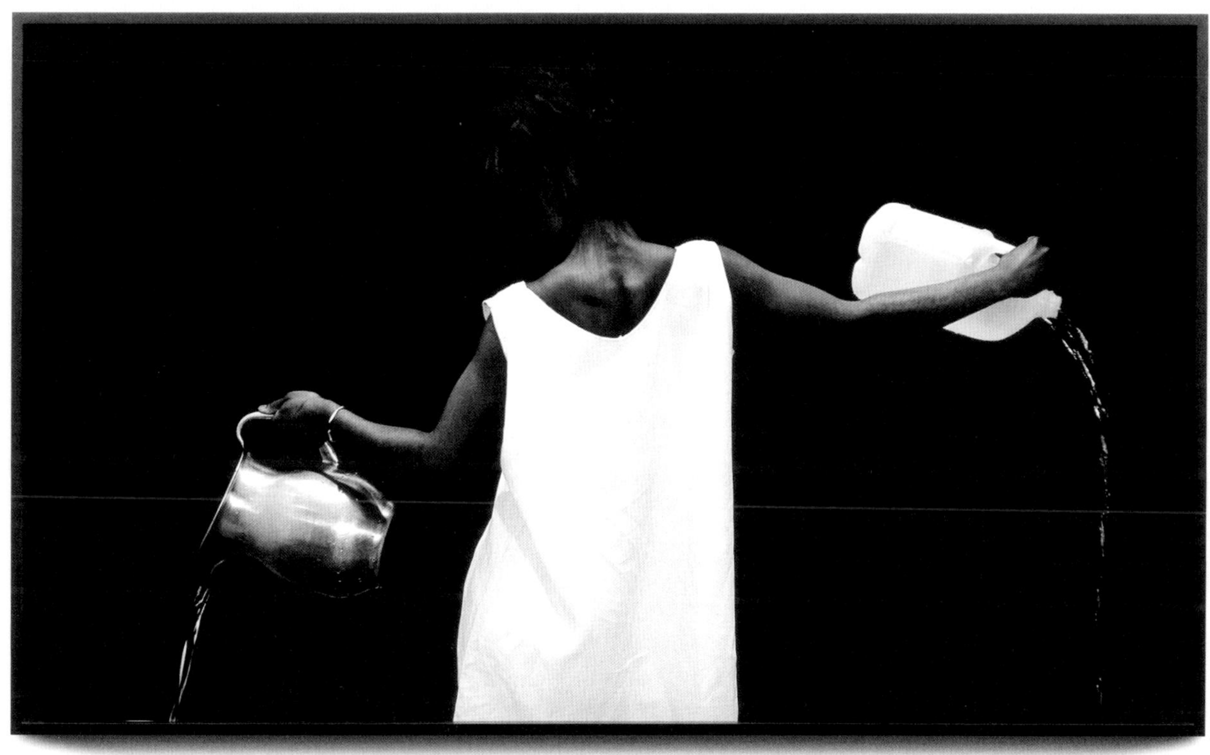

Fig. 2. Lorna Simpson, *Waterbearer*, 1986. Gelatin silver print with vinyl lettering, 59 × 80 in. (149.9 × 203.2 cm). Private collection

different iconography of race altogether. Often this involves recasting American myths and tropes by enacting them with Black figures in archetypal roles—The Cowboy, The Beauty Queen, The Girl Next Door, The Farmer—making Black American stories *The American Story.* Crucially, Sherald insists on the possibility of experiencing sublimity and the depth of everyday life through images and stories that point to its wonder and sanctity rather than its traumas. If Newman's sublime rests in the potential of individual experience to be powerful and affecting for all viewers, Sherald's arises from her paintings' potent ability to convey individual, imagined, and collective experiences of Black American life as similarly expansive and impactful for all. She refuses to engage on the field of repression and violence identified by Enwezor, turning instead to a distinctive kind of world-making and magical thinking.

In *The Boy with No Past* (2014, p. 67), Sherald imagines a youth unfettered by history, living in the moment, full of his own light. It is a conceptualization of Blackness as fundamental, boundaryless, and right, parallel to the kind of capacious completeness that scholar Kevin Quashie has so beautifully termed "aliveness."[7] Sherald's art visually enacts the same enterprise Quashie identifies in poetry—imagining a Black world that is constitutive and whole unto itself rather than defined in any way, by or against anti-Blackness. She goes beyond imagining, however, to create works that take on a quality of witnessing, revealing the aliveness in those here, now. Hers is a visual form of aliveness that speaks powerfully to Black viewers while it also, profoundly, invites viewers of any race to see the world her way. Sherald's paintings offer the sheer beauty of flesh and form rendered exquisitely against fields of vibrant color, not as cathedrals to individual experience but rather as monuments to humanity, shared and venerated.

He squints slightly in the sun, examining us, unperturbed. Relaxed and leaning elbow on knee, he stands atop a tractor rendered in toy-bright green and yellow. With a keen economy of detail—the John Deere logo, the crisp white T-shirt, denim overalls—Sherald refashions a classic American scene in *A God Blessed Land (Empire of Dirt)* (2022, pp. 130–31). The painting is, and is not, a portrait. It is based on photographs of a specific person, but he is unnamed. And as in the best portraiture, the image does more than capture a likeness. It radiates something—call it soul, spirit, or aliveness—and suggests a deeply compassionate identification of painter with subject. In nearly all of Sherald's paintings, the individual portrayed is a real person selected for something they project—a vibe, an association—that speaks to the artist and serves as a starting point for the work's narrative center. Each person is a story. For everyone she paints, Sherald chooses clothing and a setting, then photographs her subject while carefully coaching them to find a pose and facial expression that convey the narrative she imagines. The face of the farmer in *A God Blessed Land (Empire of Dirt)* is a threshold, neither an invitation nor a challenge, a study in composure that is majestic in its self-possession yet neutral enough to accept whatever meaning we might assign to it. His position on the tractor projects control, ownership, ease. The title further enriches the narrative, with its echoes of the Bible, the song "God Bless America," and territorial conquest. The image swirls with references to the history of American art and visual culture, everything from nineteenth-century paintings of agrarian landscapes and Thomas Hart Benton's romanticized rural scenes to advertisements, Walker Evans's documentary photographs of farmers, and family snapshots of people with a foot on the bumper of their shiny new car. In Sherald's hands, all these layers of visual history coalesce in a singular image that powerfully recognizes and assumes a place for Black men and women in American histories of agriculture, citizenship, land ownership, and labor.

Sherald's first contact with art came through illustrations in her family's *Encyclopaedia Britannica* set. Leonardo da Vinci made an impression, as did Michelangelo and

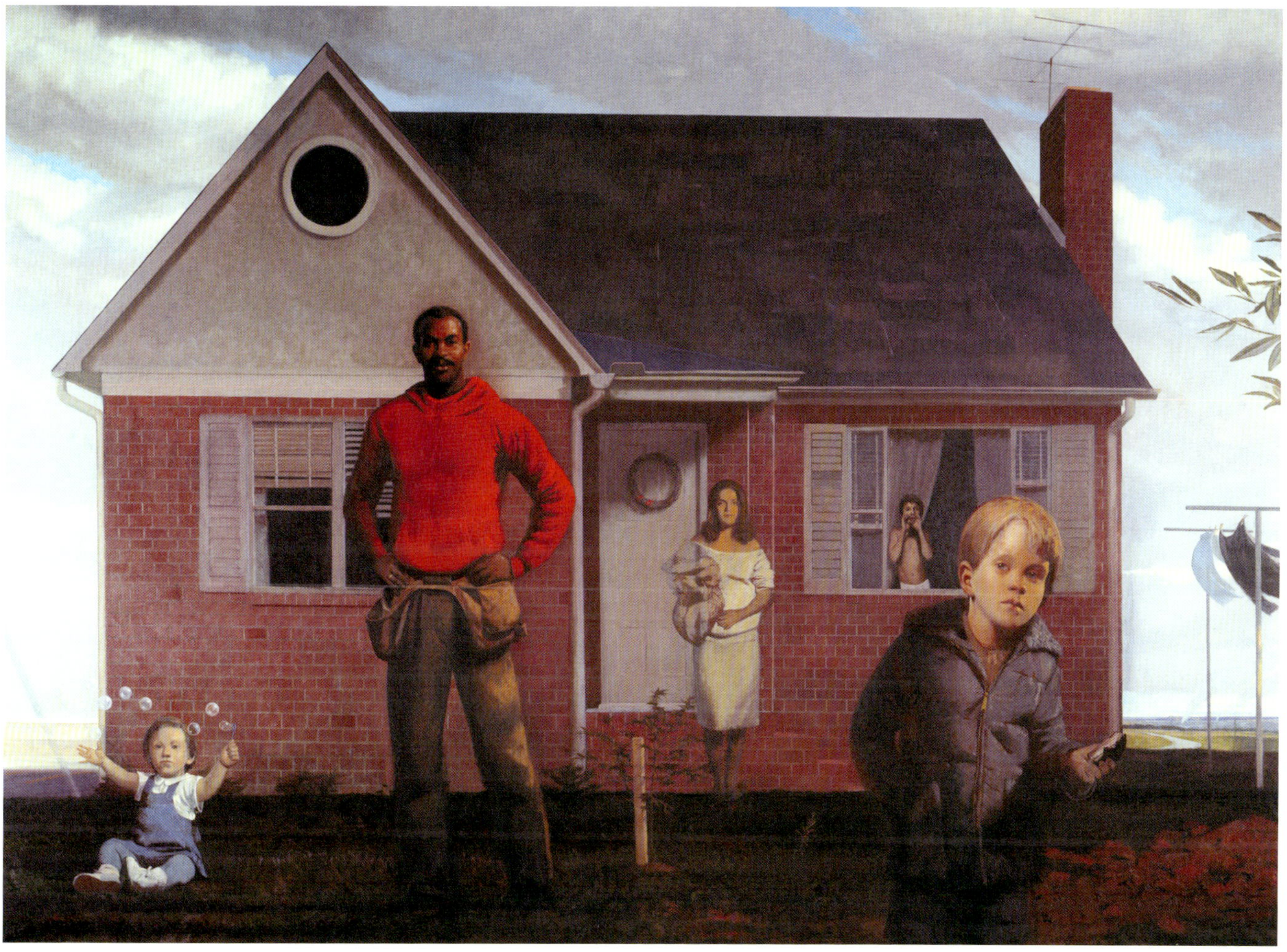

Fig. 3. Bo Bartlett, *Object Permanence*, 1986. Oil on linen, 120 × 168 in. (304.8 × 426.7 cm). Courtesy the artist, Miles McEnery Gallery, New York, and The Bo Bartlett Center, Columbus, Georgia

Rembrandt, affinities that perhaps indicate an early attraction to depictions of humanity conveyed with clarity, reverence, and emotion. Beyond the images in those volumes, her exposure to art was limited to the few religious paintings in her Columbus, Georgia, Catholic school and field trips to the Columbus Museum of Art. One such trip was the first time she saw a painting of a Black figure—Bo Bartlett's *Object Permanence* (fig. 3)—a formative experience she continues to cite in interviews.[8] It might seem surprising that the work of Bartlett, a white realist figurative painter and fellow Georgian, would become an enduring point of reference for Sherald, yet his commitment to empathetically portraying the epic in the everyday lives of his subjects clearly finds parallels in her approach. *Object Permanence* has resonated with her specifically because Bartlett depicts himself as a Black man, a move that, for Sherald, affirms the humanist potential of imagination and the power of empathetically seeing ourselves in others.[9]

As a young figurative painter looking for inspiration, Sherald simply did not encounter a lineage that included Black painters and images of Black people in the

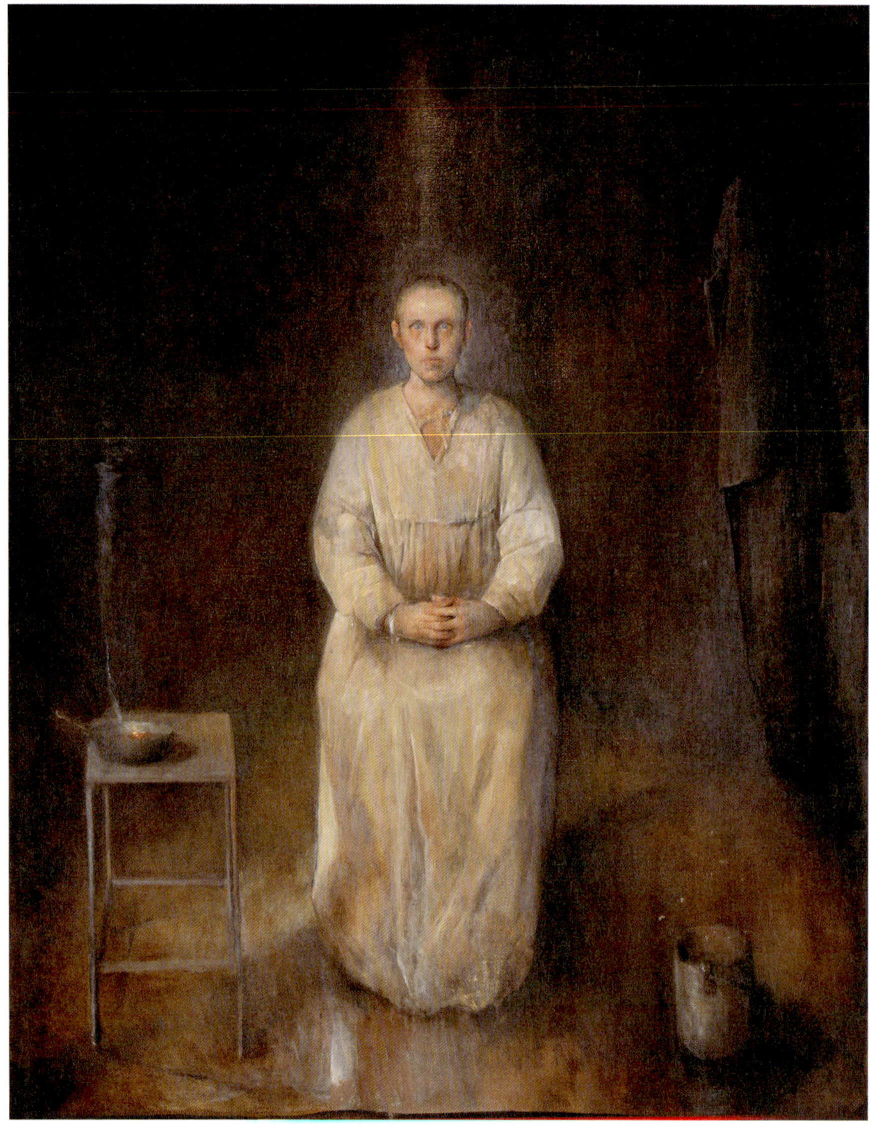

Fig. 4. Odd Nerdrum, *Death Row,* 2023. Oil on canvas, 74 × 59 in. (188 × 150 cm). Nerdrum Museum, Norway

books, community, galleries, or museums surrounding her. While she was a student at Clark Atlanta University she studied and traveled with Arturo Lindsay, a professor of painting at nearby Spelman College, and gained greater exposure to art history.[10] Through Lindsay's summer program in Portobelo, Panama—her first travel outside the US—she got to know local artists and the African diasporic community there. In graduate school at the Maryland Institute College of Art (MICA) in Baltimore,[11] she became aware of more Black artists, including Whitfield Lovell, but she did not discover the work of major figures such as Kerry James Marshall and Barkley L. Hendricks until seeing their museum exhibitions in 2004 and 2008, respectively.[12] While at MICA she became deeply interested in the work of iconoclastic Norwegian figurative painter Odd Nerdrum (fig. 4). Drawn to the mix of technical skill and psychological potency in his paintings, she secured an internship at his studio in Norway for the summer after her graduation in 2004. There she learned Nerdrum's old master–based techniques for painting light and shadow and deepened her understanding of anatomy. She gleaned additional technical knowledge by watching her fellow classmates, many of whom had studied in the rigorously traditional Accademia di Belle Arti in Florence, Italy. Unfashionable and wildly out of step with contemporary art tendencies, Nerdrum's figures have a dramatic presence and intensity that resonated with Sherald's drive to create emotionally charged figurative works. Her determination to study with him demonstrates remarkable independence of thought for a graduate student as well as a commitment to her own development irrespective of peer and market interests. Her time in Norway, at a moment when anti-American sentiment in Europe was running high due to the foreign policy of President George W. Bush, was also something of an awakening for her, as she realized that her European classmates saw her as American first and foremost, assessing nationality before race or gender. Sherald began to reconsider her own American identity, having previously felt estranged from this country's history and dominant white culture.[13]

After returning from Norway, Sherald took a two-year hiatus to care for ill family members back in Georgia. She then returned to Baltimore and to painting in 2007. Around this time she saw Kara Walker's exhibition *My Complement, My Enemy, My Oppressor, My Love* (2007–8) at the Whitney Museum of American Art in New York.[14] Walker's intense probing of US histories of slavery, racism, and the representation of Black bodies clarified Sherald's thinking about her own direction. She committed to representing Black people living their own narratives independent of these violent histories, free in body and spirit. *Hangman* (2007, p. 51) was the first of her works made with that vision in mind. Sherald has described this painting as a "reverse lynching,"[15] and indeed it stands out as her most direct visual reference to the legacy of murder and control of Black men, women, and children in the US. Like a religious painting of Christ's ascension, it shows a central figure floating, dreamlike and free from violence and harm, feet grounded without being fixed to a floor. *Hangman* was a critical step in Sherald's establishing of her work in opposition to artistic explorations of the violent histories that give rise to Enwezor's racial sublime, marking a turn toward the radical reenvisioning of Black American life for which her paintings are known today.

Well Prepared and Maladjusted (2008, p. 56) further signals the coalescence of Sherald's style and voice. It depicts a young woman wearing a stylish pink polka-dot blouse—maybe it's vintage, maybe it's designer, maybe it's her own creation. The garment is distinctive and personal, saying something about who she is. Her carefully choreographed pose—facing ahead, arms at her sides—is open, but her body language tells us very little. Her gaze does all the work, its cool regard suggesting depths of thought, history, and spirit, while also withholding. This canvas initiated the signature gray palette with which Sherald paints her subjects' skin, a technique she favors for its power to shift focus away from her figures' outward racial identities and toward their interior lives. The artistic decisions that went into *Well Prepared and Maladjusted* stemmed from decades of intersecting strands of research, life experience, and experimentation that came together in this moment. Sherald's drive to portray Black life as an open field of possibility grew out of reflection on how her perspective on her own identity had shifted as she moved through communities with different racial makeups and relationships to the diaspora, from Columbus to Atlanta, from Portobelo, Panama, and Larvik, Norway, to Lima, Peru, and Baltimore. Key catalysts also included reading books inflected with mysticism and magic realism, among them Toni Morrison's *Beloved* (1987) and Paulo Coehlo's *The Alchemist* (1988). Visiting the Ringling Circus Museum in Sarasota, Florida, in the mid-2000s led Sherald to think about the self-contained world of a traveling circus troupe and the development of the performers' characters within the ring. Perhaps most impactful on Sherald's thinking was the film *Big Fish* (2003), directed by Tim Burton. Its sprawling, fanciful narrative centers on a son coming to grips with his father's preposterous yarns while learning to believe in the power of imagination to redefine the realities of his life. The crafted universe of the film teems with Technicolor Southern small towns and eccentrics including a giant, a werewolf, and the cast of a traveling circus. Again and again Burton frames single figures against dramatic sets, establishing each character's experience within the same scene as distinct and mediated by their own imaginings (fig. 5). Also prevalent culturally at this moment was the explosion of social media sites—in 2006, MySpace was the most visited website in the US, and Facebook expanded beyond university students to all users that fall. Mobile phones with cameras became increasingly commonplace and affordable, equipping legions of people with new tools for self-fashioning and storytelling. The rise of social media fostered in its users, Sherald among them, a commensurate literacy with the staggering potential of fashion, setting, positioning, and facial expression to articulate minute shades of attitude, identity, and emotion. Connecting this loose constellation of influences is the conviction that through imagination, we can invent ourselves and generate the world we want to live in. With *Well Prepared and Maladjusted*, Sherald established her own vocabulary for this kind of world-making.

The paintings that immediately followed, such as *The Fairest of the Not So Fair*, *Pony Boy*, *The Rabbit in the Hat*, and *Puppetmaster* (all 2008, pp. 52, 57, 58, 53), draw on fantasy, fairy tales, theater, film, and literature to create distinctive worlds, incorporating surprising props and costumes that tip their narratives into fantastical

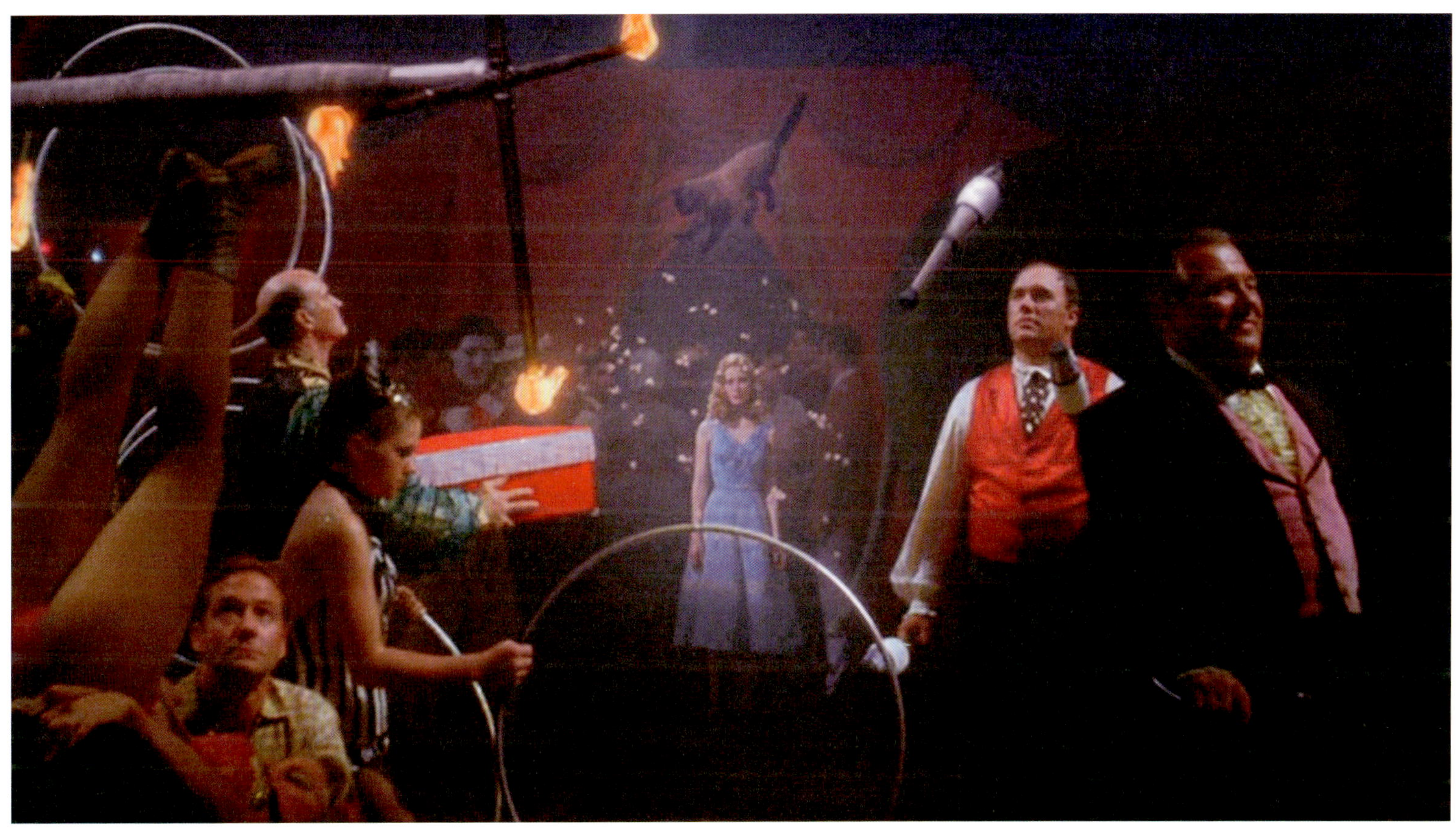

Fig. 5. Still from *Big Fish* (2003, dir. Tim Burton). Courtesy Columbia Pictures

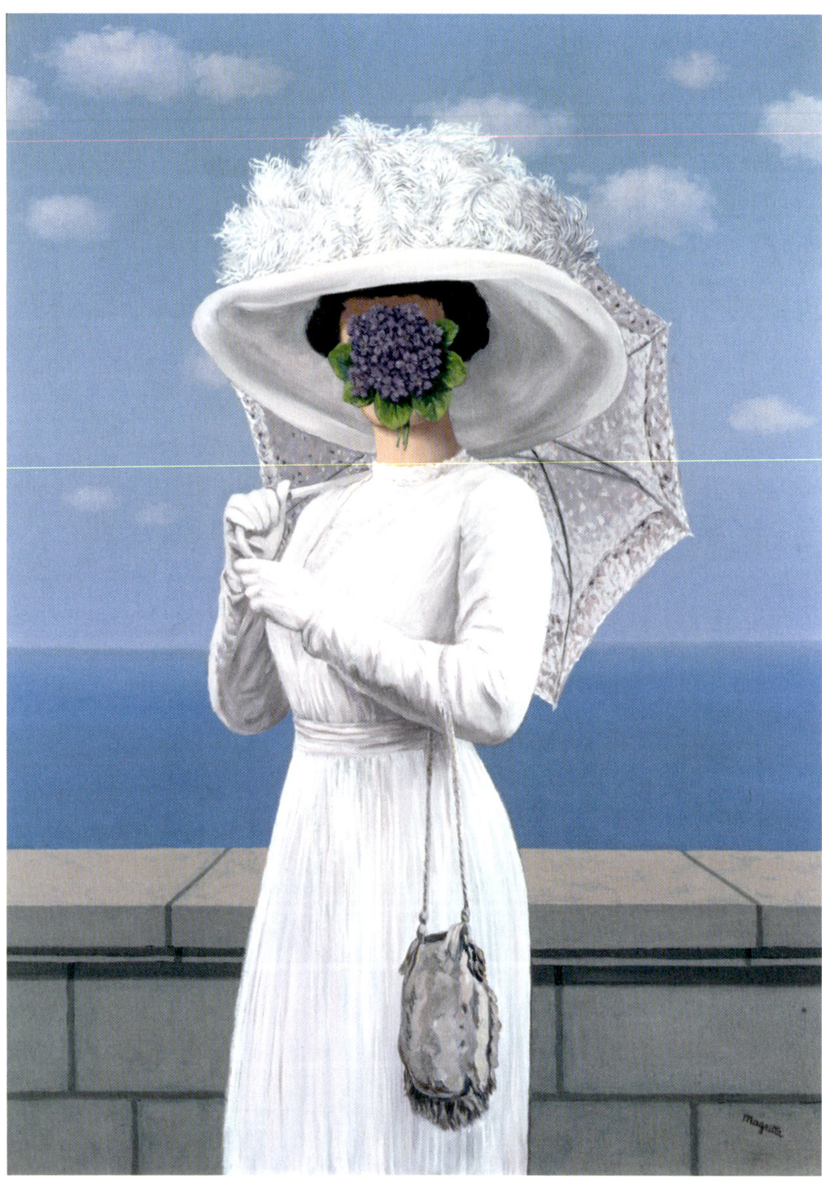

Fig. 6. René Magritte, *La grande guerre* (The Great War), 1964. Oil on canvas, 31⅞ × 23⅝ in. (81 × 60 cm). Private collection

or surreal realms.[16] No easy explanation exists for the whale hand puppet and towering hat in *Puppetmaster*.[17] Is the subject a performer? A figure in a dream? The man's untucked shirt and loosened tie—surprising for a portrait—further signal that there is complexity to his story and serve to unmoor the figure from any instinctive interpretation. On a formal level, her consistent investigation of the visual and psychological power of the singular figure against a stripped-down background echoes the conventional composition of Christian icons and paintings of saints. Perhaps more surprisingly, this format is a nod to the work of Surrealist René Magritte (fig. 6), an artist Sherald returns to frequently. Both use pared-back settings to amplify the psychological presence of their figures and disrupt the logic of the visible world. And each similarly draws on the contrast between hyperrealistically painted passages—for Sherald, faces in particular—and areas that are rendered more flatly in order to direct the viewer's focus to the former. Sherald and Magritte are likewise aligned in using clothing choices and curious objects to unsettle the possibility of straightforward narrative. Whereas many of Sherald's canvases from 2007 to 2011, including *Puppetmaster* and *Guide Me No More* (2011, p. 61), do this with overtly surreal and theatrical props and costume-like clothes, the impulse finds subtler yet still powerful expression in the paintings that have followed, such as *Miss Everything (Unsuppressed Deliverance)* (2014, p. 69), with its oversize teacup, and *Precious Jewels by the Sea* (2019, pp. 106–7), with its tiny sailboat perched on the horizon. These striking elements convey that there is more to these people and their stories than a single image can ever contain.

From the palette and composition to the stylized attire and accessories, many of Sherald's unexpected choices work specifically to confound anti-Black narratives and stereotypes that have long been embedded in American popular culture and news coverage. Sherald's strategies run parallel to Afrofuturism's imaginings of a better, more just world to come for people of African descent, yet she anchors that vision firmly in the present. The hoodie worn by the young man in *Innocent You, Innocent Me* (2016, p. 78) invokes Trayvon Martin and the racist assumptions often attached to this garment when worn by people of color, as well as its conscious adoption by some to directly challenge those associations. The vivid yellow stripes and the cartoonlike T-shirt defy expectations, and both exude the innocence of the work's title. The hoodie's even, saturated color acts as a foil to the sensitively modulated gray tones of the young man's face, heightening the tactility and vulnerability of his body. In the contrast between the two lies a challenge to recognize the potential symbolism of the sweatshirt and subjective responses to it. The hoodie is just a shirt. Meet his gaze. Do you truly see the young man within? Over and over, Sherald sets up a moment of realization, what her mentor Arturo Lindsay has referred to as a "soft slap"[18]—an instant after the attractions of richly painted detail and radiant color have drawn you in where you see something more, and are asked to process the thoughts, feelings, or preconceptions you have brought to the work. No matter our race or nationality, what we see in Sherald's paintings shows each of us something about who we are.

Innocent You, Innocent Me is one of many paintings by Sherald that speak to the vulnerability of Black youths and the preciousness of their promise. As noted above, *The Boy with No Past* (2014, p. 67) envisions the potential, freedom, and imagination of a Black boy growing up without the burden of the social injustice and racial violence that constrain and injure Black Americans in body and spirit. Another important recurring focus in Sherald's work is exploration of the way one's interior life and self-perception might shift, split, or be negated while moving through the world. This theme shines out through the titles of several of Sherald's paintings, including *Fact was she knew more about them than she knew about herself, having never had the map to discover what she was like* (2014, p. 70) and *She had an inside and an outside now, and suddenly she knew how not to mix them* (2018, p. 99). Drawn from Morrison's *Beloved* and Zora Neale Hurston's *Their Eyes Were Watching God* (1937), respectively, these titles point directly to processes of self-discovery and alienation. These paintings and others like them[19] also connect specifically to W. E. B. Du Bois's idea of two-ness or double consciousness, which he outlined in 1897 to describe his experience of navigating the world as a Black person and feeling split between trying to remain true to himself and Black culture and simultaneously conforming to the expectations of a white-dominated society.[20] The contained body language of the figures in paintings such as *Fact was . . .* and *She had an inside . . .* might be read as self-protective or reflective, suggesting a cautious navigation of the distance between the sense of self and society's expectations. In contrast, a group of works depicting confident individuals with relaxed, expressive body language bears titles that speak to self-possession. *Listen, you a wonder. You a city of a woman. You got a geography of your own* (2016, p. 84) and *Mama Has Made the Bread (How Things Are Measured)* (2018, p. 93) draw their titles from language of self-affirmation and celebration in the poems of Lucille Clifton.[21] Paintings such as these recognize and give concrete visual form to the integration of interiority and exteriority.

Beginning with *Planes, Rockets, and the Spaces in Between* (2018, p. 95), Sherald has increasingly mobilized historical images from the media and popular culture chosen specifically for their implications of Americanness. This composition points to 1960s news images of spectators watching NASA rocket launches at Cape Canaveral, Florida. *For Love, and for Country* (2022, p. 125) re-creates Alfred Eisenstaedt's 1945 photograph published in *Life* magazine of a sailor kissing a woman in Times Square to celebrate the end of World War II. *If You Surrendered to the Air, You Could Ride It* (2019, p. 105) nods to Charles Ebbets's iconic photos of steelworkers erecting New York skyscrapers in the 1920s. Images of American ambition, achievement, and power such as these are supplemented with other nuanced references to Americana—the white picket fence in *A Midsummer Afternoon Dream* (2021, pp. 118–19); the Barbie T-shirt and pink flamingo in *As American as Apple Pie* (2021, p. 123). All these works marshal a historical vocabulary of imagery to remake the idea of Americanness, expanding it to include the vast variety of Black experience and emphasizing the obvious presence of Black Americans all along, regardless of how they have or have not appeared in the national visual record. In so doing, Sherald's canvases balance realism and activism—they present a corrective vision of contemporary America and argue for the recognition of Black life as its driving force and as a primary agent of positive social change.

Sherald has frequently noted that she sees her work in the lineage of American Realism.[22] "I look at America's heart—people, landscapes, and cityscapes—and I see it as an opportunity to add to an American art narrative that was written by painters who were mostly white and male," she has observed. "The stories of American Realism recognize how America found its identity in its art."[23] Indeed, even the paintings inflected with fantasy and magic carry an equally strong realist recognition of a slice of America that previously has not been pictured in art. The best artists in this tradition—among them Isabel Bishop, Thomas Eakins, Barkley L. Hendricks, Edward Hopper, Jacob Lawrence, Archibald Motley, Alice Neel, Ben Shahn, Grant Wood, and Andrew Wyeth—invented visual languages and chose subjects to draw attention to and reframe aspects of American society and identity. Sherald cites Hopper not as an influence but as a means of both connecting her work to this lineage and declaring her aim of weaving images of Black life fully into the visual history of American identity. The association bears consideration, for both painters go beyond chronicling representative scenes to define something essential about their American moment and American culture. Hopper's images of people on street corners, in apartment windows, and at cafés and theaters created an understanding of how the sweep of mid-twentieth-century urban life in the US, with its promise of economic mobility, self-definition, and social connection, also generated economic precarity, social isolation, and dehumanization. Hopper painted as a voyeur, observing and assessing individuals living in an America defined by societal imbalances. Sherald paints as a fellow traveler, identifying with her subjects and seeing within them a whole world, a balanced America beyond any Black and white binary.

Portraiture as an act of compassionate recognition and activist substantiation also describes the work of Alice Neel, a painter whose oeuvre Sherald esteems for its authenticity and ability to capture the soul of those depicted.[24] Representing an astonishingly broad spectrum of people, from her neighbors in New York's Spanish Harlem and Andy Warhol and his coterie to political activists like Marxist feminist Irene Peslikis and civil rights leader James L. Farmer Jr. (fig. 7), Neel sought to directly challenge the human degradation she saw as resulting from segregation, capitalism, and political decision-making that put power before people.[25] Neel used the tools and techniques of her art—brushwork, color, perspective—to convey her subjects' dignity and worth through their physicality. For Sherald's subjects, although their bodies are vibrantly present and cherishingly painted, their personhood emanates from the intangible mix of body language, facial expression, clothing choices, color, and, most importantly, gaze. Sherald takes us beyond the physical to recognize in each of her subjects not just an embodied life but an inspirited one.

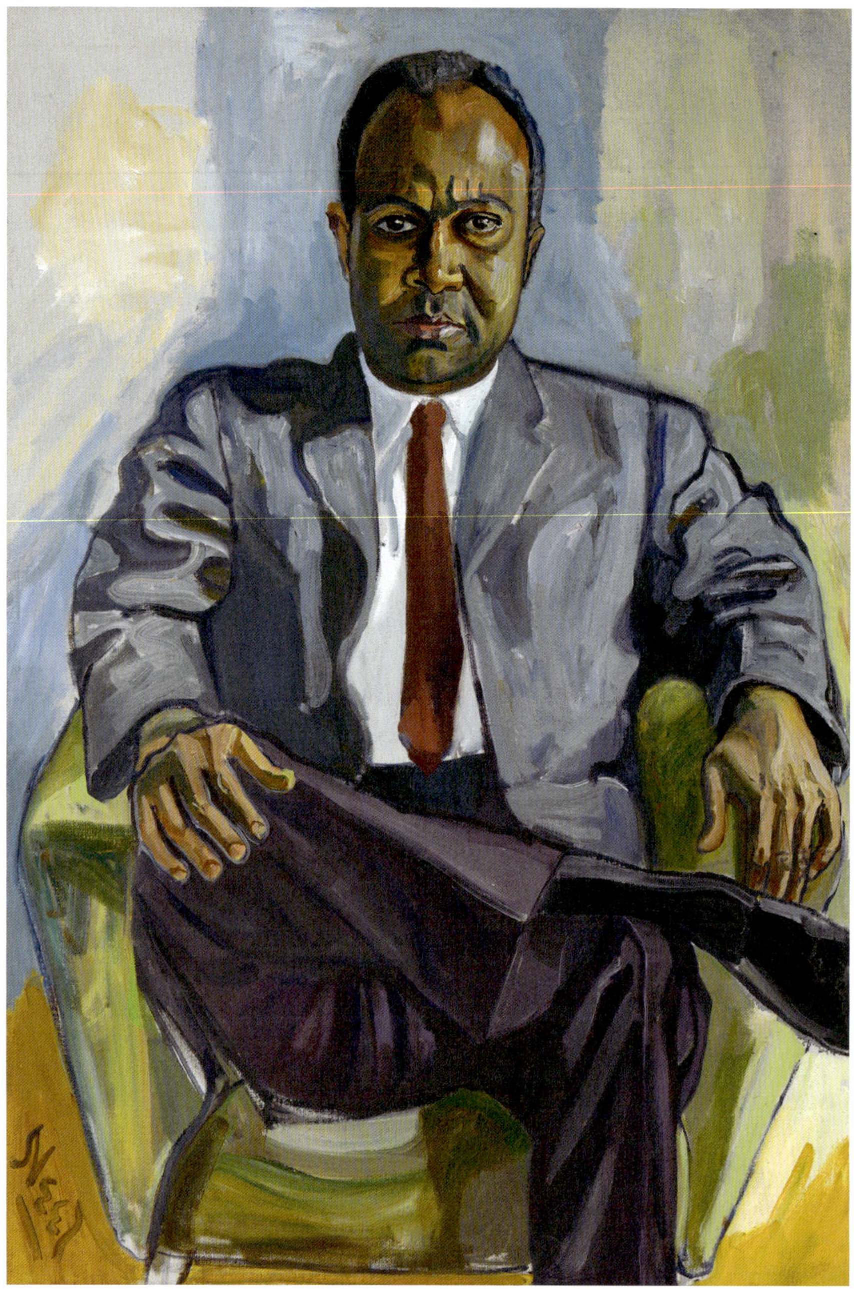

Fig. 7. Alice Neel, *James Farmer,* 1964. Oil on canvas, 43¾ × 30¼ in. (111.1 × 76.8 cm). National Portrait Gallery, Smithsonian Institution, Washington, DC, gift of Hartley S. Neel and Richard Neel

The most powerful tool in Sherald's possession for establishing this quality of aliveness is facial expression. Sherald institutes a way of seeing that enfolds rather than differentiates: her unparalleled ability to paint subtle, vitally expressive faces results again and again in an exchange between viewer and subject that asks that we behold rather than look.[26] The gaze of every figure she portrays is magnetic and just ambiguous enough to invite curiosity and imaginings of a backstory, a mood, a life lived. Every countenance she renders carries a sense of the momentary and of intent—our gaze has been met, yet the terms of the exchange are still open for discussion. When the works are experienced in person, this effect is redoubled due to the artist's practice of hanging the canvases such that viewers encounter the faces of her subjects at or close to eye level (noticeably lower than the conventional height used by most art museums and galleries). These paintings radically challenge viewers, especially non-Black viewers, to take stock of any preconceptions they may carry into their reading of the work. They invite all of us to see differently, to observe as a form of receiving or accepting grace.

Sherald's strategy of portraying unnamed figures in imagined narratives with evocative, open-ended titling makes her works accessible, even universal. Without the viewer's engagement, these stories are incomplete. This titling practice can also be read as a tactic for protecting the privacy of those who have lent themselves and their likenesses to her craft.[27] In a social media and news landscape filled with avid coverage of Sherald's work, her sitters retain their agency in deciding whether or not to be known to the public. Notably, with *Michelle LaVaughn Robinson Obama* (2018, p. 101) and *Breonna Taylor* (2020, p. 117), the two high-profile instances where Sherald completed commissions of identified subjects, she made their portraits with the clear intent to go beyond the public portrayals and media narratives surrounding these women and instead give full, nuanced voice to their lived humanity. Michelle Obama's portrait captures not simply her likeness but her poise, style, wit, and gravitas. Commissioned for the cover of *Vanity Fair* magazine in summer 2020 (p. 30), *Breonna Taylor* makes palpable the life of this vibrant young woman who was killed by police in Louisville, Kentucky, in March 2020, an event that fueled the eruption of widespread social unrest over racial injustice and policing. Sherald approached the portrait as a means of giving Taylor an ongoing, vital presence in the world—one that runs counter to the national narratives around the tragedy of her murder. With these works, arguably the two most widely recognized and socially impactful paintings created in the past fifty years, Sherald made her mark as an indelible force in American culture, influencing discourse around Black achievement and excellence, gender roles, social justice, and police violence. Sherald's groundbreaking portrait of this country's first Black first lady has entered the national consciousness with particular force, demonstrating the power of Sherald's art to impact public dialogue and opinion around what it means to be an American. A photo of a two-year-old Black girl gazing awestruck at Obama's portrait shortly after it was unveiled in 2018 rocketed across social media and national news outlets, capturing the depth of change represented by Sherald's painting and the profound effect it already was having on the American people. The snapshot instantly became iconic, crystallizing a moment in American history much like Ebbets's steelworkers or Eisenstaedt's kiss in Times Square.[28]

Given Sherald's commitment to expanding notions of Americanness and challenging common perceptions of Black American life—along with the deep resonance of her work within American art—there could not be a more fitting title for this survey than *American Sublime.* Just as the defining figures of American Realism delineated and made visible elements of American identity, Sherald's paintings build a more complete picture of the extraordinary richness, range, and complexity of Black American life in the twenty-first century. Crucially, her works go beyond representation to prompt reflection on how Black Americans have been misrepresented and call for a resetting of established understandings of race in the United States. Perhaps the American sublime that Sherald proposes is one that turns the idea of the sublime back on itself. Rather than experiencing awe and terror before the natural world or works of art, she suggests that we find the sublime in the interior, in deep reflection on the history of this country and the vibrant interior lives of the Americans she paints.

NOTES

1. The Romantic sublime derives, of course, from the well-known aesthetics of Edmund Burke, particularly his *A Philosophical Enquiry into the Origins of Our Ideas of the Sublime and Beautiful* (New York: Harper and Brothers, 1863). Burke's writings have been dissected extensively in relationship to twentieth-century art and Barnett Newman's ideas of the sublime, as well as related texts by Robert Rosenblum and Jean-François Lyotard. The latter three authors' writings, as well as many other considerations of the sublime, are usefully collected in Simon Morley, ed., *The Sublime* (London: Whitechapel Gallery; Cambridge, MA: MIT Press, 2010).

2. On pages 32–37 in this volume, Elizabeth Alexander further discusses the ways these types of paintings in the US were intertwined with the doctrine of westward expansion and how they disregarded the enslaved labor and displacement of Native peoples involved in accomplishing that movement. Also inherent in such paintings is American mythologizing of the individual, in the form of the implied bravery, self-sufficiency, and perseverance of those who undertook exploration of the West.

3. Barnett Newman, "The Sublime Is Now," part of "The Ides of Art: 6 Opinions on What Is Sublime in Art?," *Tiger's Eye* 1, no. 6 (December 1948): 51–53.

4. Ibid., 53.

5. Okwui Enwezor, "Repetition and Differentiation: Lorna Simpson's Iconography of the Racial Sublime," in *Lorna Simpson* (New York: Harry N. Abrams, in association with the American Federation of Arts, 2006), 103–31.

6. Ibid., 113.

7. See especially the introduction in Kevin Quashie, *Black Aliveness, or a Poetics of Being* (Durham, NC: Duke University Press, 2021), 1–14. Quashie has also written about the nature of beauty and about beauty as proxy for being in Sherald's work: see "In Praise of Mere Beauty," in *Amy Sherald: The World We Make* (New York: Hauser & Wirth, 2022), 129–44.

8. See, for example, Mary Carole McCauley, "Equipped with a New Heart, Baltimore's Amy Sherald Gains Fame with Surreal Portraiture," *Washington Post*, December 21, 2016. See also Jenna Wortham, "'I Want to Explore the Wonder of What It Is to Be a Black American,'" *New York Times Magazine*, October 8, 2019.

9. Sarah Cascone, "What Amy Sherald Is Looking At: The Painter on 8 Cultural Touchstones that Inspire Her, from Wes Anderson to W. E. B. Du Bois," *Artnet News*, September 12, 2019, https://news.artnet.com/art-world/amy-sherald-cultural-inspirations-1648324.

10. I am grateful to Arturo Lindsay for sharing his many recollections of Sherald's student years and their travel together to Portobelo, Panama; Lindsay, in conversation with the author, January 12, 2024. Calida Rawles also generously discussed her memories of Sherald and their time together as students in Lindsay's painting classes and Portobelo; Rawles, in conversation with the author, January 26, 2024.

11. Sherald's time in Baltimore was critical to her development as an artist, both for its impact on her work and for the deeply supportive community of artists and friends surrounding her there. The richness of that experience falls outside the scope of the present essay but is worthy of lengthy consideration at a future date. I offer warm thanks to Leslie King Hammond, Amy Raehse, Myrtis Bedolla, and Cara Ober for

contributing their time and thoughts toward research for this project.

12. Sherald visited the exhibition *Kerry James Marshall: One True Thing, Meditations on Black Aesthetics* while it was on view at the Baltimore Museum of Art from June through September 2004. She saw the exhibition *Barkley L. Hendricks* at the Studio Museum of Harlem during its run from November 2008 to March 2009.

13. Sherald, in conversation with the author, January 12, 2024, Jersey City, New Jersey.

14. See Philippe Vergne and Sander L. Gilman, eds., *Kara Walker: My Complement, My Enemy, My Oppressor, My Love*, exh. cat. (Minneapolis: Walker Art Center, 2007).

15. "Amy Sherald, In Depth by Joan Cox," interview in *Bmore Art,* November 12, 2012, https://bmoreart.com/2012/11/amy-sherald-in-depth-by-joan-cox.html.

16. The props also echo the attributes of Catholic saints, often included in paintings as symbols of their life stories and reminders of their identities for worshippers.

17. The puppet and hat were made by Sherald's friend and fellow MICA graduate Valeska Populoh for a performance of her own. She also created the jacket in *Pony Boy,* at Sherald's request. I am grateful to Populoh for sharing her insights into this critical period of Sherald's development. Populoh, in conversation with the author, February 1, 2024.

18. Lindsay, in conversation with the author, January 12, 2024.

19. Other works that express this theme include *They Call Me Redbone, but I'd Rather Be Strawberry Shortcake* (2009, p. 59), *Well Prepared and Maladjusted* (2008, p. 56), and *Try on dreams until I find the one that fits me. They all fit me.* (2017, p. 92).

20. W. E. B. Du Bois, "The Strivings of the Negro People," *Atlantic Monthly* 80 (August 1897): 194–98.

21. Clifton's *What the mirror said* (1980) and *Good Times* (1969), respectively.

22. Philip Kennicott, "Painting Michelle Obama Brought Amy Sherald Fame. Now, the Artist Wants to Make Works 'To Rest Your Eyes,'" *Washington Post,* May 14, 2018. See also Amy Sherald, "I Always Want the Work to Be a Resting Place for Black People," in "Nine Black Artists and Cultural Leaders on Seeing and Being Seen," interviews by Noor Brara, *T: The New York Times Style Magazine*, June 24, 2020.

23. Amy Sherald, in "A Conversation Between Amy Sherald and Marc Payot," *Ursula*, September 2, 2019, https://www.hauserwirth.com/ursula/24748-conversation-amy-sherald-marc-payot/.

24. Precious Adesina, "'Her Authenticity Is an Inspiration': Why Alice Neel's Soulful Portraits Have Found New Resonance with Artists and Audiences Today," *Artnet News*, April 25, 2023, https://news.artnet.com/art-world/alice-neel-barbican-hot-off-the-griddle-2287221.

25. In 1950, Alice Neel stated, "There isn't much good portrait painting being done today and I think it is because with all this war, commercialism and fascism, human beings have been steadily marked down in value, despised, rejected and degraded." Alice Neel, quoted in Mike Gold, "Alice Neel Paints Scenes and Portraits from Life in Harlem," *Daily Worker* (New York) 27, no. 258 (December 27, 1950): 11.

26. This idea of beholding comes from Quashie, who defines it as way of looking as a shared relationality, where the subject or speaker in a text guides the looking. Quashie contrasts beholding with a specular way of looking that seeks to find and secure difference. Quashie, *Black Aliveness*, 3–4.

27. Hilton Als has noted Neel's extraordinary capacity to earn the trust of women of color in order to paint them semi-clothed, calling privacy one of the few defenses against racism. Hilton Als, "Alice Neel's Portraits of Difference," *New Yorker*, April 19, 2021.

28. See, for example, Michael S. Rosenwald, "'A Moment of Awe': Photo of Little Girl Captivated by Michelle Obama Portrait Goes Viral," *Washington Post*, March 4, 2018.

Chasing Happiness

DEBORAH WILLIS

What is called the imagination (from image, magi, magic, magician, etc.) is a practical vector from the soul. It stores all data, and can be called on to solve all our "problems." The imagination is the projection of ourselves past our sense of ourselves as "things." Imagination (image) is all possibility, because from the image, the initial circumscribed energy, any use (idea) is possible. And so begins that image's use in the world. Possibility is what moves us.

—Amiri Baraka[1]

Standing in front of Amy Sherald's paintings I experience moments of isolation as well as a sense of belonging. Just as I was born to photograph, Sherald was born to paint.[2] While I use photographs as inspiration for storytelling, Sherald reimagines her subjects through them, engaging the almost alchemical process Amiri Baraka describes to explore the magic potential of image making. Her paintings take me vividly back to childhood and Saturday afternoons in summer, as in *A Midsummer Afternoon Dream* (2021, pp. 118–19): bare shoulders, blue dress, flowers, bicycle, and bright colors. I see in Sherald's work explorations of pleasure, community, style, politics, and constructions of beauty. These are themes commonly found in our family photo albums, which likewise re-create memories of love; they also collectively compel us to contemplate the complexities of life in Black America. Sherald recalls that as a young girl, there were no painted portraits in her home. It was family photographs (fig. 1) that connected her with her heritage and gave her "a deep sense of self, of dignity, and of how to be, how to become."[3] Today, photographs guide the becoming of her paintings.

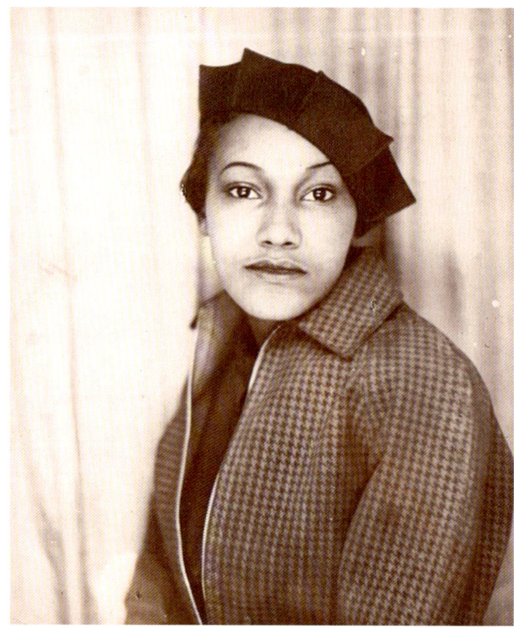

Fig. 1. Family photograph of Sherald's grandmother, Jewel Hendricks, ca. 1930

Painters have used photographs to construct their canvases since photography's invention in the nineteenth century. Continuing in this tradition, Sherald looks to photographs as sources of inspiration through which to define and imagine her subjects. As a figurative painter, she draws from vernacular photography, iconic images in the history of photojournalism, and her own photographs of people she intends to paint. She then re-creates and recontextualizes these individuals on canvas through details of pose, gesture, clothing, and visage; recalling, reminding, and conjuring narratives, whether from history or chance meetings. A signature element of her works is their attentiveness to the exchange of gazes: her subjects' eyes meet the viewer's directly or, more rarely, look away, as in *Saint Woman* (2015, p. 73). Sometimes they are covered, as in *The Boy with No Past* (2014, p. 67). Sherald's compositions merge encounters on street corners, personal memories, and specific photographic objects, creating deeply nuanced portraits of everyday life. In doing so, they lead us through a journey of new possibilities.

Over the course of her career, Sherald has become a keen observer of diverse peoples and developed a distinctive concept of portraiture. She has said that "portraiture as a genre has come to have a new face" as it offers "a way to reclaim time and space within an art historical narrative that is mostly starkly European. It no longer belongs to the social elite. Artists of color are using portraiture to author a narrative of people that art history was written without. It speaks to the human condition and holds up a mirror to life. It now employs colorful reflections and representations of everyday people on the walls of museums where there [were] once misrepresentations."[4] Sherald's paintings extend the stories that portraiture can tell. She combines dress, color, light, and modes of expression to bring her subjects to life. Both period clothing and leisure dress fascinate her, and this is particularly reflected in her explorations of women. Her work reveals that the women who capture her eye are steadfast in their commitment to style, even when trauma is the backstory to a particular narrative. In paintings such as *Well Prepared and Maladjusted* (2008, p. 56) and *The Bathers* (2015, pp. 74–75), Sherald distills memories collected over time to depict subjects who are consistently in dialogue with ideas about self-fashioning and self-awareness. As she has observed: "The people I find seem to possess a kind of presence that feels nostalgic. They are how we saw ourselves in our future, long ago when life was unsure, and freedom came at a cost."[5]

Sherald does not typically connect her work to specific political events. But following the death of young Breonna Taylor, a Black medical worker who was shot and killed in her bed by police officers in Louisville, Kentucky, on March 13, 2020, she felt a strong call to re-image Taylor's life on canvas. "I knew I had to do it," Sherald says. "I knew it was a way to focus not on her death but . . . on her aliveness and what her life meant." *Breonna Taylor* (2020, p. 117) is the result of a unique process of considering the lived experience of a deceased person and conjuring her memory through line, color, and form. It is also exceptional in that it was not based on a photograph taken by the artist. Sherald began by looking for source images "that had not been floating around social media." In the end, she selected a well-known selfie

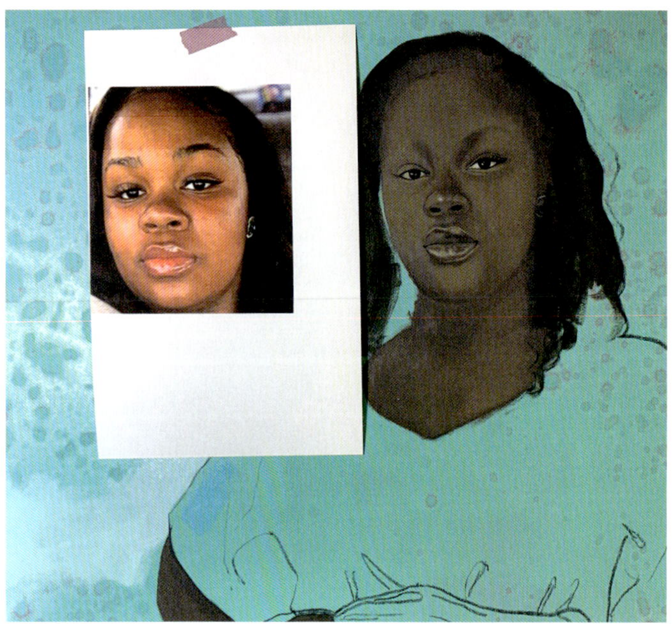

Fig. 2. In-progress photo of Sherald's *Breonna Taylor* (2020, p. 117) and the selfie by Taylor that Sherald used as a source for the painting, 2020

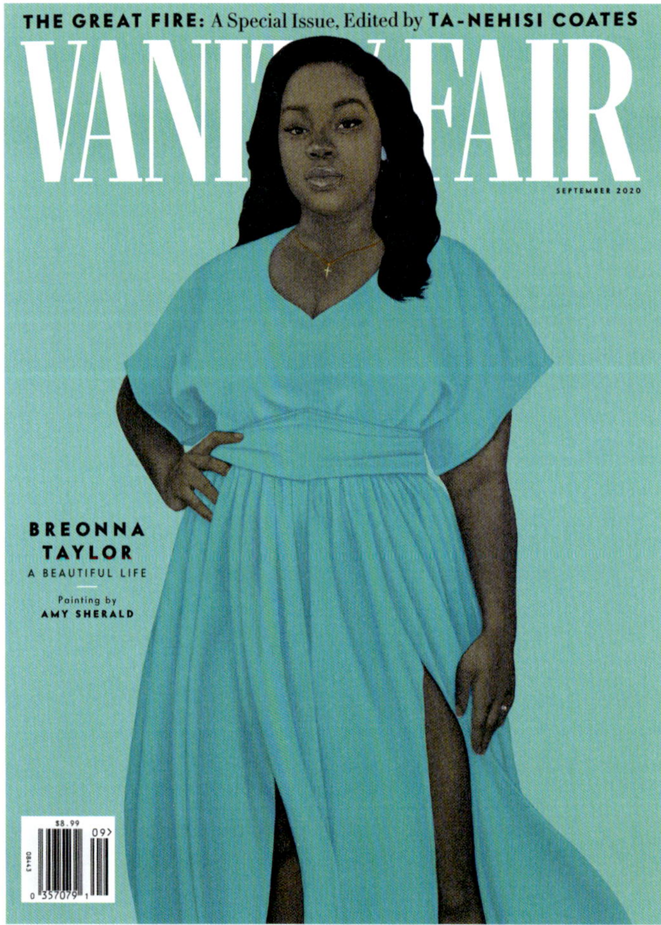

Fig. 3. *Breonna Taylor* on the cover of *Vanity Fair,* September 2020

Taylor had taken in her car (fig. 2). Sherald wanted the painting to embody a moment of "freedom and power." She explains, "I wanted to leave her family with that memory. Not that it can erase the tragedy that happened, but to offer them some kind of solace in the way that she's represented in the world now."[6]

Breonna Taylor was published on the cover of *Vanity Fair* in September 2020 (fig. 3), accompanied by an article in which Taylor's mother, Tamika Palmer, recounts her daughter's story to writer and activist Ta-Nehisi Coates.[7] Sherald recalls struggling to select the colors for Taylor's dress and the painting's background, noting that she tried several colors before deciding on blue. Sherald observes, "There's something about blue that's very powerful, that's very spiritual, that's very otherworldly, but, yet of the earth. It's infinite in its capacity to hold energy. . . . It didn't confine her. I wanted people to feel that she was floating inside of a space that you could be in as well as stand outside of, and just have your moment of solace."[8]

While the portrait of Taylor is distinctive, Sherald's paintings are consistently both conceptual and representative, entering into art historical silences and critically engaging the visual archive of American history to tell Black stories. She is cognizant of the diversity of Black American identity and insists that its expansiveness be represented. A sense of narrative play threads throughout her work, conveyed by clothing choices, bicycles, playground slides, and balloons. Freedom is conceptualized through home ownership, the idyllic white picket fence, and an American flag–patterned button-down worn by a young man in a cowboy hat. Sherald's image making not only constructs narratives of joy and ancestry but also, and perhaps most saliently, reiterates the chase for happiness, staging and restaging her personal encounters while reimagining the perceived viewer's desire to locate pleasure in these hostile times.

NOTES

1. LeRoi Jones [Amiri Baraka], "The Revolutionary Theatre," *Liberator*, July 5, 1965.

2. Amy Sherald discusses her sense of vocation in "Enduring Blackness: A Decade of Black Portraiture[s]: Paris 2013–2023," a panel discussion moderated by Cheryl Finley, Musée du quai Branly – Jacques Chirac, Paris, May 30, 2023, https://www.youtube.com/watch?v=nGPUd53OSGs.

3. Amy Sherald, remarks during "Portraiture at the Intersection of Art and History: A Conversation between Deborah Willis, Amy Sherald, and Bisa Butler," part of *The Simmons Talks*, National Museum of African American History and Culture, Washington, DC, March 16, 2023, https://nmaahc.si.edu/events/simmons-talks-portraiture-intersection-art-and-history-conversation-between-deborah-willis.

4. Ibid.

5. Amy Sherald, in "A Conversation Between Amy Sherald and Marc Payot," *Ursula*, September 2, 2019, https://www.hauserwirth.com/ursula/24748-conversation-amy-sherald-marc-payot/.

6. All quotations in this paragraph are from Sherald, "Portraiture at the Intersection of Art and History."

7. Ta-Nehisi Coates invited Sherald to create the *Vanity Fair* cover.

8. Sherald, "Portraiture at the Intersection of Art and History."

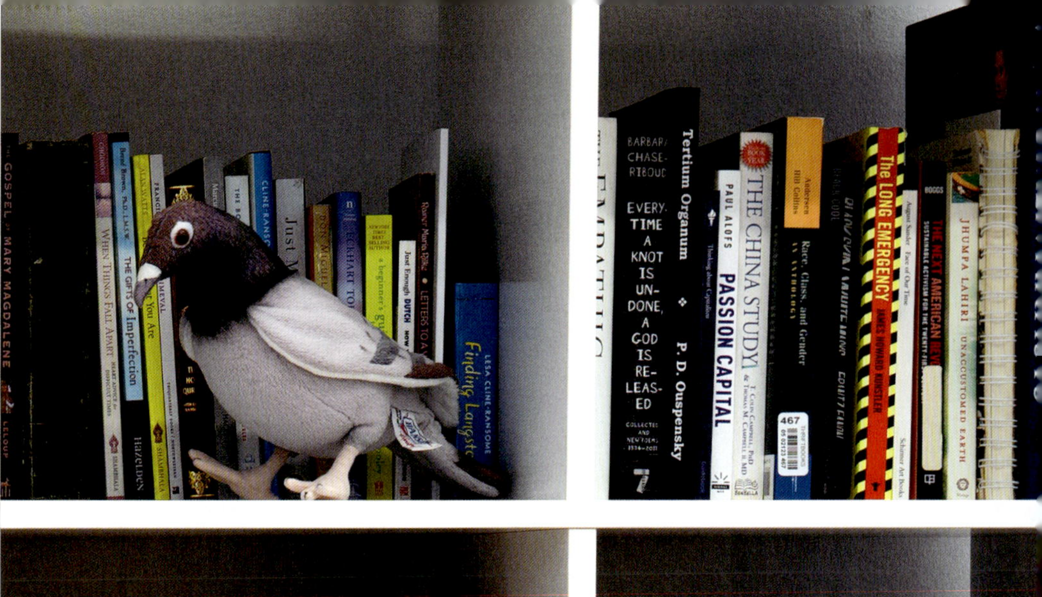
Mary Magdalene
Things Fall Apart
The Gifts of Imperfection
Finding Langston
Lesa Cline-Ransome
Every time a knot is undone, a god is released
Tertium Organum
P. D. Ouspensky
Passion Capital
Paul Alofs
The China Study
The Long Emergency
Jhumpa Lahiri
Unaccustomed Earth

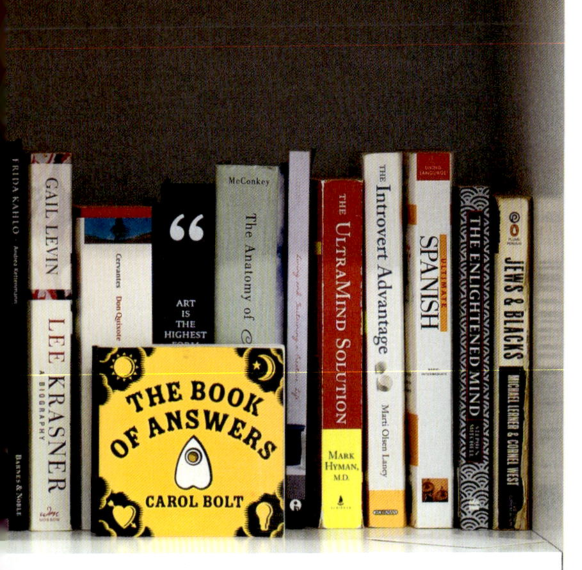
Frida Kahlo
Gail Levin
Lee Krasner
Art is the highest
The Anatomy of
The Book of Answers
Carol Bolt
The UltraMind Solution
Mark Hyman, M.D.
The Introvert Advantage
Marti Olsen Laney
Spanish
Jews & Blacks

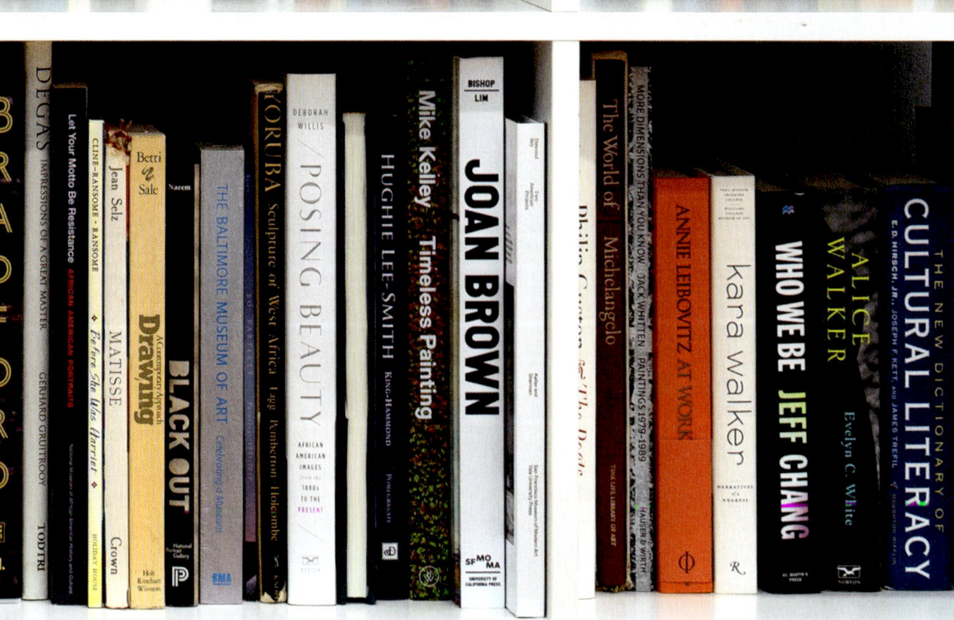
Bradford
Degas
Let Your Motto Be Resistance
Matisse
Drawing
Black Out
The Baltimore Museum of Art
Yoruba Sculpture of West Africa
Posing Beauty
Deborah Willis
Hughie Lee-Smith
Mike Kelley Timeless Painting
Joan Brown
The World of Michelangelo
Annie Leibovitz at Work
kara walker
Who We Be
Jeff Chang
Alice Walker
The New Dictionary of Cultural Literacy
Lines
Shantell Martin

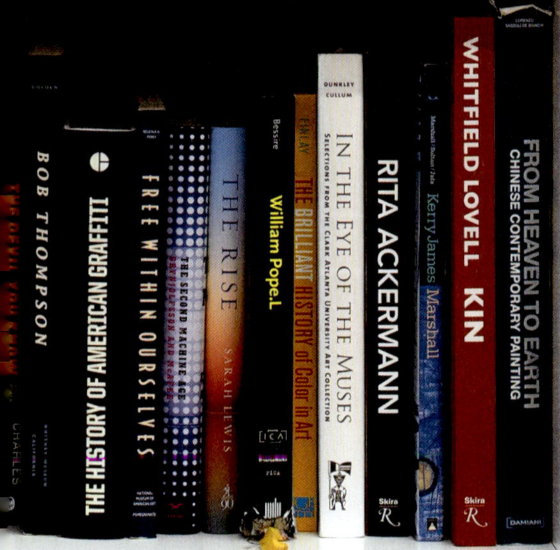
Bob Thompson
The History of American Graffiti
Free Within Ourselves
The Rise
Sarah Lewis
William Pope.L
The Brilliant History of Color in Art
In the Eye of the Muses
Rita Ackermann
Kerry James Marshall
Whitfield Lovell Kin
From Heaven to Earth
Chinese Contemporary Painting

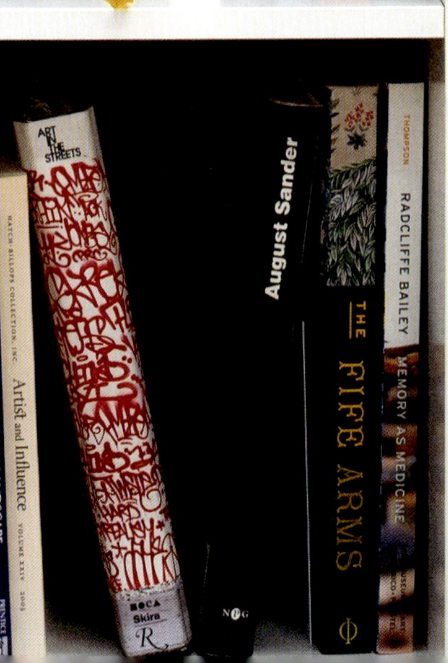
Southern Accent
Vivian Maier Street Photographer
Philip Guston: Painter 1957–1967
Collage Techniques
The Restless Urban Landscape
Artist and Influence
August Sander
The Fife Arms
Radcliffe Bailey
Memory as Medicine

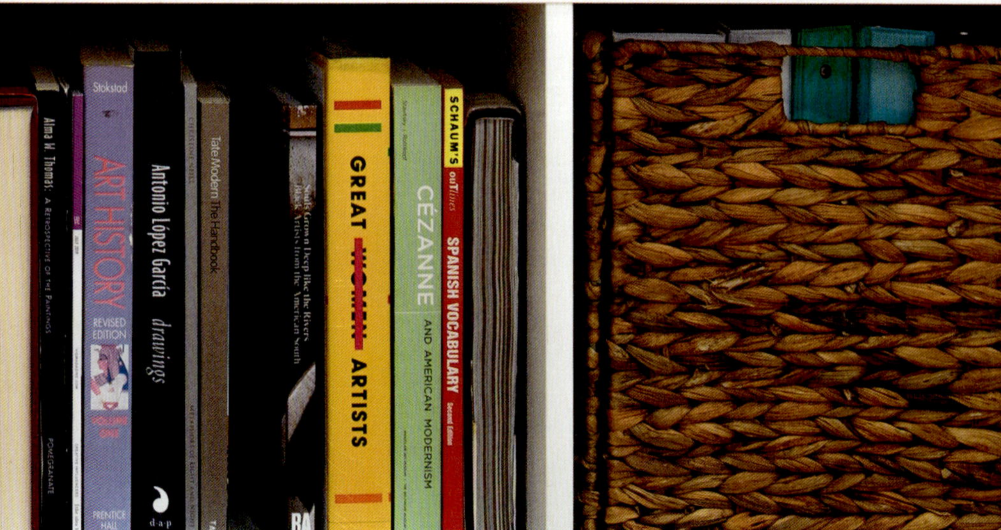
Art History
Antonio López García drawings
Tate Modern The Handbook
Great Women Artists
Cézanne and American Modernism
Schaum's Outlines
Spanish Vocabulary

Everyday Sublime

ELIZABETH ALEXANDER

Wonders do not confuse. We call them that
And close the matter there. But common things
Surprise us.

—Gwendolyn Brooks, "The Artists' and Models' Ball (For Frank Shepherd)"

Consider the painter in her studio. For countless hours and days and weeks and months and years she stares at nothing and everything and out of that, creates worlds. There are shapes and shadows in her head, wordless feelings, colors and proportion. And then there is the challenge of the craft itself, of getting the paint on the canvas and making it do miraculous things.

Art is also made from other art, so in the painter's head there are other paintings, music, literature, and many other miraculously made things. I picture all that shape, sound, and image as an ever-whirling Rolodex that the painter's mind stops imperceptibly to borrow from and transform. I know that poets work this way, and that we are not always aware of how this process works—the vast filing cabinet of inspiration that we use and sometimes do not even see we have sourced until the work is long done. That is the magic of making and one of the pleasures of thinking long about great art.

To sit with Amy Sherald's paintings is to experience the sublime in the commonplace of everyday people illumined by their wondrous interiority. Sherald usually chooses the compelling constraints of single-sitter portraiture, at a scale that is near-human but also dramatic and presentational. The viewer is always brought face to face, eye to eye, soul to soul, with people. Beholding her paintings is an uncanny encounter, because of how she takes us to great depths of experiencing oneself in the presence of a fellow soul. Her people convey quiet, yet they are clearly storied. The sense of recognition is uncanny. They are a level removed from intimates and do not feel like a sister or brother but rather a cousin, neighbor, congregant, classmate. Sherald conveys universes in the self.

I am honored to experience a kinship with Amy Sherald. We are a painter and a poet in a long, quiet conversation that is happening even when we are not spending time together, which we have had scant but meaningful opportunity to do. Our conversation is often as quiet as a poem or a painting can be, and yet I feel its constancy. I have written to her great painting *What's precious inside of him does not care to be known by the mind in ways that diminish its presence (All American)* (2017, p. 89) in my book *The Trayvon Generation* (2022).[1] Her subjects are usually unnamed, but she brings history into her paintings with a subtle restraint that I find both fascinating and generative.

Sherald has told me that my book *The Black Interior* (2004) has been meaningful to her, and I feel that the paintings brought together in this book are in conversation with this passage in particular:

> Social identity, in unfettered dream space, need not be seen as a constraint but rather as a way of imagining the racial self unfettered, racialized but not delimited. What I am calling dream space is to my mind the great hopeful space of African American creativity. Imagining a racial future in the black interior that we are constrained to imagine, outside of the parameters of how we are seen in this culture, is the zone where I am interested in African American creativity. "The black interior" is not an inscrutable zone, nor colonial fantasy. Rather, I see it as inner space in which black artists have found selves that go far, far beyond the limited expectations of what black is, isn't, or should be.[2]

The sublime dream space in Sherald's paintings is the measure of the depth of her exploration of Black interiors and their—our—heretofore unseen visual possibilities. We see her unshakeable belief that Black people can fill the frame, are worthy subjects, and are infinite behind their carefully presented exteriors that vanquish stereotypes.

Sherald has told me that my collection of poems *American Sublime* (2005) sparked the title of her exhibition. I love that allusion, and also that she inhabits the verse in a quite different place than where I wrote it. The painter and the poet aspire to make new art that continues to take form after we have put it into the world. The living creatures that are her paintings bring the poetry to new life and conversation.

The title poem of my *American Sublime* references those nineteenth-century American landscape paintings that were influenced by ideas of "westward expansion" and the majesty and awe beheld in nature. These paintings are wholly without figures—without the self that is so prominent in Sherald's work.[3] In the poem, I write from the paradox of an American sublime that overlooked the larger and, to my mind, primal American matter of slavery and Native displacement. Sherald is peopling an American history that is riven and characterized by violence and displacement, one by one, soul by soul, at the level of the intimate that makes up our collective humanity. For her paintings, I see "American Sublime" as a marker that these people together begin to make what Robert Hayden's poem "[American Journal]" calls the "multi people," in wonder, awe, and regarded with profound interest.

On this round of looking, and looking, I am taken in by the interplay of her titles with the paintings. Though her subjects are mostly unnamed, there is great specificity in the titles, as though you walked into the middle of a book, or someone's dream. I think her titles—allusive, cryptic, distilled, often referential—are small poems unto themselves that offer a runway to enter and contemplate the paintings. They give us a glimpse of the artist's mind and the noise inside that she alchemizes into resolution. Sherald has a sensitivity for literary language of a certain kind: excerpts of language that are as distilled as a line of poetry. The elliptical power of the titles mirrors the modus of the paintings. You are given the language itself, but the language is a phrase—not a full sentence but something in the middle, oblique and evocative. The mystery is not to deliberately obscure but rather to open the vastness of our interiors, to invite you in but also to interrupt the assumption that anyone can be known at a glance. I hear in my head Walt Whitman's words from "Song of Myself": *I am large, I contain multitudes.* Sherald's literariness as a painter is different from what I am calling her poetics.

Let us consider her titles themselves, and some of their sources. I get the sense that libraries are always in Sherald's head and part of the substance with which she makes her work. She is in conversation with many writers in the Black tradition. For example, several of her works take titles from Toni Morrison's *Beloved*. They do not replicate the context of Morrison, though, they are a reinterpretation, the sounds Sherald hears in her head—perhaps even without pausing to name it—as she paints and creates inner worlds and words for her subjects.

Here is a sampling of Sherald's titles with literary sources:

> *If You Surrendered to the Air, You Could Ride It*: Morrison, *Song of Solomon*
> *Hope Is the Thing with Feathers (The Little Bird)*: Emily Dickinson
> *There Is No Charm Equal to Tenderness of Heart*: Jane Austen, *Emma*
> *As Soft as She Is . . .* : Sappho

It is worth quoting the Sappho in its entirety. "Soft as she is" comes from the pithy poem "Blame Aphrodite":

It's no use
Mother dear, I
can't finish my
weaving
            You may
blame Aphrodite

soft as she is

she has almost
killed me with
love for that boy.

Perhaps lesbian desire and a love triangle are the backstory to the painting, as in the poem, where the speaker is undone by unrequited love and confesses it to her mother. Or perhaps the Sappho was nowhere in Sherald's mind, but the phrase she distilled has familiarity and resonance: "soft as she is." Maybe the poem is merely the music in this beholder's head.

She had an inside and an outside now, and suddenly she knew how not to mix them: Zora Neale Hurston, *Their Eyes Were Watching God*. Hurston's Janie is one of the great female protagonists of American literature, and in the book she returns to her front porch in her old hometown to tell her best friend, Pheoby, of her coming-of-age and the story of her life blossoming into womanhood and loves. That moment of coming to consciousness, of understanding herself as a woman in the world—as she had earlier in the book come to understand herself as "colored"—is a moment of interior revelation that Sherald's painting captures.

Those are just a few of Sherald's engagements. There is much more to say and research about her literariness and how literary words bring us into the images. If you will permit me an excursion, the poet I see as most akin to Sherald and who best illustrates her painter's poetics is Gwendolyn Brooks. I feel this comparison—this conversation—richly illuminates the poetics of this painter of sublime interior everyday wonder. Sherald, like the great Brooks, is a genius of American sublime interiority. Putting Brooks next to Sherald's paintings I think reveals aspects of the power of Sherald's work and certain characteristics I see there. Just listen to some of these Brooks lines, and imagine them as titles of Sherald paintings:

> *But in the crowding darkness not a word did they say*
>
> *Abortions will not let you forget*
>
> *I've stayed in the front yard all my life.*
> *I want a peek at the back.*
> *Where it's rough and untended and hungry weed grows.*
> *A girl gets sick of a rose*
>
> *However even without lipstick she is lovely and it is no*
> *wonder that the preacher (at present) is a*
> *synonym for her telephone*
>
> *Life must be aromatic.*
> *There must be scent, somehow there must be some*
>
> *I love those little booths at Benvenuti's*

He grew up being curious
And thinking things are various.

Bessie of Bronzeville visits Mary and Norman at a Beach-house in New Buffalo

Bronzeville Woman in a Red Hat

Somehow to find a still spot in the noise
Was the frayed inner want . . .

He feared most of all the choices, that cried to be taken

In Brooks, as in Sherald, there is formality, longing, restraint, and the rigorous act of profound looking and beholding, almost divining, inner lives.

Sublime: elevated or lofty, characterized by grandeur and awe. *Sublime*: renders and regards things at their finest. *Sublime* also refers to the act of converting something to higher worth, from vapor to solid. This is the painter's and the poet's work, to "give to airy nothing / a local habitation and a name," as Shakespeare's Theseus says in *A Midsummer Night's Dream*. The painter thus elevates the subject to "a high degree of spiritual purity or excellence."

Everyday people are beheld in their full interiority in Sherald's paintings. They exist on the exalted spirit plane of sacred humanity, each as important as the next. "The light in me recognizes the light in you," we say at the end of yoga practice in the new age transliteration of the Sanskrit word *namaste*, and that is what it feels like to spend time in the sacred human plane of Amy Sherald's paintings.

NOTES

1. Elizabeth Alexander, *The Trayvon Generation* (New York: Grand Central Publishing, 2022), 43.

2. Elizabeth Alexander, *The Black Interior* (St. Paul, MN: Graywolf Press, 2004), 5.

3. Elizabeth Alexander, "American Sublime," in *American Sublime* (St. Paul, MN: Graywolf Press, 2005), 89.

Monumental Time

RHEA L. COMBS

I do not define time, space, place and motion, as being well known to all. Only I must observe, that the common people conceive those quantities under no other notions but from the relation they bear to sensible objects. —Isaac Newton[1]

To transgress we must return to the body. —bell hooks[2]

Images can change the world. —Amy Sherald[3]

Before ever meeting Amy Sherald, I was familiar with her work. A mutual friend shared a digital photograph of one of her paintings and wanted my opinion. Our friend was uncertain if it was the artist or the painting they were attracted to. I assured them it was both. Upon seeing the image, I was struck by the technical precision and care Sherald gave to the subject. Staring into the eyes was hypnotic—all sense of time and place was lost. Never mind the styling was impeccable, with a slight sense of humor, and the bright, vivid colors bold and playful.

The painting was *They Call Me Redbone, but I'd Rather Be Strawberry Shortcake* (2009, p. 59). It feels unapologetic, but not polemical or dogmatic. There are equal parts sass and innocence associated with the tilt of the head, the slanted part, and the long, black pigtails bound together by red-and-white bows. The youthful face holds an endearing and steady gaze against the dazzling yellow dress that is accentuated by bright strawberries as the young girl's hands dig deeply into her pockets. This simple, elegant painting tells a rich, dynamic story about the awkward, self-conscious feeling many young girls and women experience when subjected to unwanted advances and objectifying, gazing eyes. It simultaneously critiques colorism, a phenomenon known within the Black community for privileging lighter skin tones as more attractive. ("Redbone" is a common euphemism, particularly in the South, for someone who has fairer skin, often with reddish undertones.) Seeing Sherald's work for the first time, it felt new yet familiar—as if the painter was letting the world see moments common to some and unknown to many others.

Photography, essential to Sherald's practice, is how she begins her paintings. "I consider my paintings to be a meditation on photography," she explains. "It's offered me another way to see portraiture beyond the reign of European painting, because, when the camera was invented, so was the opportunity for us to become the authors of our own narratives."[4] Early African American photographers throughout the United States used the power of mechanical reproduction to create dignified images of Black people as a counterbalance to many prevalent, stereotypical portrayals. A prominent display during the *Exhibit of American Negroes* at the 1900 Paris Exposition, where African American scholar W. E. B. Du Bois presented images of respectable African Americans, has served as inspiration for Sherald. With assistance from his students at Atlanta University (now Clark Atlanta University, where Sherald attended college), Du Bois showed maps, graphs, and charts demonstrating progress among African Americans in Georgia as well as more than 350 photographs that offered "a narrative of Black agency."[5] The portraits of finely dressed men, women, and children—many of them unsmiling and with a direct gaze—are part of a narrative through line in which Sherald's work is situated. Du Bois, along with early Black photographers such as C. M. Battey (another Georgia-born artist), offers an important perspective in understanding Sherald's praxis.

Sherald is originally from Columbus, Georgia, and there is a Southern dignity coursing through many of her paintings. The posture, styling, and refinement in them feels not only personal but rooted in a politics of respectability reflective of an interior strength seen among many nineteenth- to mid-twentieth-century images of Black people made by African Americans. Reflecting on Sherald's paintings, I am also reminded of the work of Southern image maker Henry Clay Anderson, who photographed the everyday life of Black Mississippians from the late 1940s through the mid-1980s. Anderson believed that "a photographer understands that pictures will show what is in the person . . . making pictures is a lot like telling a story."[6] There is power in celebrating small, unassuming moments, and when looking at Sherald's paintings this holds true. Sherald brings out what is in the person, their dignity and self-possession—an essence.

Sherald's *Welfare Queen* (2012, p. 63), for instance, could have been inspired by the young woman in Anderson's *Indoor portrait of young couple at Coleman High School Prom* (fig. 1). The etymology of the phrase "welfare queen" involves a derogatory origin story in the United States that dates to the early 1960s and has been used as a political dog whistle to demonize large groups of people. Over the years, the term became racist shorthand for Black single mothers. Still today, "welfare queen" is an entrenched idea that conjures visions within the racial imagination of the "angry Black woman" who has numerous unruly children and no partner, and who relies on government entitlements while taking advantage of the tax system by misappropriating resources. Sherald's painting challenges this misconception and turns it on its axis. Again, like with *They Call Me Redbone, but I'd Rather Be Strawberry Shortcake*, she takes a term familiar to some and offers a revisioning. The title, then, is a double entendre subverting stereotypical narratives. Standing against a crimson background and wearing a blue dress, pearl-drop earrings and pearl necklace, a tiara, and white opera gloves, this dignified figure is an American beauty like the young woman in Anderson's photograph. Furthermore, Sherald's use of a monochromatic background in the portrait allows for a timelessness that transports the viewer from the mid-twentieth century to the present, with pit stops along the way in the Reagan era of the 1980s and the Clinton era of the 1990s.

Meanwhile, a 1958 portrait by Anderson of Douglas Burns, Alfred A. Neal, and Charles Henry Sayles sitting on a porch (fig. 2) could be a complement to the figures in Sherald's *The Boy with the Big Fish* (2016, p. 83), *Pony Boy* (2008, p. 57), and

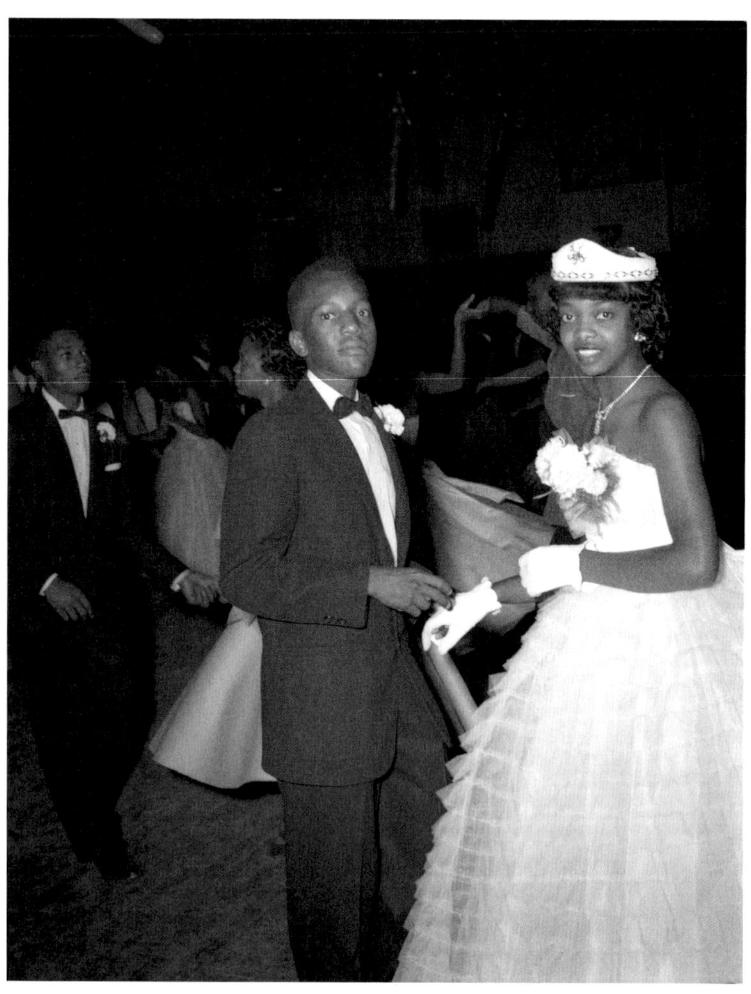

Fig. 1. Henry Clay Anderson, *Indoor portrait of young couple at Coleman High School Prom,* ca. 1960. Gelatin silver print, 5 × 4 in. (12.7 × 10.2 cm). Smithsonian National Museum of African American History and Culture, Washington, DC

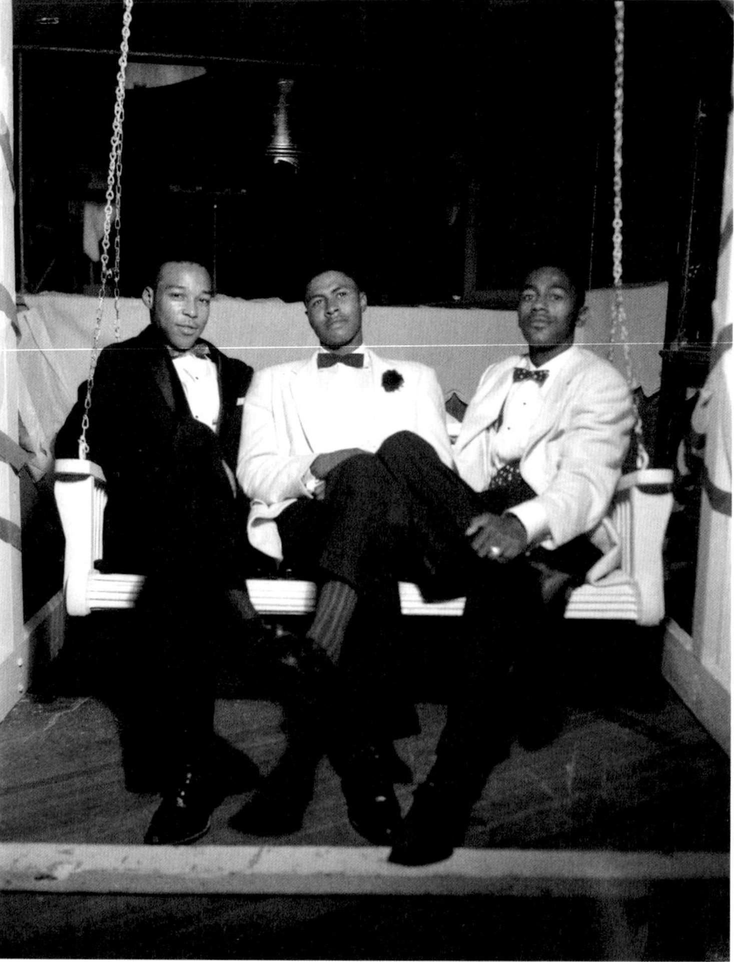

Fig. 2. Henry Clay Anderson, *Portrait of three young men sitting on a porch swing,* 1958. Gelatin silver print, 5 × 4 in. (12.7 × 10.2 cm). Smithsonian National Museum of African American History and Culture, Washington, DC

The Rabbit in the Hat (2009, p. 58) when they all get together for a night out. Sherald finds her models either by walking up to strangers to ask if she can photograph them, or, more recently, by utilizing casting companies. However, the "speculative history" and "critical fabulation," to borrow ideas posited by scholar and cultural theorist Saidiya Hartman, of pairing Sherald's work with that of someone like Anderson points to the power of the archive and offers a reminder that the past is prologue.[7] The flattening of time and space that occurs when studying a Sherald painting is in large part because the figures feel humane, familiar, and affirming.

Another part of this hypothetical consideration asks us to explore the nature of time—which is perhaps humankind's greatest remaining mystery, since it is not fixed nor does it pass uniformly. Scientists have long debated time; it is elusive. For some, it is a measurement of change; for others, the phenomenon occurs whether or not one sees change happening. These enduring ideas of time, space, and place appear often in discussions of African American art, particularly within Afrofuturism, a perspective that "seeks to weave together contemporary notions of freedom with both past experiences and future possibilities."[8] Within the context of Sherald's work, the concept of time and Afrofuturism applies to her approach to painting. Her canvas becomes a portal for space travel. The application of grayscale to create skin tones that are juxtaposed against a bold and vibrant full-color palette, for instance, challenges the limiting strictures of race, class, and gender—and their sociocultural historical underpinnings—while simultaneously serving as an homage to early photography. Her work, therefore, offers an imaginary place and time where the social construction of race vis-à-vis skin tone is not paramount.

Time, as we know, is not a renewable resource. Birth and death, past and present—these things are deeply interconnected and also apparent in an Amy Sherald painting. As a result her art feels urgent and ageless. It interrogates contemporary conversation and notions of time, as seen most evidently in a painting literally titled *The Boy with No Past* (2014, p. 67), or in the tender work *Planes, Rockets, and the Spaces in Between* (2018, p. 95), where one subject in a cool, bright, multicolored summer dress stares at the viewer while the other gazes at a rocket ship launching into outer space—possibly reminding the viewer "there are Black people in the future."[9] Moreover, many of her paintings engender nostalgia and moments of respite that honor the beauty and power of a Black quotidian existence (either experienced or longed for), as seen in *The Bathers* (2015, pp. 74–75), *Precious Jewels by the Sea* (2019, pp. 106–7), *As American as Apple Pie* (2021, p. 123), and *A Midsummer Afternoon Dream* (2021, pp. 118–19). Through her meticulous paintings, Sherald creates liminal spaces that offer viewers an unparalleled chance to travel beyond the limitations of history and the constrictions of the corporeal into a space of unrequited possibility.

In some of Sherald's newer works, while her impeccable precision in painting persists, idyllic settings—of the sort that could have been plucked from a family scrapbook or a futuristic fantasy of a brighter tomorrow—replace the clean backgrounds around the central figure. The very nature of their monumental scale (re)claims space that for centuries of art history has been contested and denied to certain people. *A God Blessed Land (Empire of Dirt)* (2022, pp. 130–31) serves as such an example. Instead of the languid settings of the farm paintings and romanticized depictions of peasant life often associated with artists like Vincent Van Gogh (fig. 3) or Jean-François Millet, Sherald has created a scene where a Black male farmer is centered, self-possessed, and standing atop a tractor. Arms folded, his forehand rests on his knee. This bearded man, with his short Afro, perfectly cuffed denim overalls, clean white T-shirt, and brown boots, meets the viewer with an assured and direct gaze. The composition presents a contemporary sensibility to a figure who looks as if he could be posing for a Ralph Lauren photo shoot. The pink steering wheel, a stark contrast to the huge black-and-yellow tires and green tractor body emblazoned with "John Deere" provides a sense of modern-day whimsy. Thin, black-and-white rope that nearly fades into the powder-blue sky penetrates the background as if it is a reminder of the real-life boundaries and restrictions imposed on Black farmers. A delicately placed red tie also peeks from the left edge of the canvas—perhaps a warning sign to "not pass."

In addition to serving as an homage to Sherald's upbringing in the South, where farming and landownership by Black farmers has a long and storied history, *A God Blessed Land (Empire of Dirt)* acknowledges a past and present where the land has been a deeply contested terrain. Generations of African Americans who endured chattel slavery and postbellum sharecropping, coupled with current-day African American farmers who are being systemically excluded from federal programs, have made Black people's relationship with the land complicated, and farming a precarious

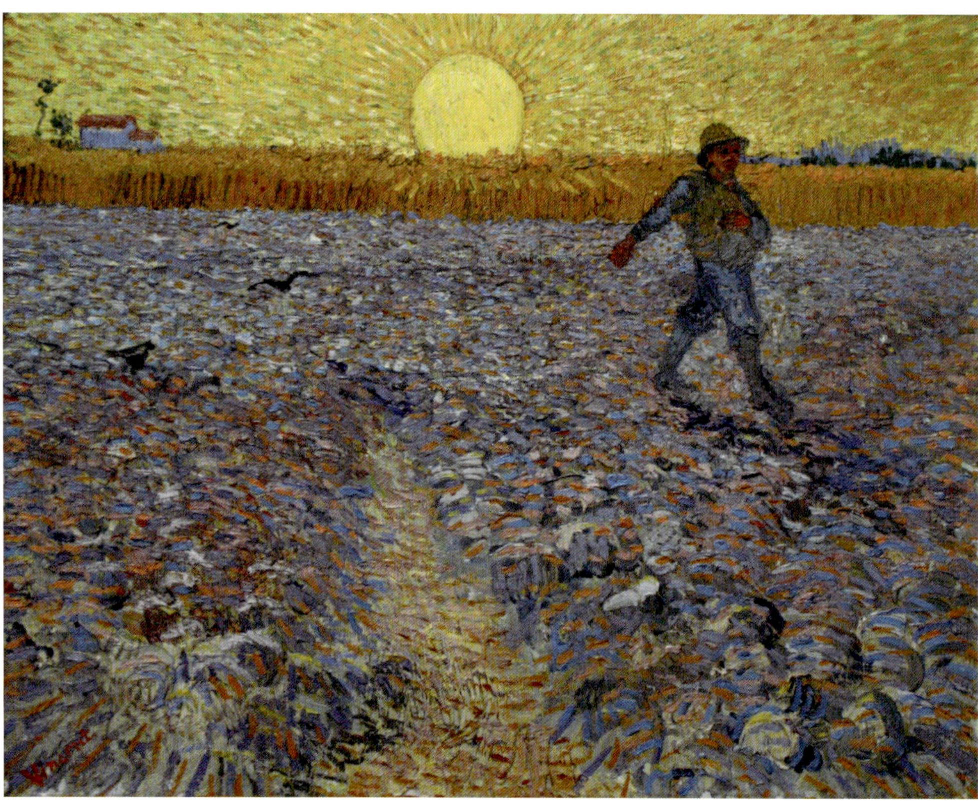

Fig. 3. Vincent Van Gogh, *The Sower*, 1888. Oil on canvas, 25¼ x 31⅝ in. (64.2 × 80.3 cm). Kröller-Müller Museum, Otterlo, the Netherlands

proposition. However, as Sherald explains, "Farming has been a birthright, and food and farming have long been a form of resistance and ritual."[10] By creating this large-scale painting that visually inserts Black farmers into this narrative, Sherald makes the viewer reckon with historical absences. Moreover, the contemporary styling offers an imaginary or aspirational future where the Black farmer is "king of the (dirt) hill": proud, self-assured, and full of swagger.

Portraiture, a genre called "an exhausted form" by some, traditionally has been used to represent a niche of an elite class of individuals where privilege and exclusion are its refrain.[11] As the poet Elizabeth Alexander notes, "The black body has been misrepresented, absented, distorted, rendered invisible, exaggerated, made monstrous in the Western visual imagination."[12] Fortunately, many contemporary portraitists are offering countervailing narratives to address this long reign of absence, Sherald notwithstanding. By deliberately centering the Black body (although not placing emphasis on various skin tones within the Black community) with dignity, power, and grace, and while honoring her Southern identity, Sherald acts like a woman on a wire—successfully walking the tightrope between past, present, and future. Her appreciation for history in all its murkiness allows Sherald to dream a brighter, more humane tomorrow. And her keen awareness of the precarity of time has resulted in bountiful, enduring paintings that situate Sherald within the cannon of art history and make her one of the finest painters of the modern era. By positioning the figurative subject as not only out front but also monumental, her portraits become timeless, transgressive acts that expand the conversation beyond the strictures of the canvas.

NOTES

1. Isaac Newton, *Newton's Principa: The Mathematical Principles of Natural Philosophy*, trans. Andrew Motte (1726; New York: Daniel Adee, 1846), 77.

2. bell hooks, "Being the Subject of Art," in *Art on My Mind: Visual Politics* (New York: The New Press, 1995), 133.

3. Amy Sherald, in *Art in the Twenty-First Century*, season 11, "Everyday Icons," aired April 7, 2023, on PBS, https://art21.org/watch/art-in-the-twenty-first-century/s11/everyday-icons/.

4. Amy Sherald, in "60 Seconds with Amy Sherald," The Columbus Museum, May 20, 2020, video, 2:13 min., https://youtube/ZNlVZAT2Xqk?si=V9FzoKbW-mK7FRTk.

5. Aldon Morris, "American Negro at Paris, 1900," in *W. E. B. Du Bois's Data Portraits: Visualizing Black America; The Color Line at the Turn of the Twentieth Century*, ed. Whitney Battle-Baptiste and Britt Rusert (Amherst, MA: W. E. B. Du Bois Center at the University of Massachusetts Amherst, 2018), 27.

6. "Oh Freedom! Rev. Henry Clay Anderson," Smithsonian American Art Museum, accessed April 25, 2024, https://americanart.si.edu/education/oh-freedom/rev-henry-clay-anderson.

7. Saidiya Hartman, "The Anarchy of Colored Girls Assembled in a Riotous Manner," *South Atlantic Quarterly* 117, no. 3 (July 2018): 465–90.

8. Kevin M. Strait and Kinshasha Holman Conwill, eds., *Afrofuturism: A History of Black Futures* (Washington, DC: Smithsonian Books, 2023), 11.

9. This phrase was part of a project developed between 2012 and 2020 by interdisciplinary artist and cultural producer Alisha B. Wormsley that was inspired by Afrofuturist artists' and writers' reclamation of space, time, and a rightful place for Black bodies and Black communities.

10. Amy Sherald, in Jo Lawson-Tancred, "'As an Empath, Portraiture Works for Me': Amy Sherald on How She Makes Space for Black Histories in Her First U.K. Show," *Artnet*, October 11, 2022, https://news.artnet.com/art-world/profile-amy-sherald-uk-show-fall-2022-2187619.

11. Kerr Houston, "A Sense of Human Connection: The Work of Amy Sherald," *Bmore Art: A Journal of Art + Ideas*, no. 5 (Spring 2018): 13.

12. Elizabeth Alexander, *The Black Interior: Essays* (St. Paul, MN: Graywolf Press, 2001), 5.

Beyond Flesh

DARIO CALMESE

I was given a thorn in my flesh, a messenger of Satan, to torment me. Three times I pleaded with the Lord to take it away from me. But he said to me, "My grace is sufficient for you, for my power is made perfect in weakness." Therefore I will boast all the more gladly about my weaknesses, so that Christ's power may rest on me. That is why, for Christ's sake, I delight in weaknesses, in insults, in hardships, in persecutions, in difficulties. For when I am weak, then I am strong.
—2 Corinthians 12:7–10

Amy Sherald wants us to get out of our flesh.

"A doughnut? They're vegan." Sitting across from each other at a small, round table under the double-height concrete ceiling of her cavernous studio, Amy shares her exquisite taste for gluten-free pastries along with an even more exquisite taste for life. And by "exquisite," I don't mean fanciful or elegiac. I mean the manifestation of an inner, subconscious desire for an encounter that will make your mouth water; that will break your heart open. I'm speaking of the *sublime*: the overwhelming and terrifying awe one feels in the face of ineffable greatness, and the resultant residue, after having survived the encounter. Making it to the other side of one's confrontation with terror? That's called grace. The residue? We call that beauty.

Amy has been playing life on hard mode.

Years waiting tables post Clark Atlanta University. The loss of her brother at the age of thirty-seven to lung cancer. The religion of her youth, now classified in some circles as a cult. Writing grant applications in her hospital bed while recovering from heart transplant surgery in order to afford the now necessary lifetime supply of anti-rejection pills. And she made it to the other side. She survived the encounter. Her exquisite sojourn of grace—what one would call, in the gospel tradition, "trials and tribulations"—becomes our revelation of beauty; artifacts of surrender.

"I listen to Goapele's 'Closer to my dreams' for ten minutes every morning," she explains. Noted.

We're now standing in front of a corkboard full of thumbtacked sheets of paper printed with various ephemera; some serving as references for future compositions ("I use photography as a sort of sketchbook"), others existing to simply "think about." These motley collections of references serve as focusing devices for thought and reflection over time; let's call them thematic mandalas. One image in particular catches my eye. It's an archival image of one of the eight stainless-steel eagles that protrude from the sixty-first floor of the Chrysler Building in New York City. It hasn't made it into a formal work; and yet, its influence resonates throughout her oeuvre.

With the sprawling scape of Manhattan Island and the East River beneath, the polished steel eagle head reigns prominent in the foreground; its welding scars create a Frankenstein-like quality in this American symbol of freedom. Hollow. Cold. Pieced together. A stand-in for American mythmaking, historical narrative, and state power, this static and lifeless eagle—unlike its natural counterpart—cannot soar high, it cannot see far, and it will never touch down onto the land of the free and the home of the brave; and well, maybe that's the point. Even its national anthem, as the character Belize states in Tony Kushner's *Angels in America* (1991), "set the word 'free' to a note so high nobody can reach it. That was deliberate." Indeed, sixty-one stories is pretty damn high. Empire and capitalism are sustained by the hodgepodge externalization of what we already possess inside of us.

However, this is not Amy's American vision. Far from lofty national expressions of freedom, her subjects offer us the only true freedom guaranteed to any of us . . . the freedom to be(come). Clad in garments selected by (and at times designed by) the artist, her portrait subjects reside fully within themselves, often returning the viewer's gaze with a look of soft internal comfort, groundedness, and self-assurance. There is no pretense here. No unreachable heights. One recalls the gazes of Renty and his daughter Delia, of Jem and Fassena, models selected by nineteenth-century Harvard professor Louis Agassiz to prove his theory of polygenesis (tl;dr different races were different species). However, their piercing gazes defied the assignment, reversed the power dynamic, and reclaimed their internal agency; their ground of being.[1] In Sherald's portraits, the edges of their gazes have softened, lightened, and diffused over time, the essential will-to-be remaining.

Whether perched on the summit of a playground slide (*Kingdom*, 2022, p. 135), sitting atop a flange at a construction site (*If You Surrendered to the Air, You Could Ride It*, 2019, p. 105), or dipping a lover in a kissing embrace (*For Love, and for Country*, 2022, p. 125), the people in Sherald's paintings repopulate the archive of American iconography for a new generation of citizens, and from the point of view of those who were not always constitutionally seen as such.

> God created black people and black people created style.
> —George C. Wolfe, *The Colored Museum*

Far from the reaches of frivolity—a domain to which fashion is usually relegated—Black Americans have continually engaged the fashion object beyond its utilitarian function into a device of "self-expression, identity, and self-authorship," as stated by scholar Van Dyk Lewis.[2] As a form of identification, self-actualization, and agency, Sherald's vibrant and sumptuous portraits reveal swirling and fantastical interiorities that cannot help but burst forth onto the skin. Whether a young woman in a simple polka-dot belted dress (*The Girl Next Door*, 2019, p. 110) or a young man sporting a bowler hat stacked high with peonies and roses (*Try on dreams until I find the one that fits me. They all fit me.*, 2017, p. 92), Amy breaks the fourth wall of the subject's imagination; transforming the viewer's passive gaze and inviting active participation. What can we imagine *together*?

But these are not imaginary people, oh no. Beneath the layers of cloth lie real flesh, blood, and bone; actively churning, evolving, and expanding in real time. And herein lies the beauty of a rendered figure: it holds the paradox of both aliveness and effigy; suspending time just enough for it to disappear altogether. Past, present, and future collapse into an eternal now; bolstered on all sides by what has been and what will be. And by engaging the fashion object in this way, Ms. Sherald becomes an architect, constructing a visual dialogue about space; the space between skin and cloth, and the space between that cloth and the viewer's gaze. How tenuous is the distance between who we are, who we want to be, and how we are perceived? The fashion object is transubstantiated into a semipermeable membrane between the gaze and the content it holds.

> But certainly for the present age, which prefers the sign to the thing signified, the copy to the original, fancy to reality, the appearance to the essence, . . . illusion only is sacred, truth profane.
> —Ludwig Feuerbach, *The Essence of Christianity*

The flesh, too, fails to escape this conundrum. Like the cacophony of meaning mapped onto the welded steel eagle atop the Chrysler Building and tacked onto Amy's studio reference board, we have been conditioned to confuse the sign for what is signified; content with the illusion of appearances. Although our flesh—a carbon raiment for our spiritual self—is merely a thin membrane between our interiority and the expanse of the universe, we insist on dragging our pasts with us—individually and collectively—visually forcing one another into ill-fitting clothes, unaware that what appears to be a current state of being is simply old news. We greet each other as corpses, unaware of the unfolding before us. Luckily, Amy's work does the heavy lifting for us.

Rendered in tones of gray, inspired by the faded black-and-white images found in her childhood home, Amy dissolves the flesh and removes the sign, allowing us space to contemplate the ever-evolving essence of what is signified; that which is self-signified. Although the figure remains, the instantly recognizable tonality of flesh in Amy's work forces the tense of the viewer's present projections back to the past; back to the what-has-been, or what-I-was-told-has-been, or, in the case of Breonna Taylor (*Breonna Taylor*, 2020, p. 117), what-could-have-been. Identity is not something you are but something you hold, something you wear. Labels like wife, mother, Black, Asian, American, lawyer, cisgendered . . . all exist outside of the self—like clothing on garment racks—and will remain for others to assume and try on after the demise of our mortal coil.

Every man has a place
In his heart, there's a space
And the world can't erase his fantasies
—Earth, Wind, and Fire, "Fantasy"

As I make my way back to the train station, I contemplate Amy's insistence that we "get out of our flesh," replete with biblical undertones. It strikes me that in the twelfth chapter of 2nd Corinthians, the thorn Paul speaks of is the flesh itself; a sign mistaken for what embodiment signifies. What becomes possible when our identities, both assumed and projected, are stripped away from us and rendered in the past tense? Well . . . everything. And therein lies the terror. And the awe. When the membrane that falls between the self and the universe is dissolved, one's imagination becomes intergalactic; time dissolves and space does indeed become the place. Plenty good room indeed.

By evoking the Black body as a site for exploring what's on the other side of confronting the terror of becoming, Amy Sherald provides a window into the beauty that awaits us all; we just have to trust that grace will see us through the resistance and the machinations of our reluctance. Because Black imagination is not tied to the flesh but is a way of navigating existence; expanding beyond what is and existing as the interstitial space in which all that is resides.

NOTES

1. See Ilisa Barbash, Molly Rogers, and Deborah Willis, eds., *To Make Their Own Way in the World: The Enduring Legacy of the Zealy Daguerreotypes* (Cambridge, MA: Peabody Museum Press, 2020).

2. See Van Dyk Lewis, "Dilemmas in African Diaspora Fashion," *Fashion Theory* 7, no. 2 (2003): 163–90.

Plates

Hangman, 2007

Oil on canvas, 100 × 67 in. (254 × 170.2 cm)

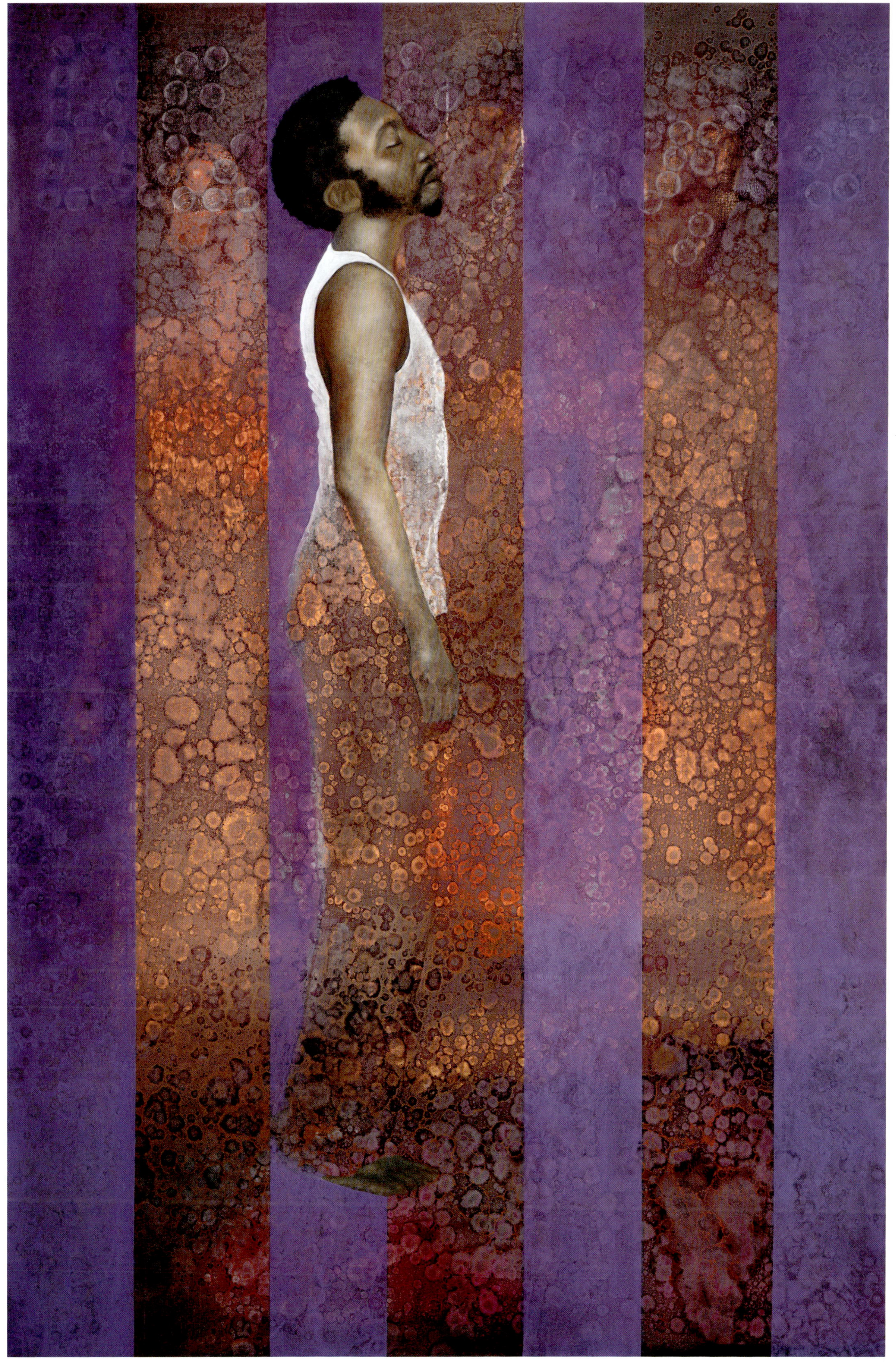

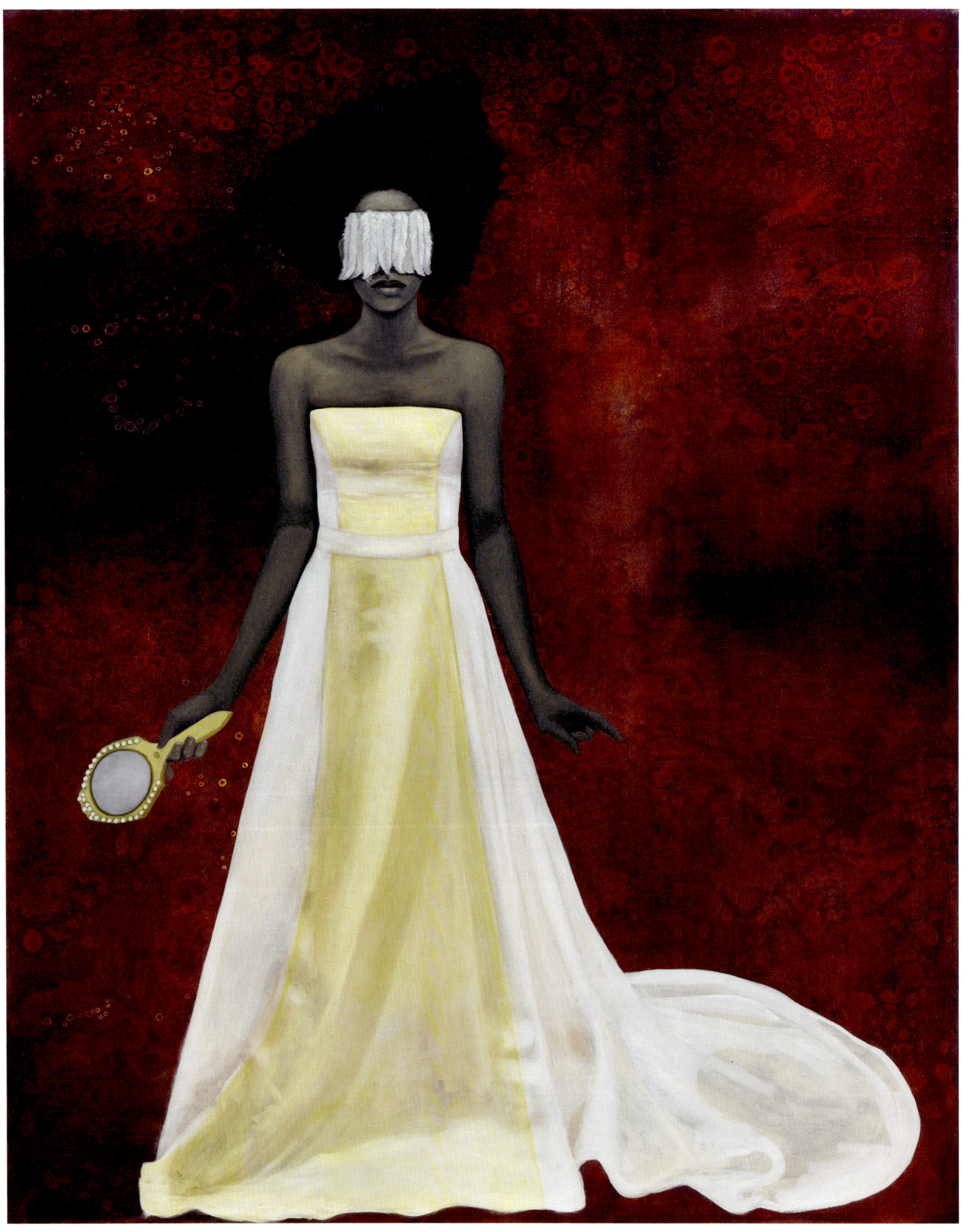

The Fairest of the Not So Fair, 2008
Oil on canvas, 54 × 43 in. (137.2 × 109.2 cm)

OPPOSITE
Puppetmaster, 2008
Oil on canvas, 72 × 51 in. (182.9 × 129.5 cm)

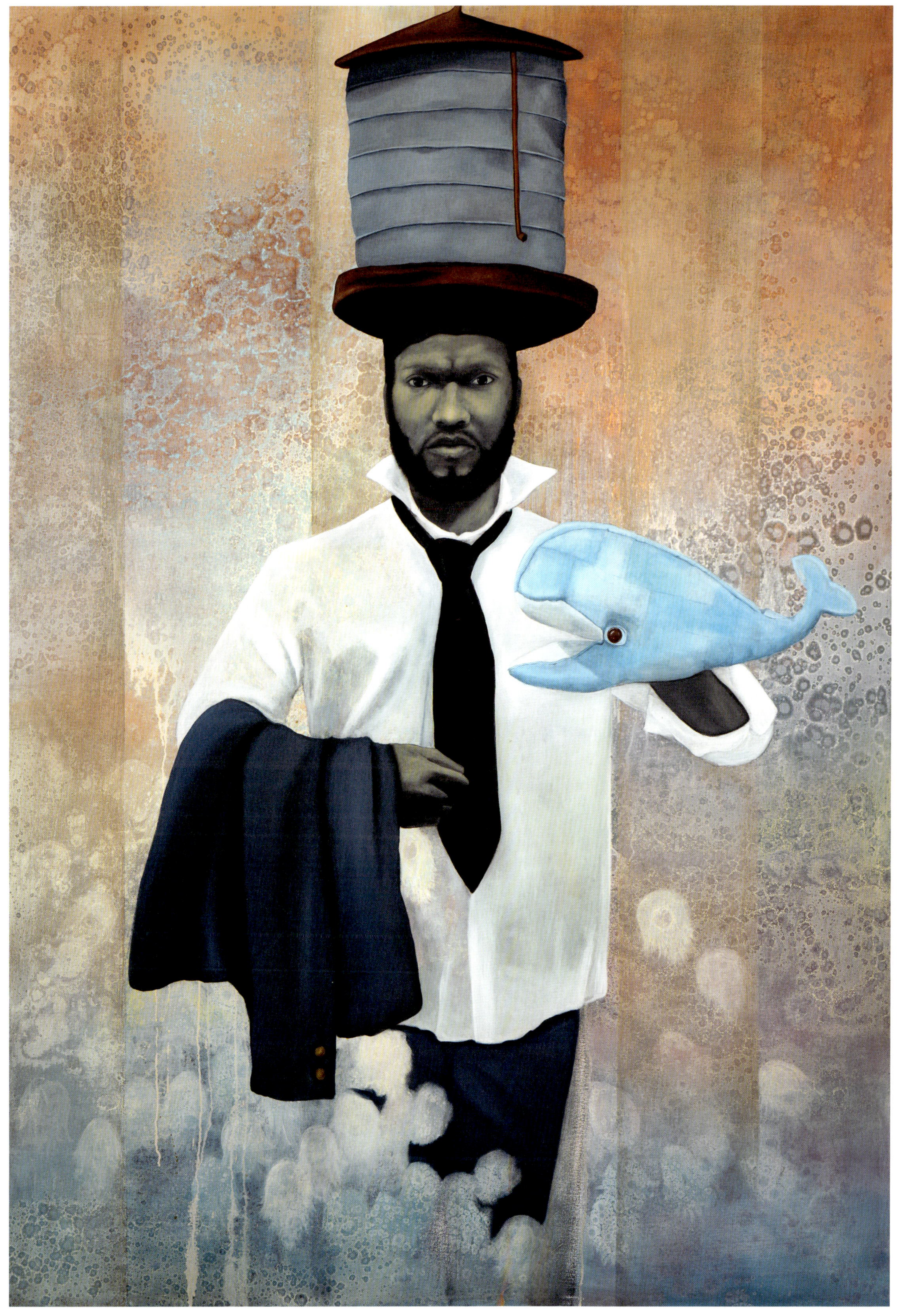

Equilibrium, 2008

Oil on canvas, 100 × 67 in. (254 × 170.2 cm)

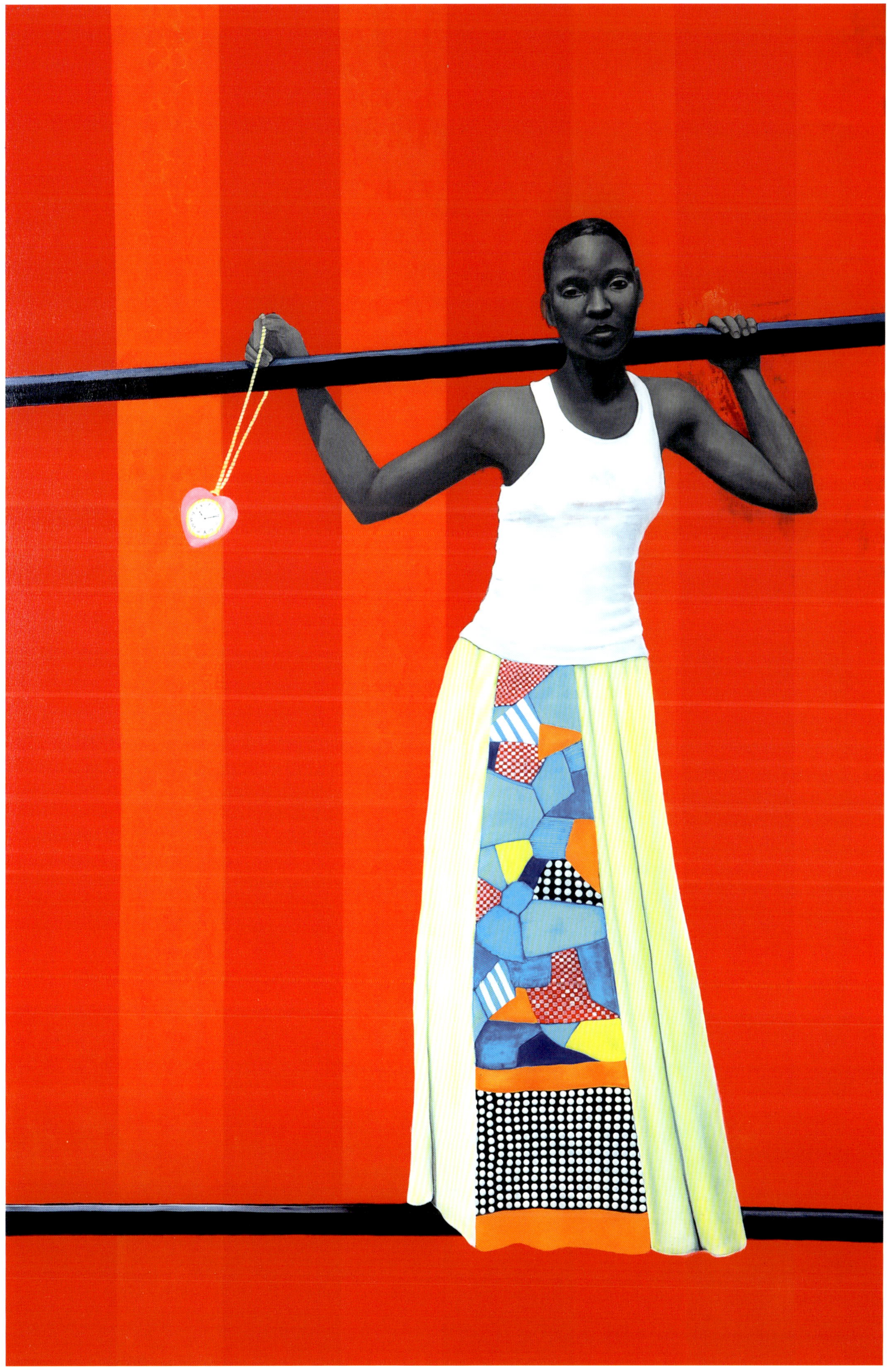

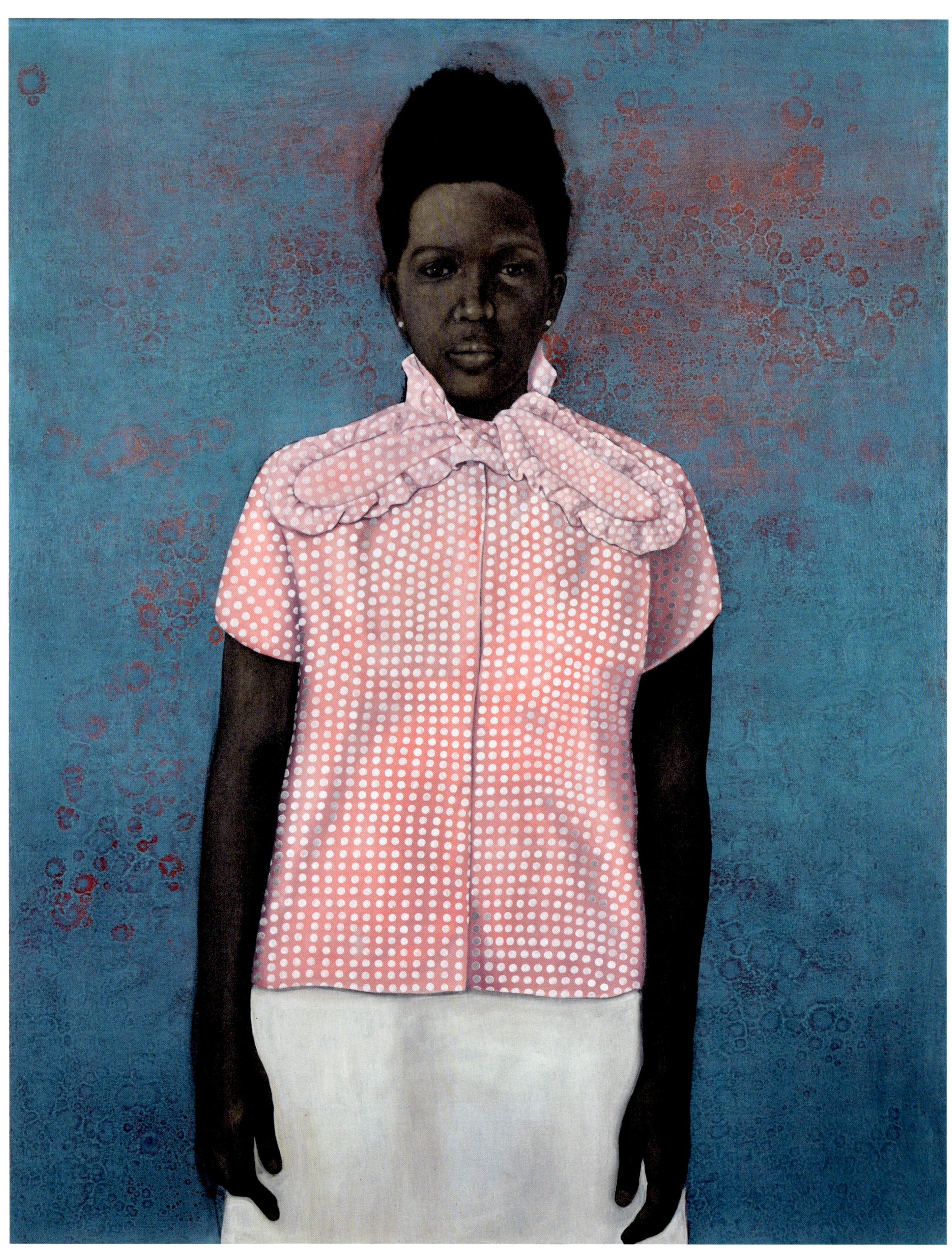

Well Prepared and Maladjusted, 2008
Oil on canvas, 54 × 43 in. (137.2 × 109.2 cm)

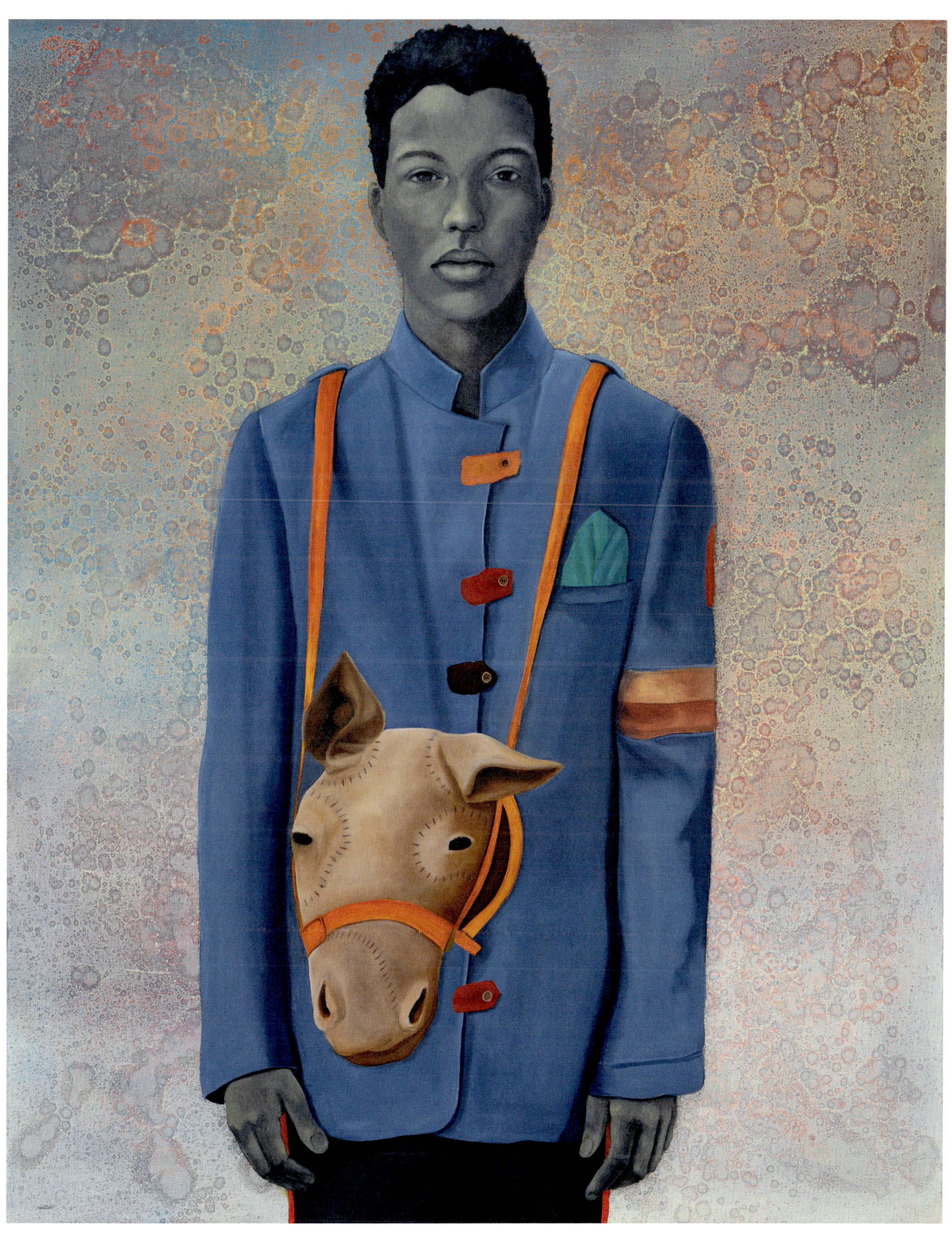

Pony Boy, 2008

Oil on canvas, 54 × 43 in. (137.2 × 109.2 cm)

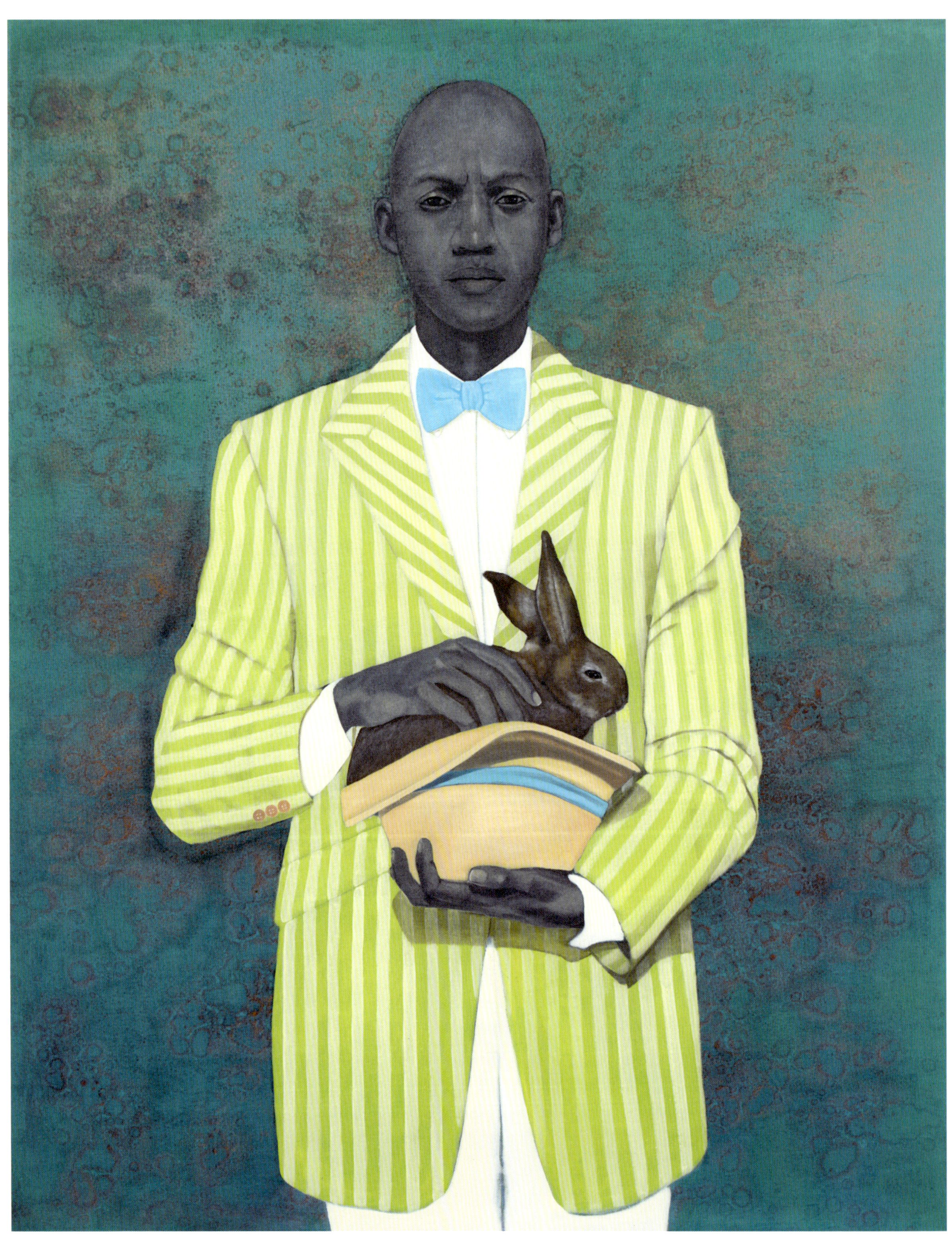

The Rabbit in the Hat, 2009

Oil on canvas, 54 × 43 in. (137.2 × 109.2 cm)

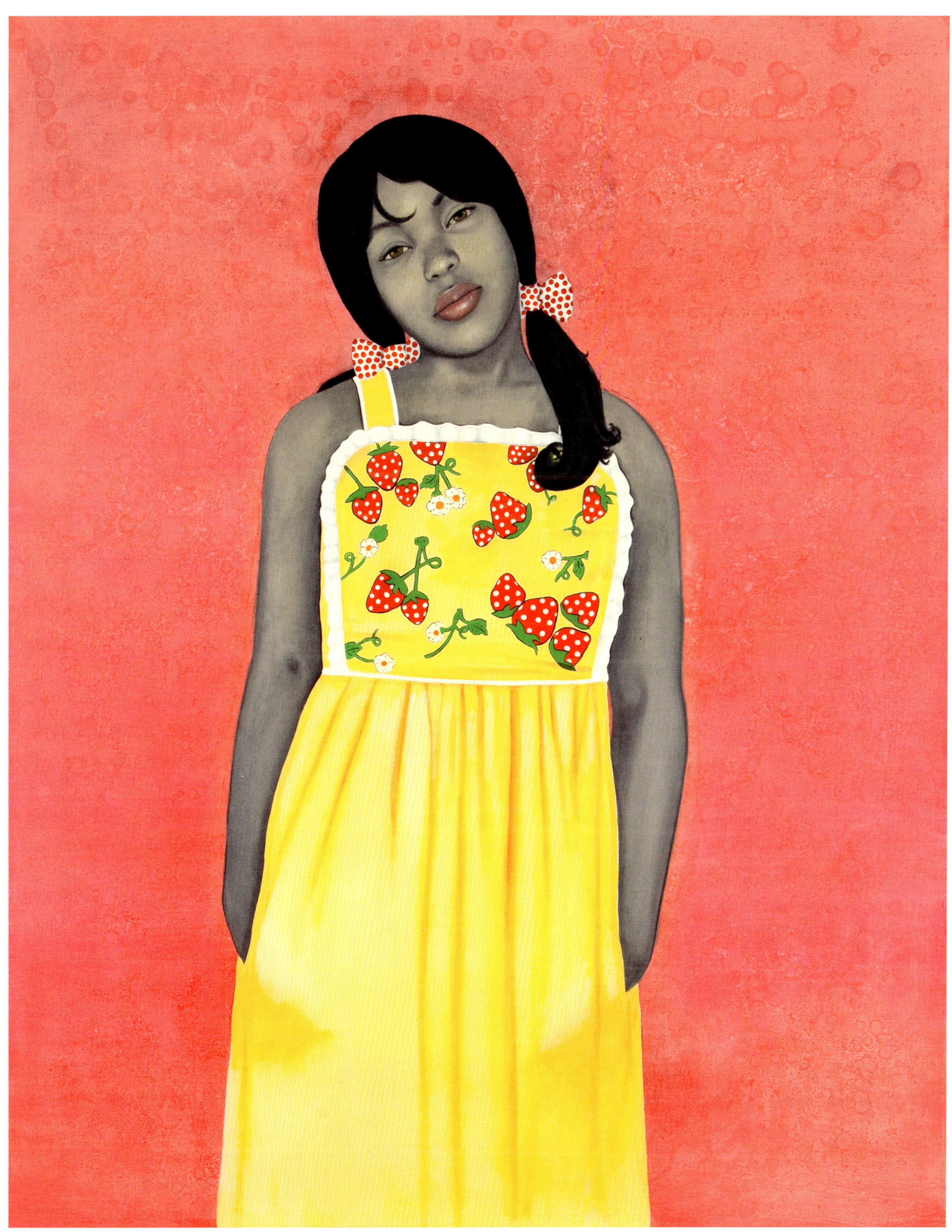

They Call Me Redbone, but I'd Rather Be Strawberry Shortcake, 2009
Oil on canvas, 54 × 43 in. (137.2 × 109.2 cm)

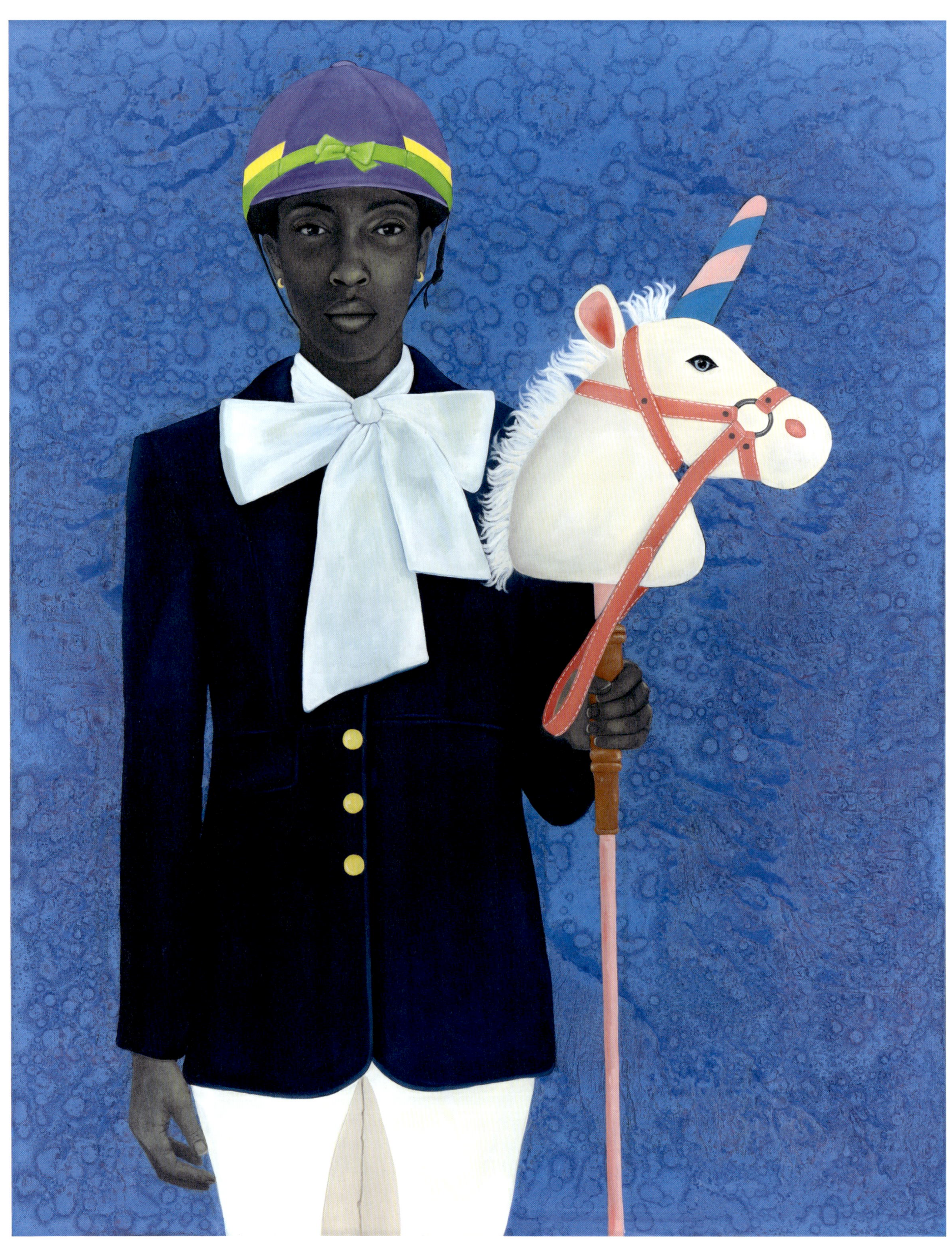

It Made Sense . . . Mostly in Her Mind, 2011
Oil on canvas, 54 × 43 in. (137.2 × 109.2 cm)

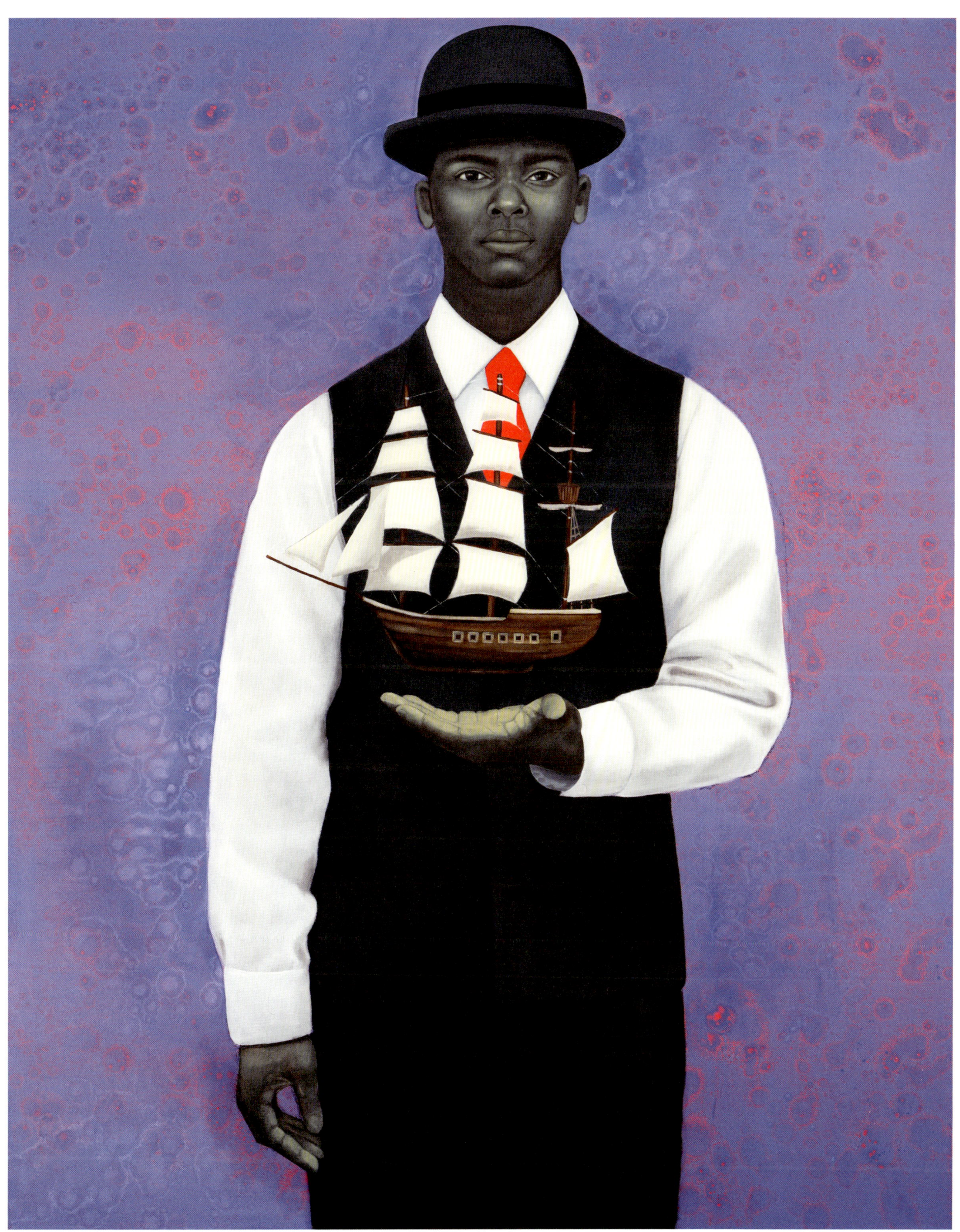

Guide Me No More, 2011

Oil on canvas, 54 × 43 in. (137.2 × 109.2 cm)

Welfare Queen, 2012

Oil on canvas, 54 × 43 in. (137.2 × 109.2 cm)

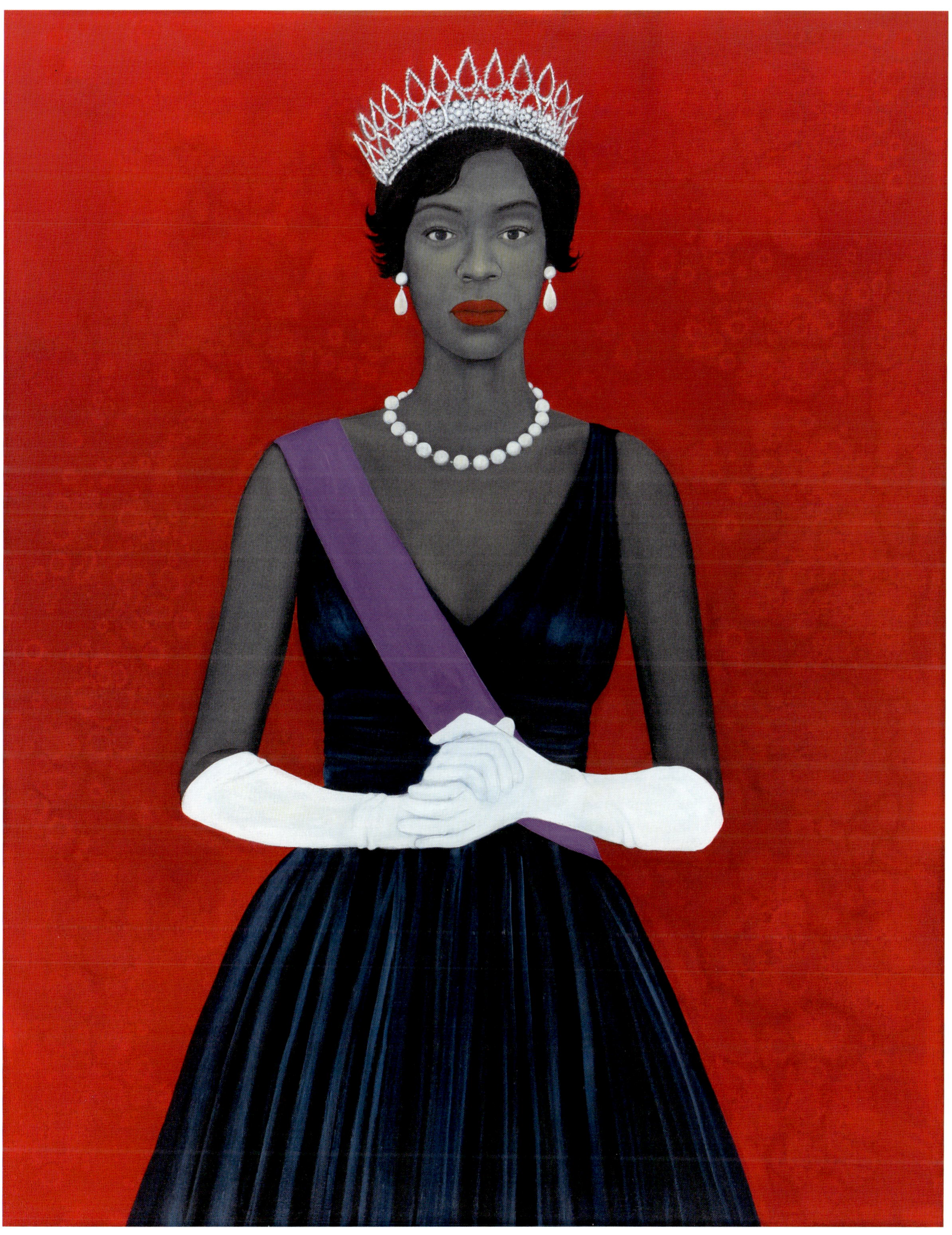

Grand Dame Queenie, 2012

Oil on canvas, 54 × 43 in. (137.2 × 109.2 cm)

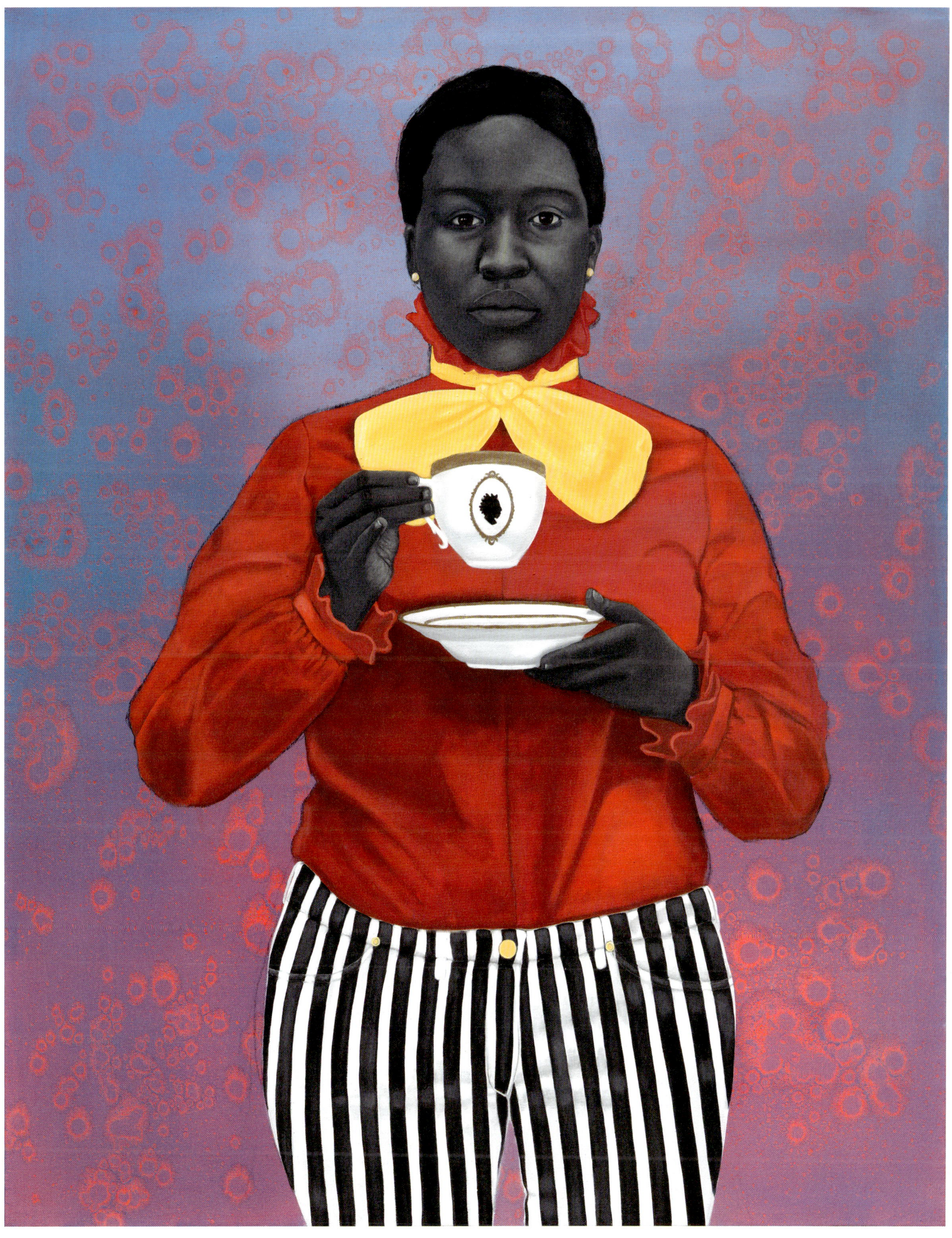

The Boy with No Past, 2014

Oil on canvas, 54 × 43 in. (137.2 × 109.2 cm)

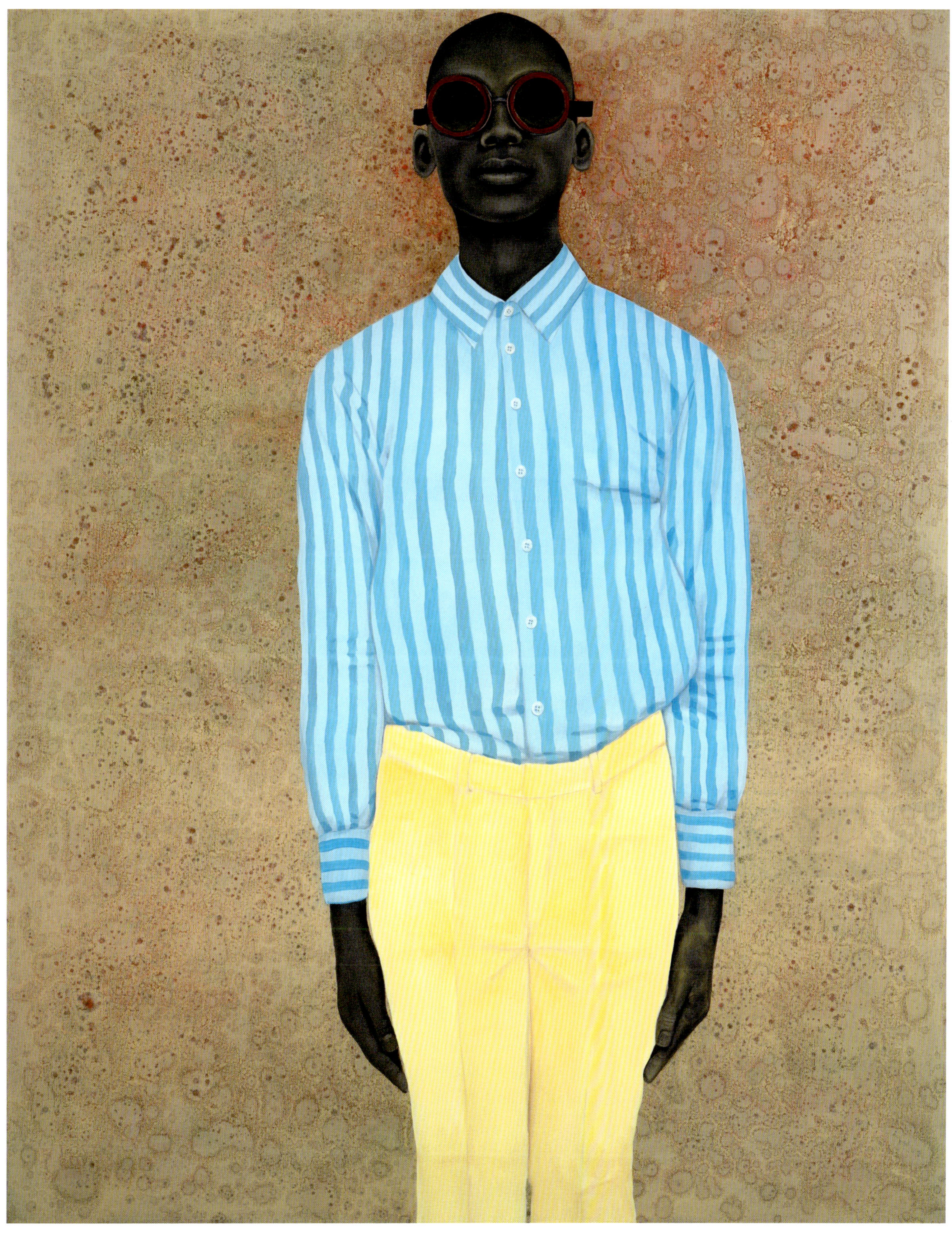

Miss Everything (Unsuppressed Deliverance), 2014

Oil on canvas, 54 × 43 in. (137.2 × 109.2 cm)

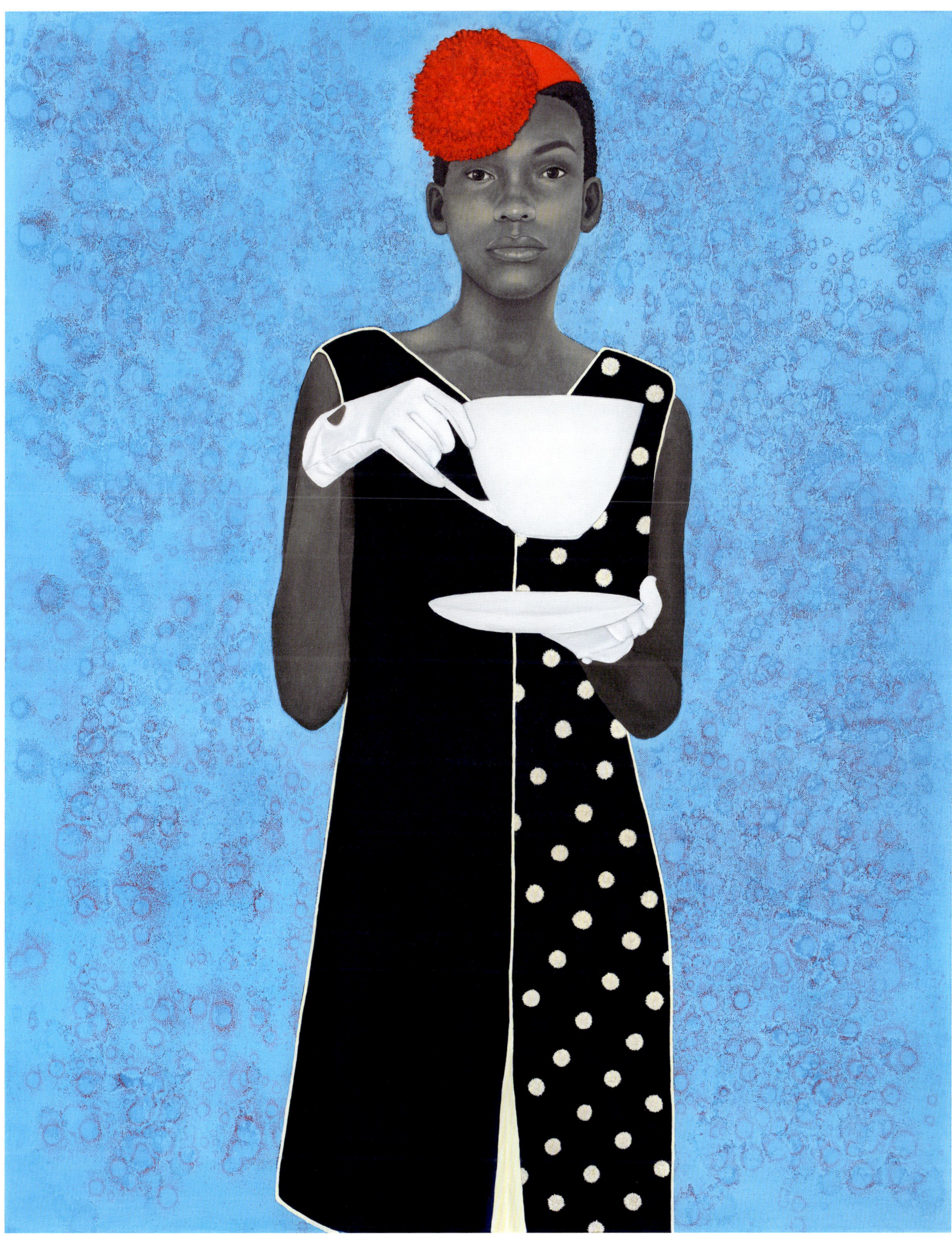

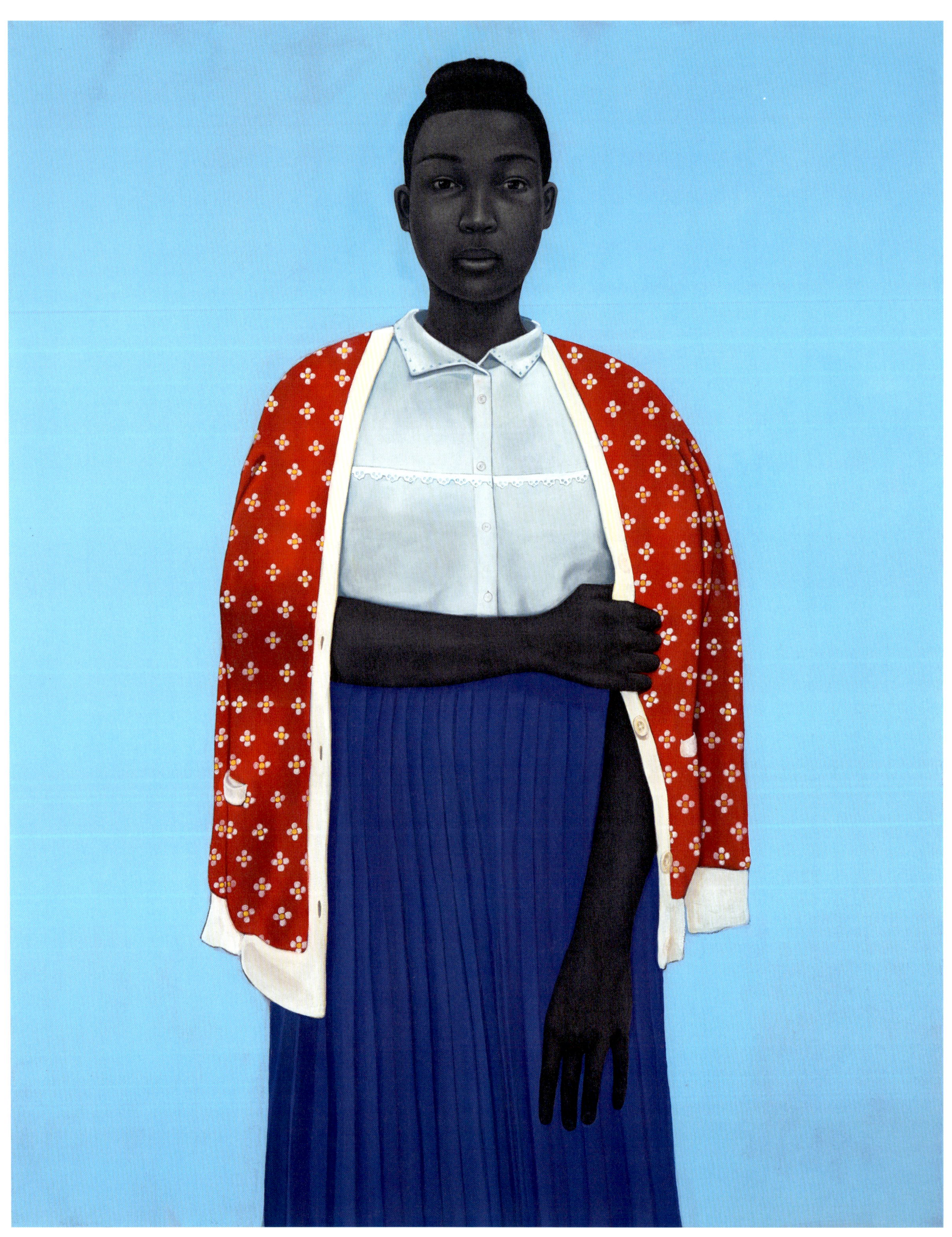

Fact was she knew more about them than she knew about herself, having never had the map to discover what she was like, 2014
Oil on canvas, 54 × 43 in. (137.2 × 109.2 cm)

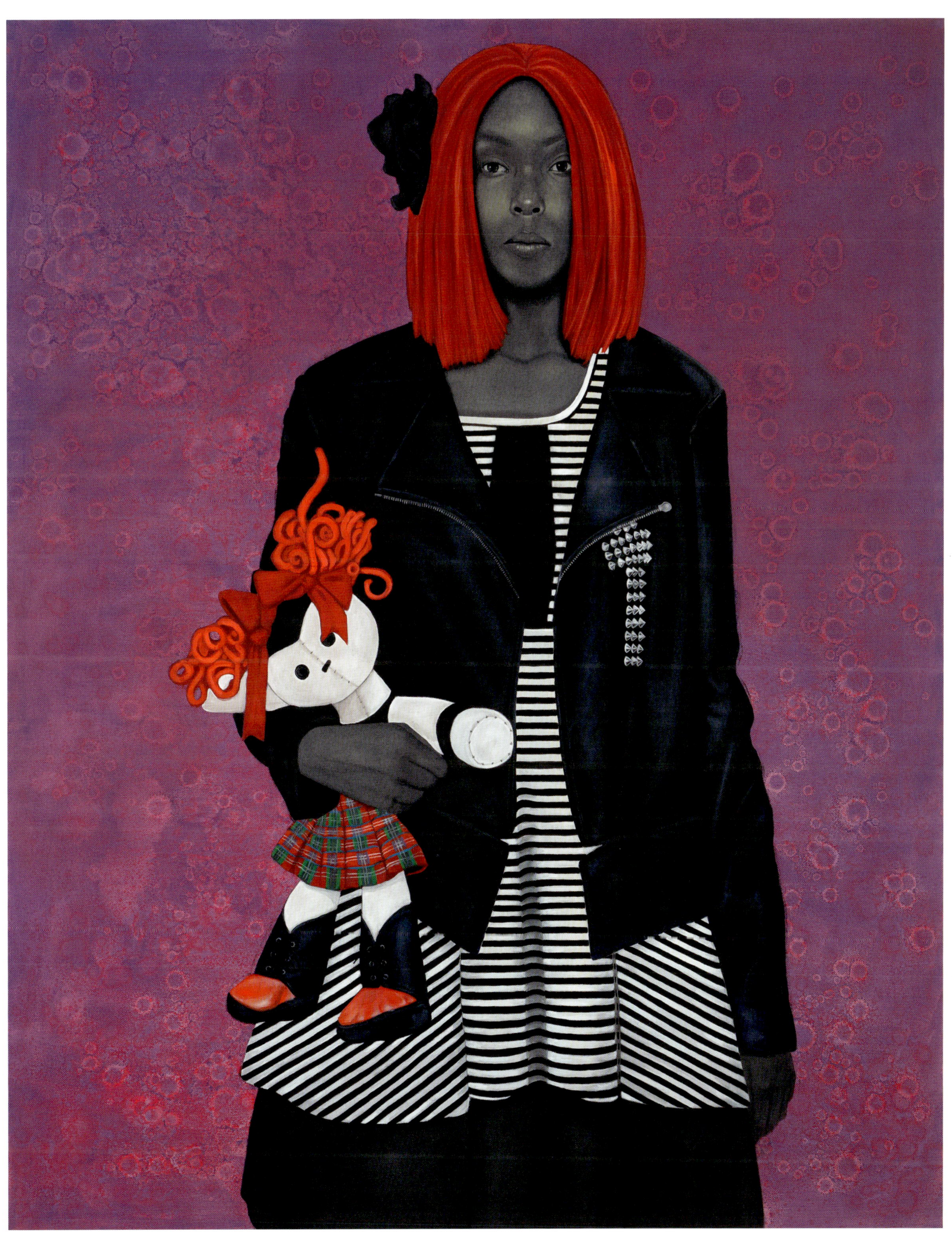

Freeing herself was one thing, taking ownership of that freed self was another, 2013
Oil on canvas, 54 × 43 in. (137.2 × 109.2 cm)

Saint Woman, 2015

Oil on canvas, 54 × 43 in. (137.2 × 109.2 cm)

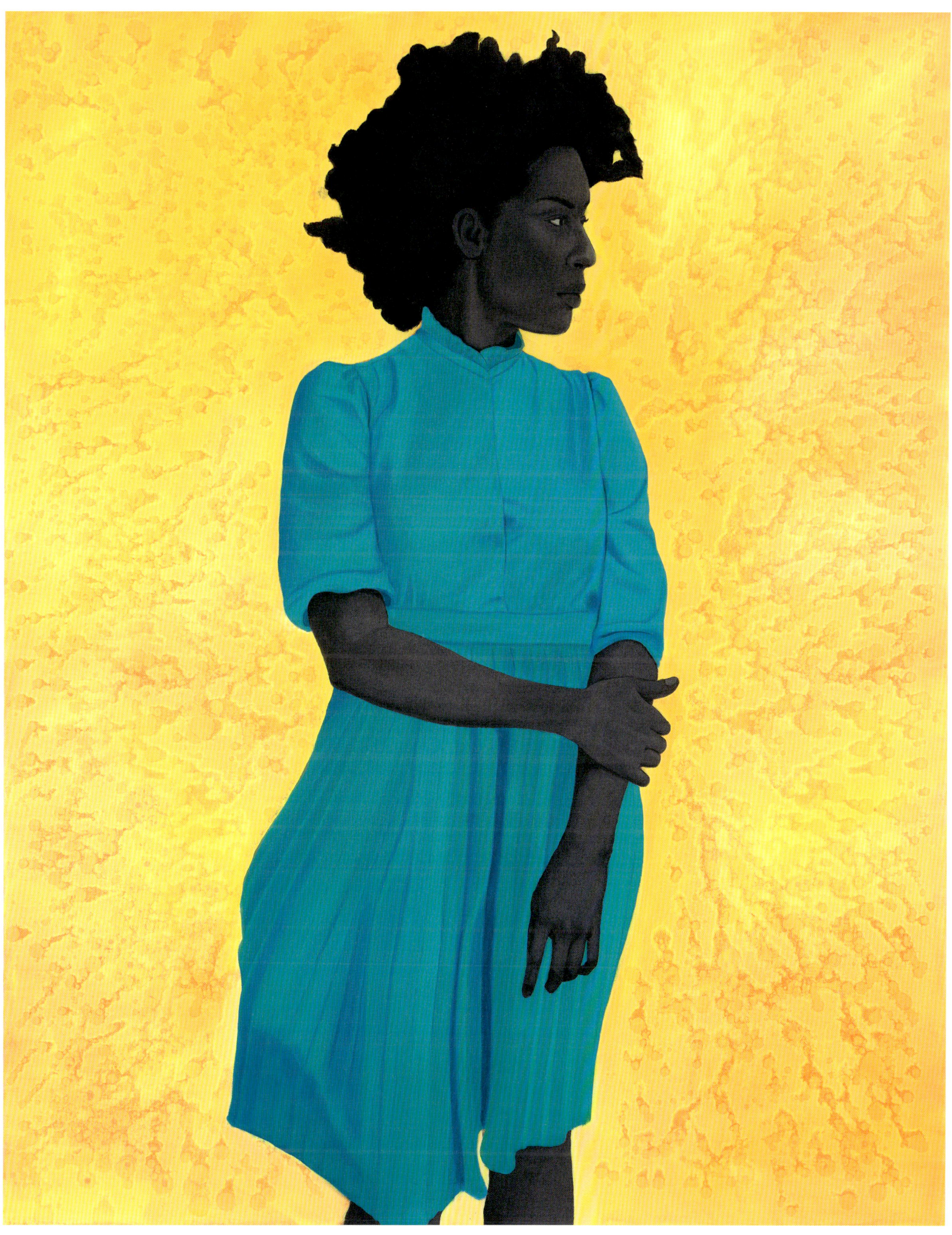

The Bathers, 2015
Oil on canvas, $72\frac{1}{8}$ × 67 in. (183.2 × 170.2 cm)

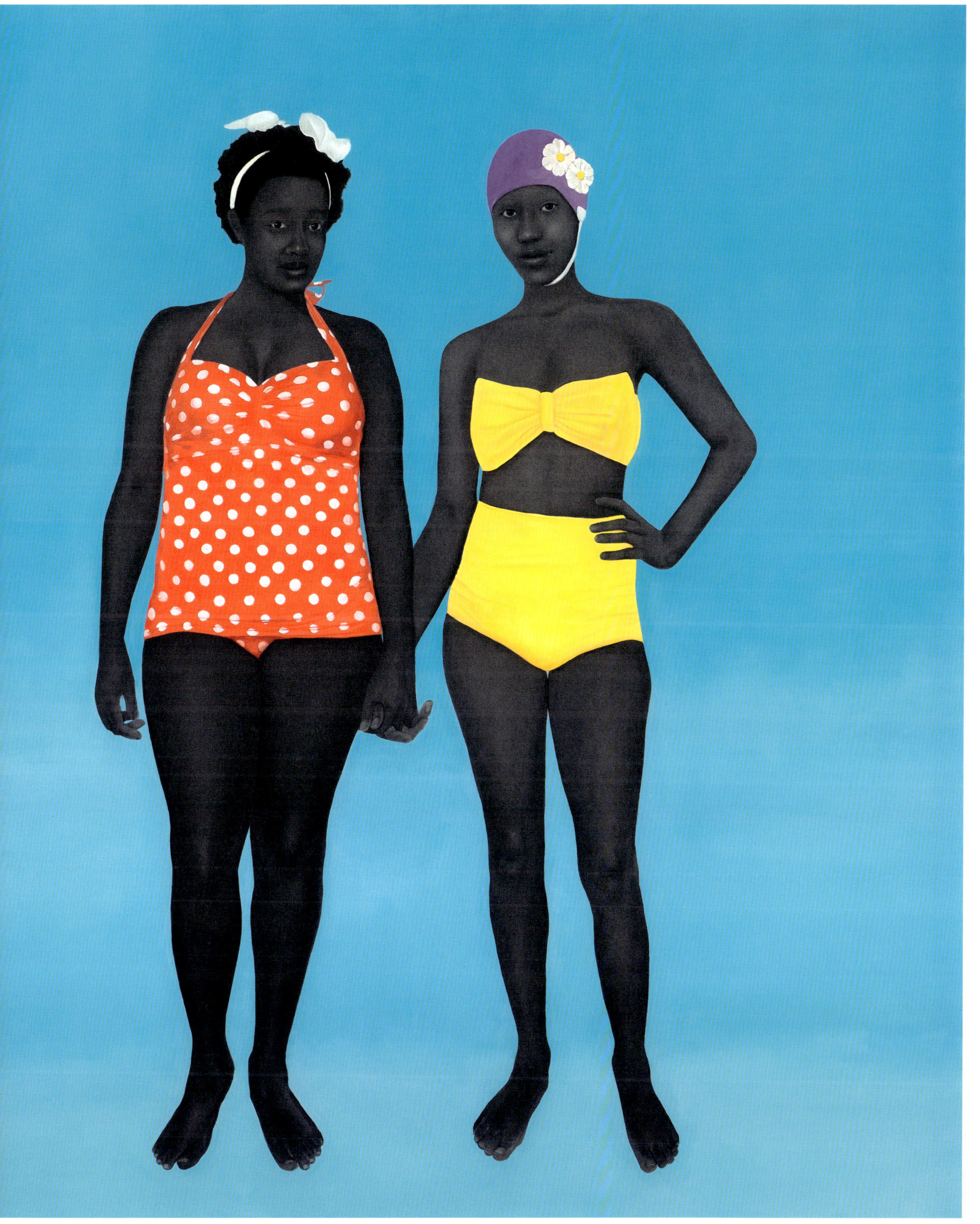

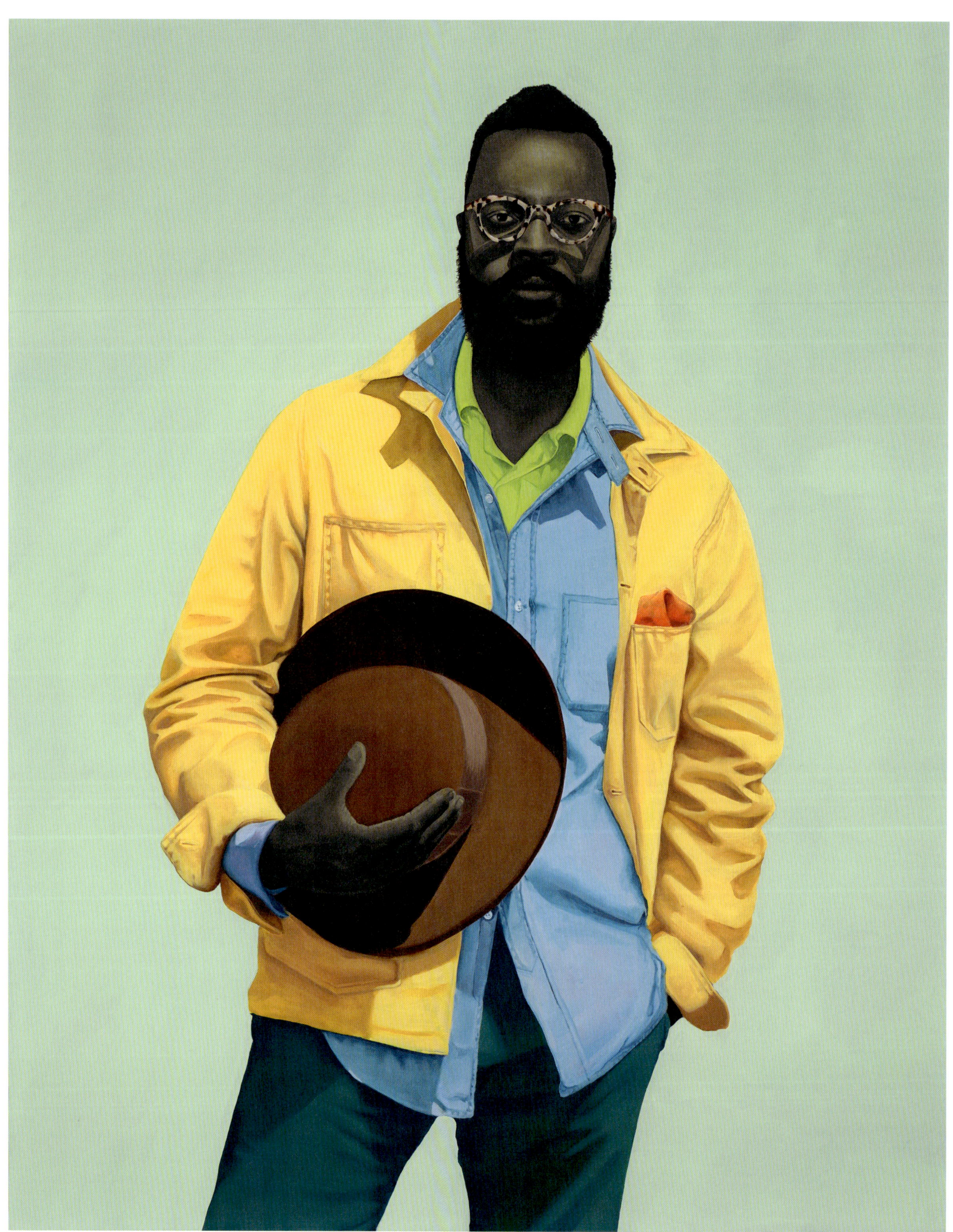

A Golden Afternoon, 2016
Oil on canvas, 54 × 43 in. (137.2 × 109.2 cm)

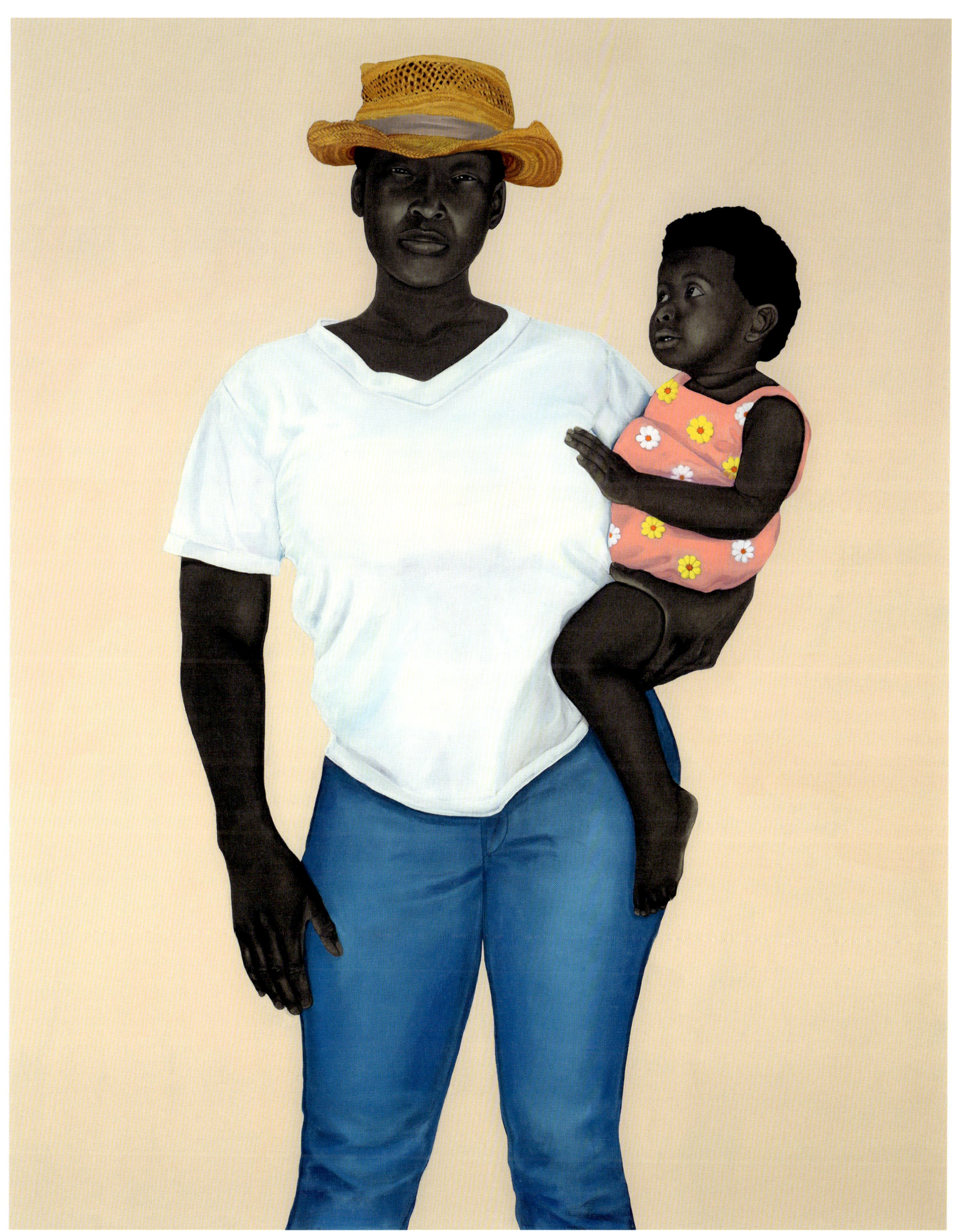

Mother and Child, 2016
Oil on canvas, 54 × 43 in. (137.2 × 109.2 cm)

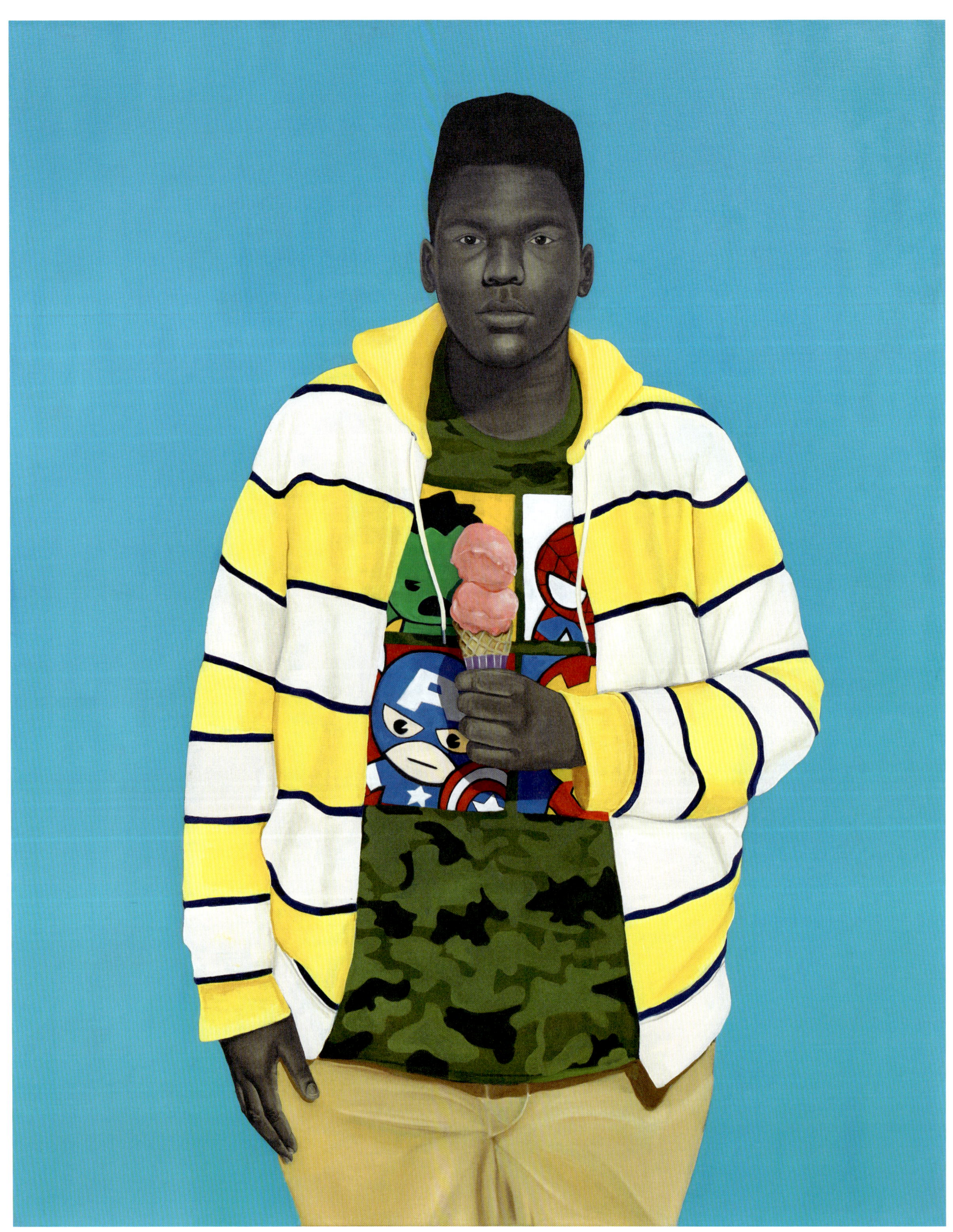

Innocent You, Innocent Me, 2016

Oil on canvas, 54 × 43 in. (137.2 × 109.2 cm)

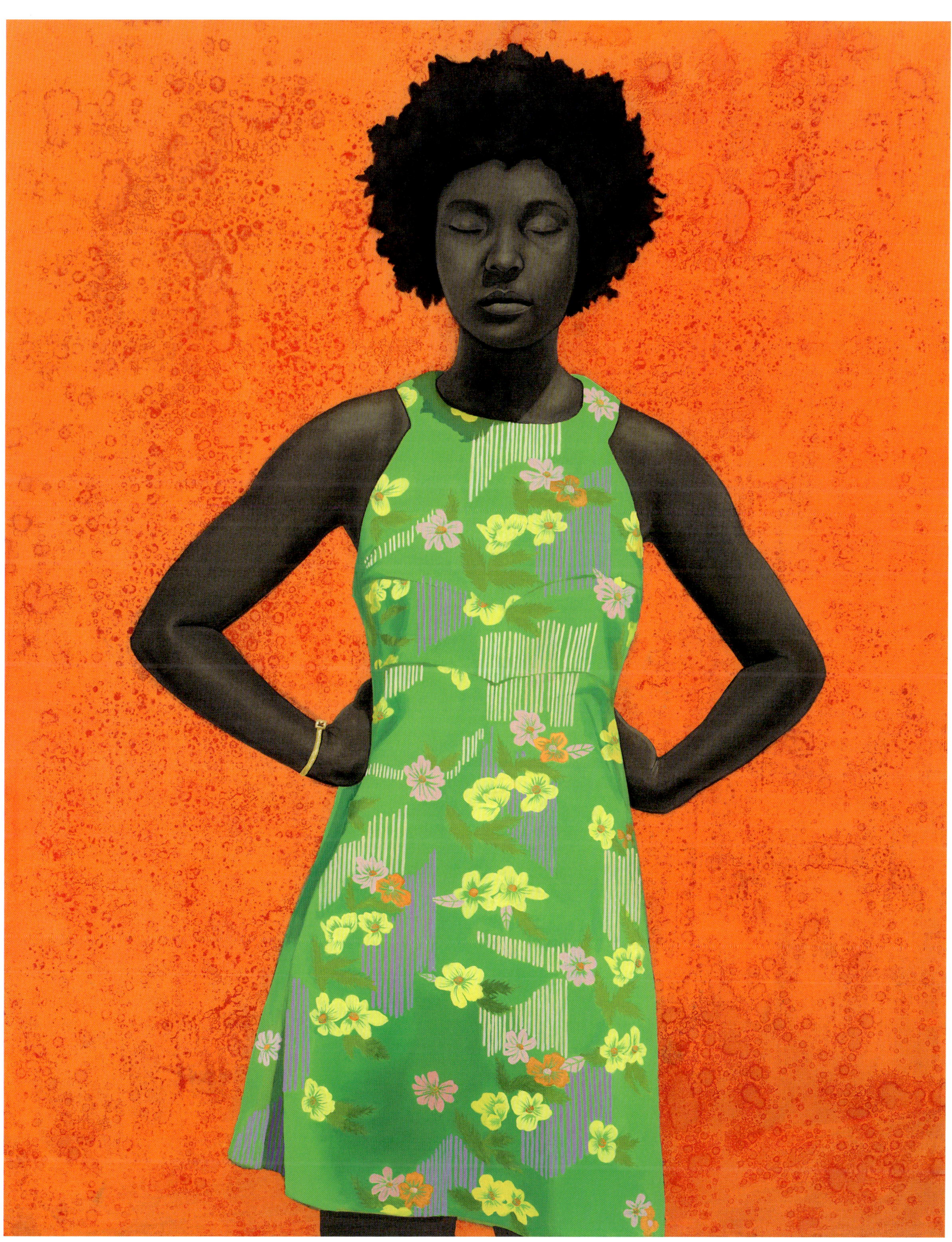

The Make Believer (Monet's Garden), 2016

Oil on canvas, 54 × 43 in. (137.2 × 109.2 cm)

Pilgrimage of the Chameleon, 2016

Oil on canvas, 72 × 51⅛ in. (183 × 130 cm)

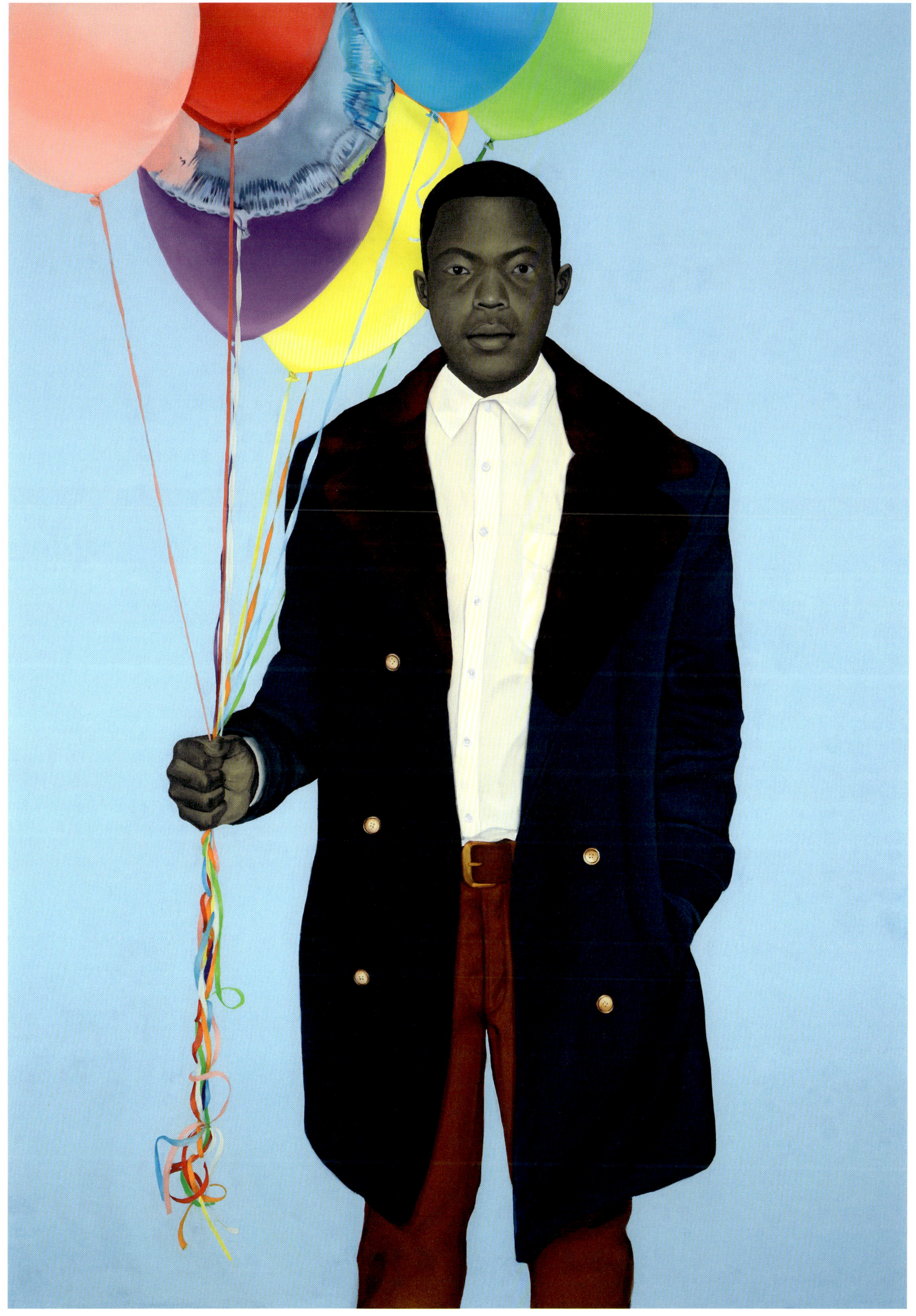

The Boy with the Big Fish, 2016

Oil on canvas, 54 × 43 in. (137.2 × 109.2 cm)

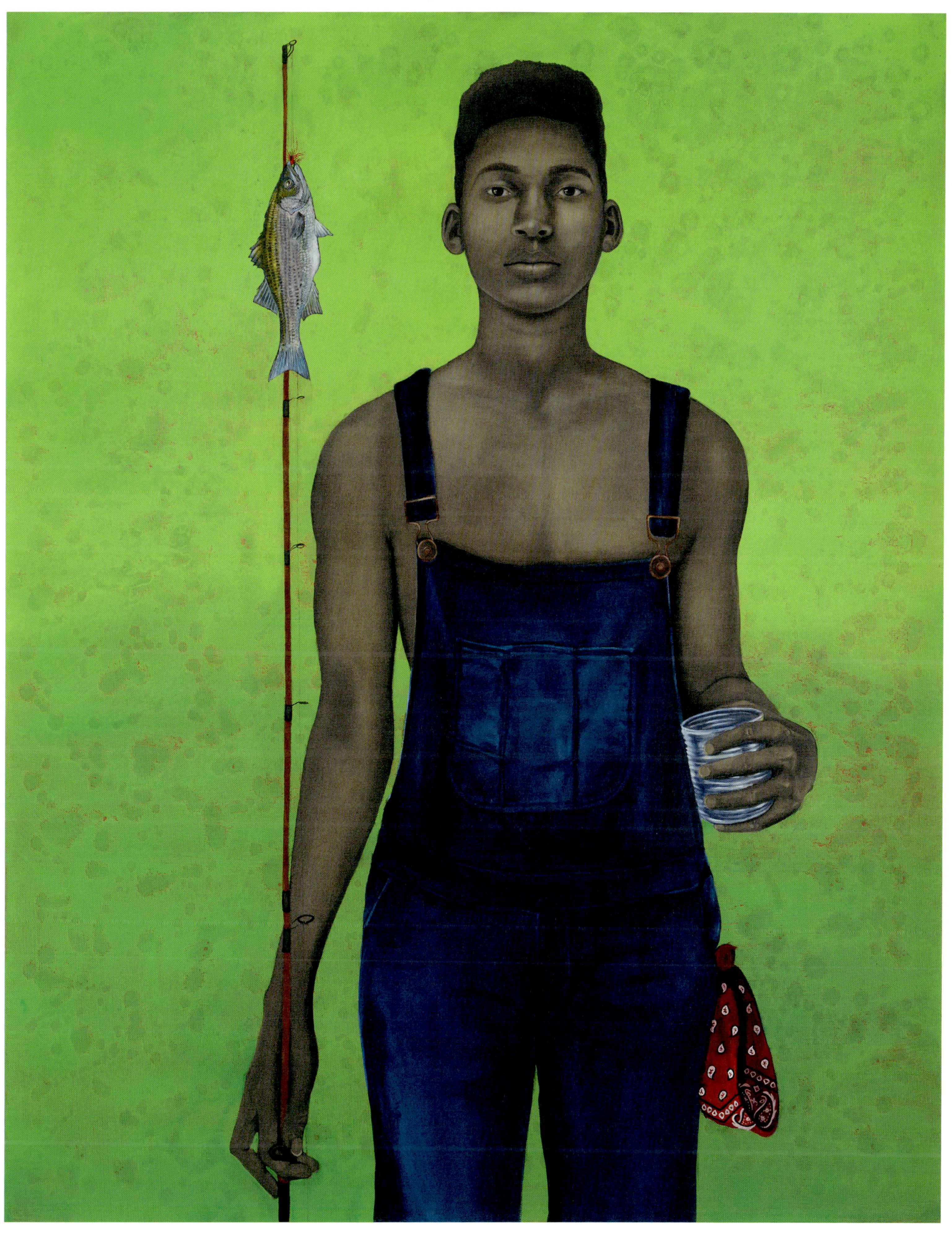

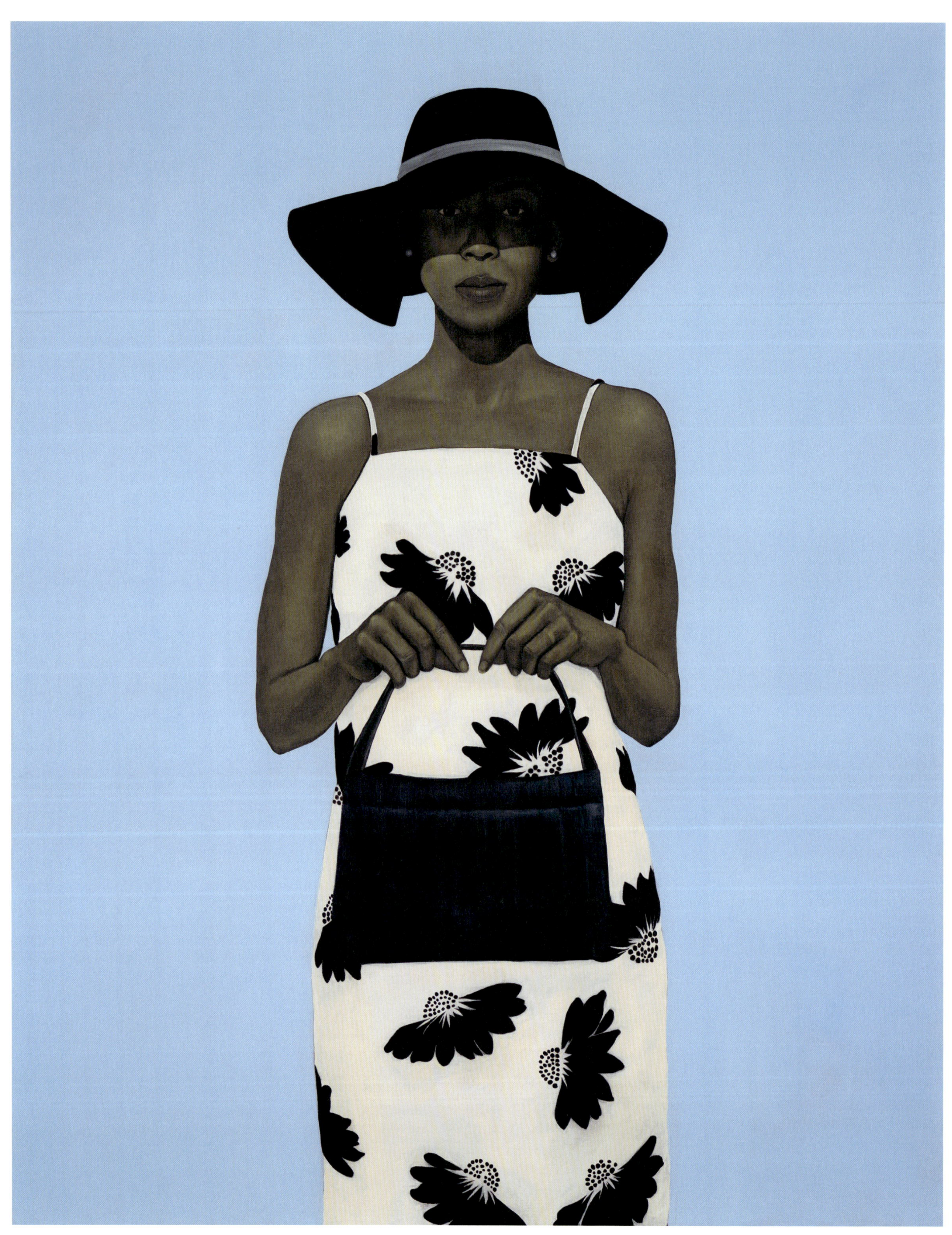

Listen, you a wonder. You a city of a woman. You got a geography of your own, 2016
Oil on canvas, 54 × 43 in. (137.2 × 109.2 cm)

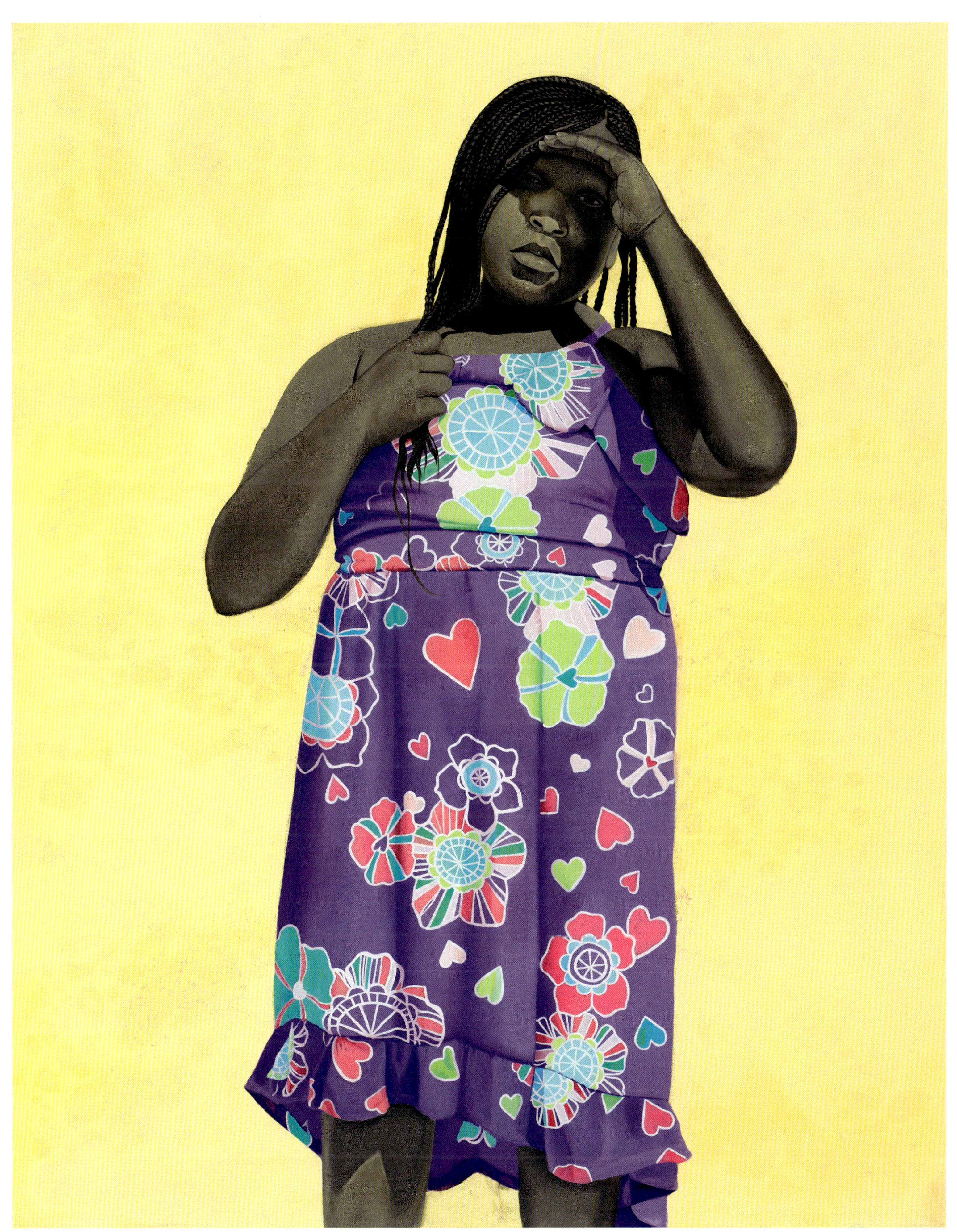

All Things Bright and Beautiful, 2016
Oil on canvas, 54 × 43 in. (137.2 × 109.2 cm)

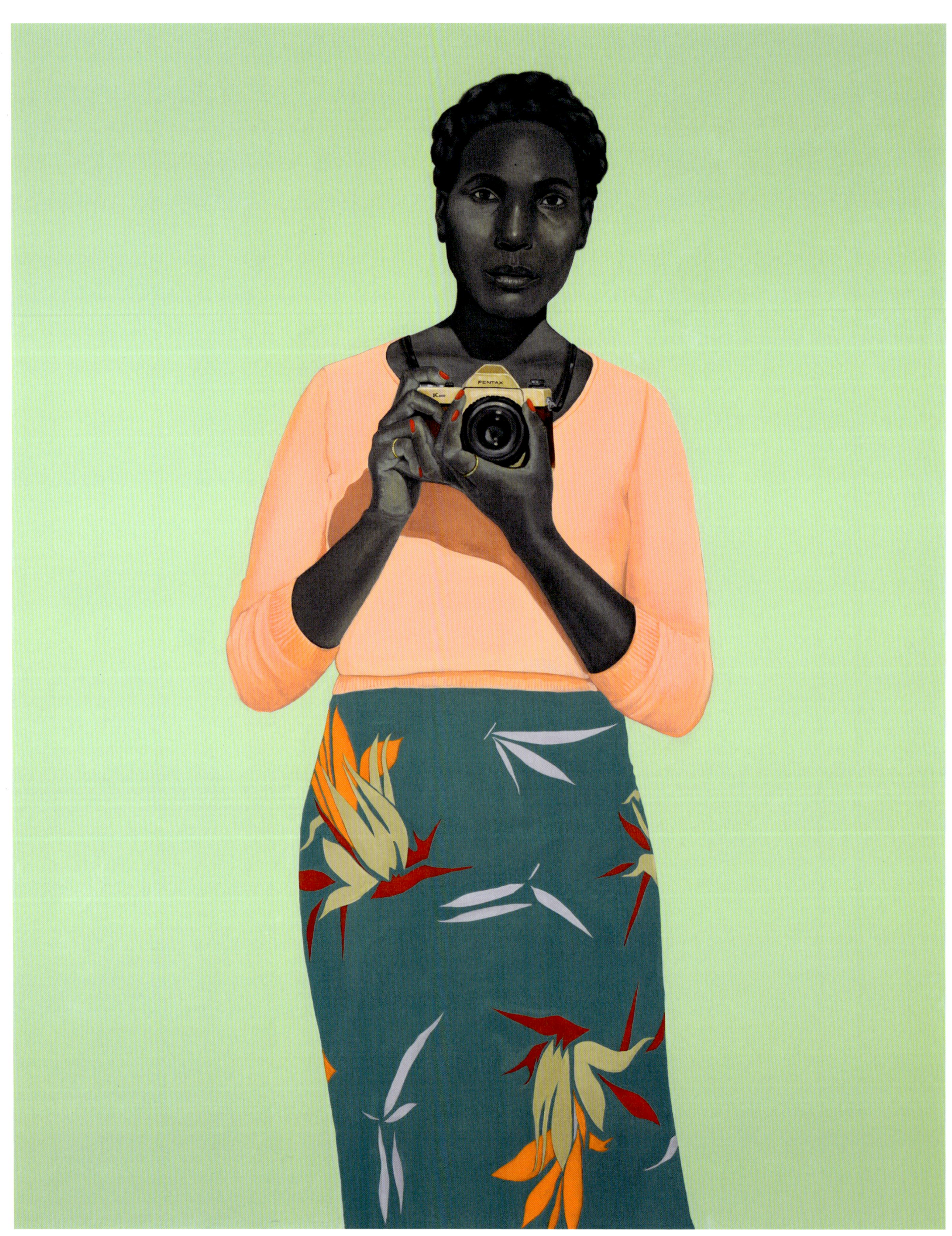

What's different about Alice is that she has the most incisive way of telling the truth, 2017

Oil on canvas, 54 × 43 in. (137.2 × 109.2 cm)

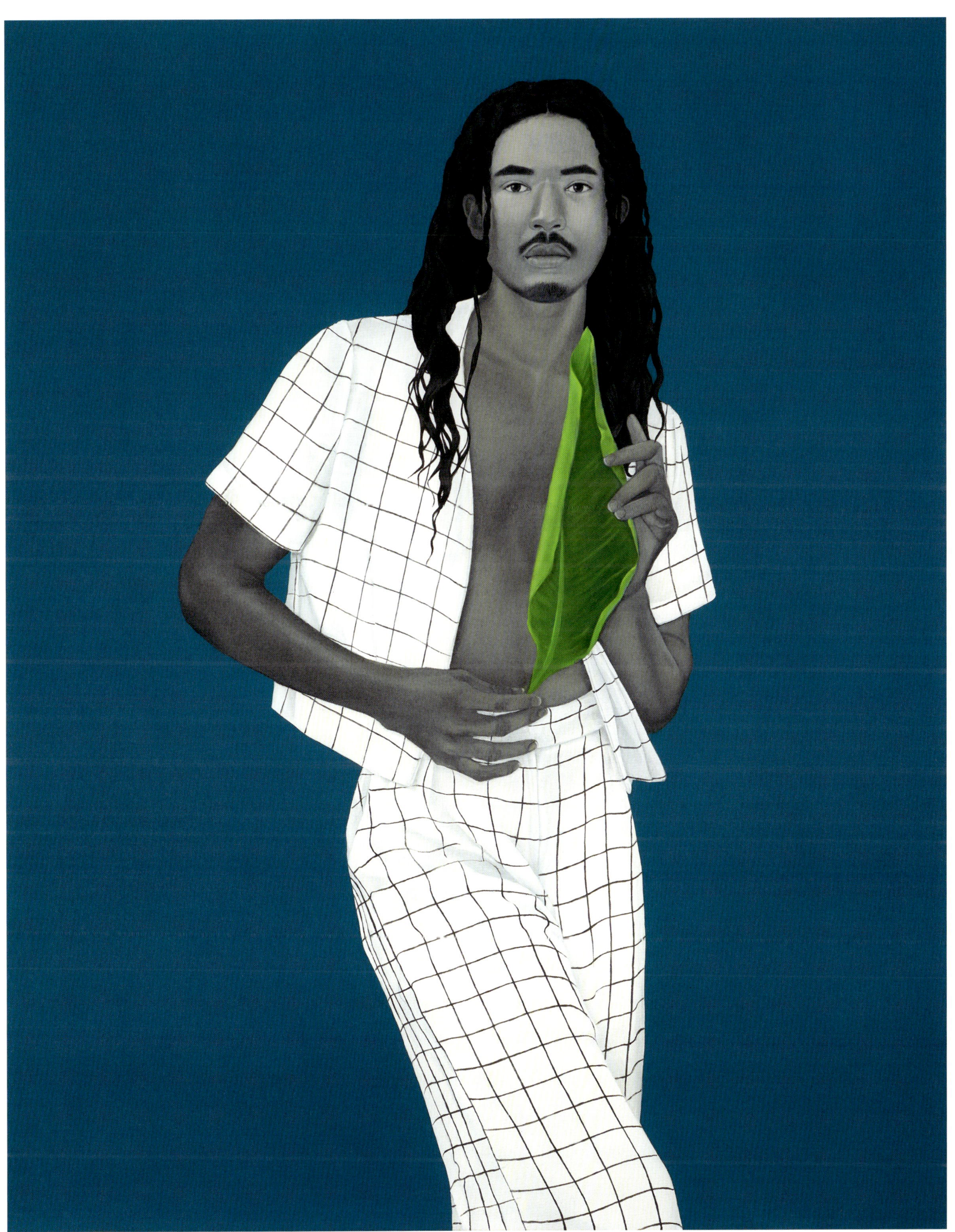

The Lesson of the Falling Leaves, 2017
Oil on canvas, 54 × 43 in. (137.2 × 109.2 cm)

What's precious inside of him does not care to be known by the mind in ways that diminish its presence (All American), 2017
Oil on canvas, 54 × 43 in. (137.2 × 109.2 cm)

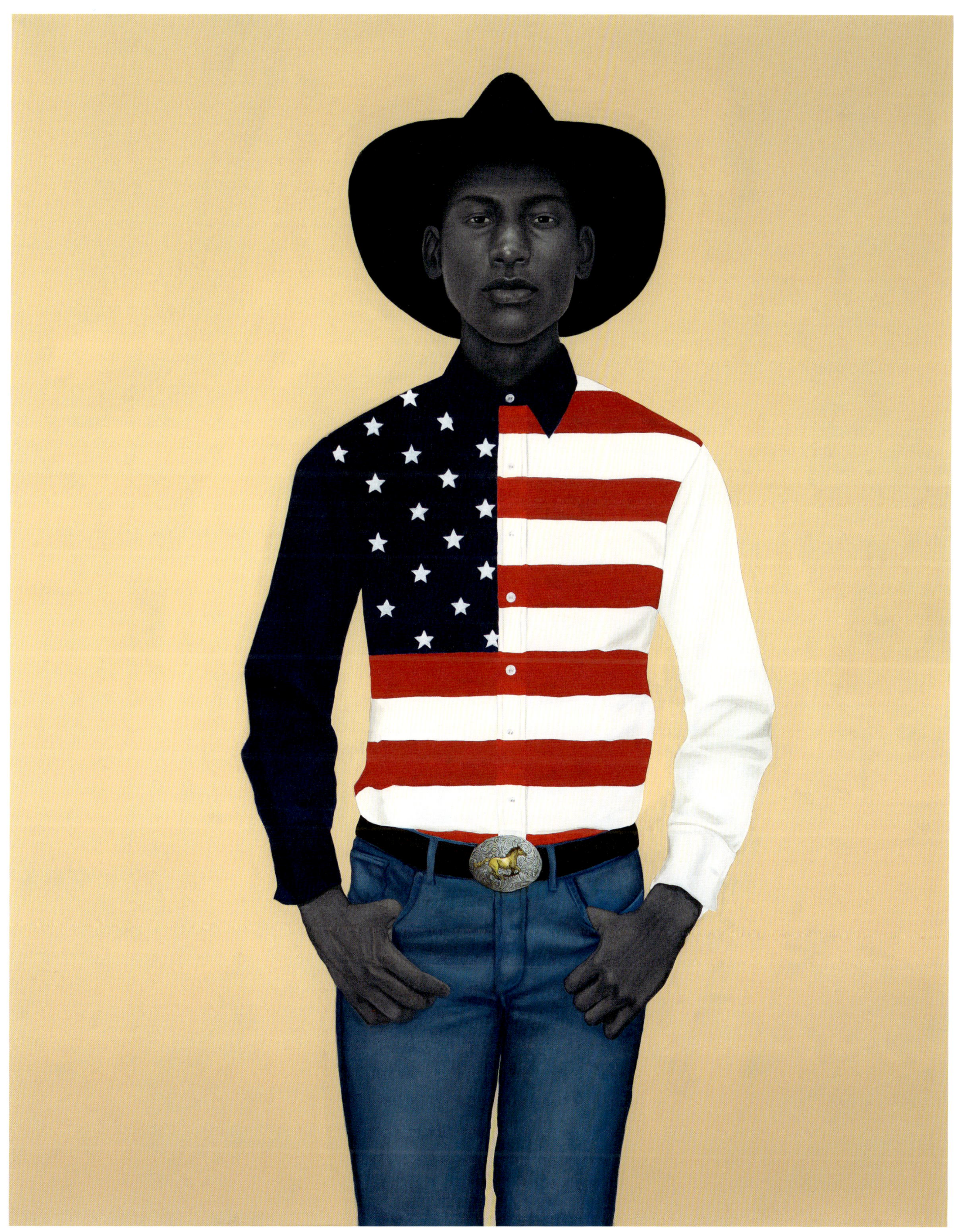

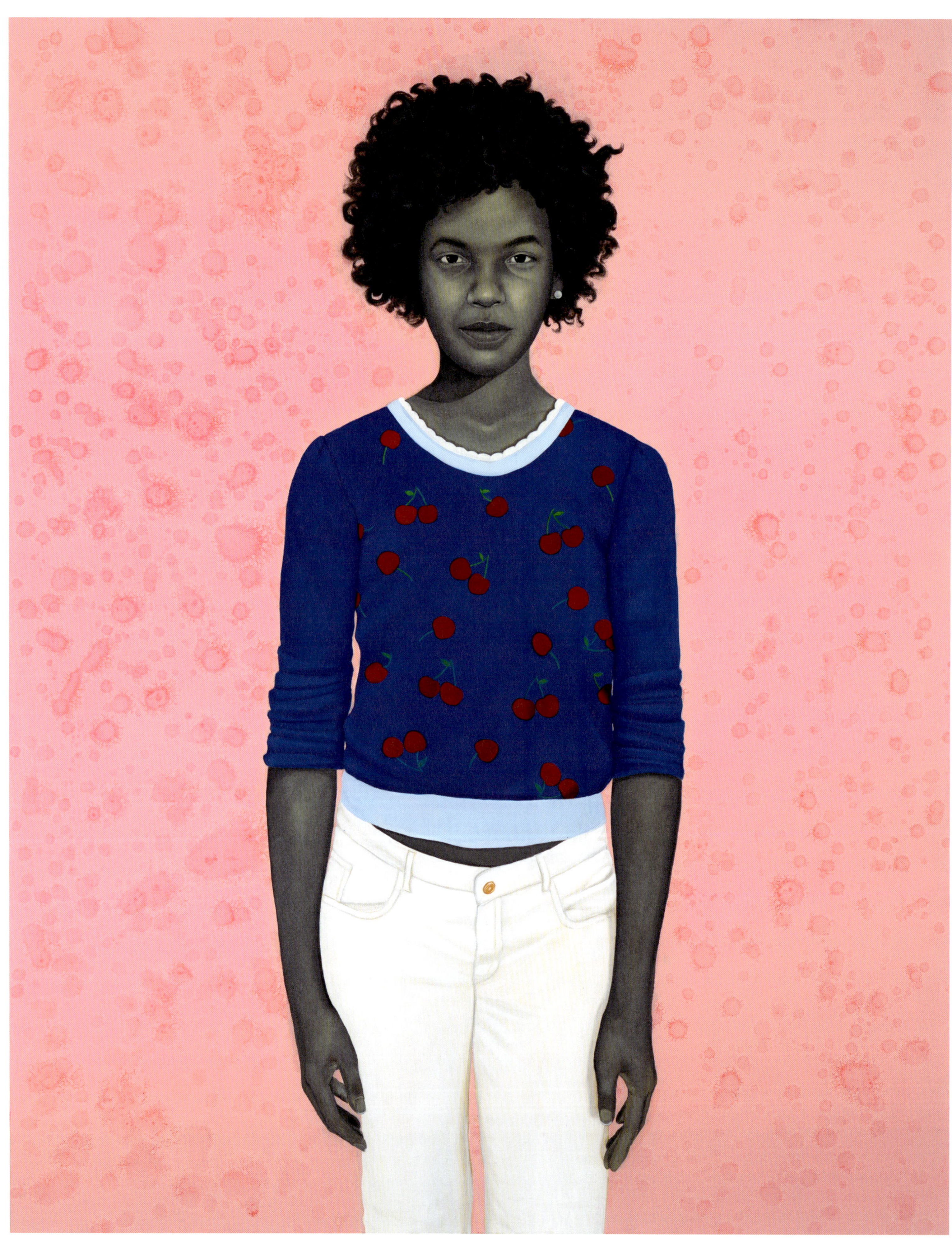

Light Is Easy to Love, 2017
Oil on canvas, 54 × 43 in. (137.2 × 109.2 cm)

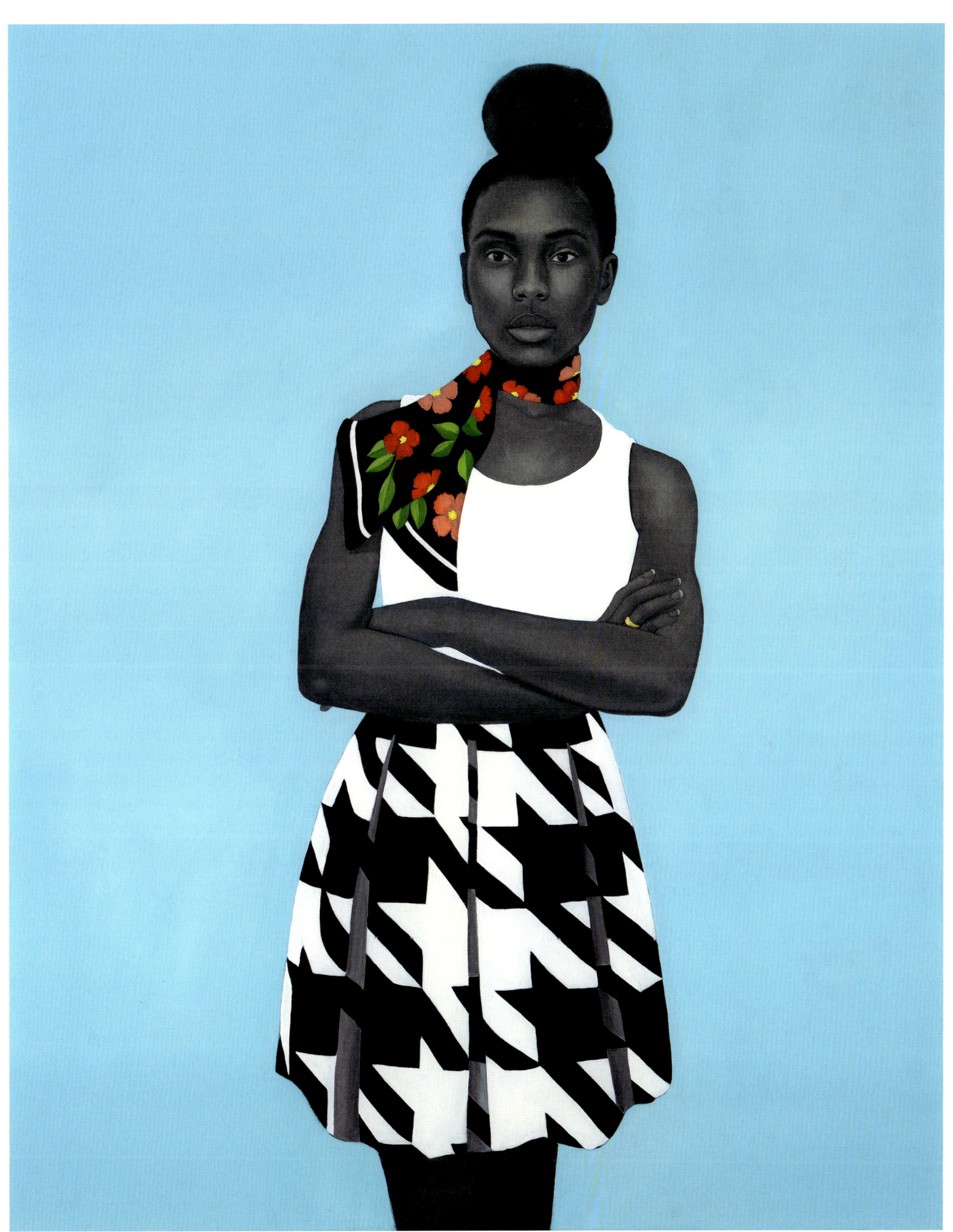

A Clear Unspoken Granted Magic, 2017
Oil on canvas, 54 × 43 in. (137.2 × 109.2 cm)

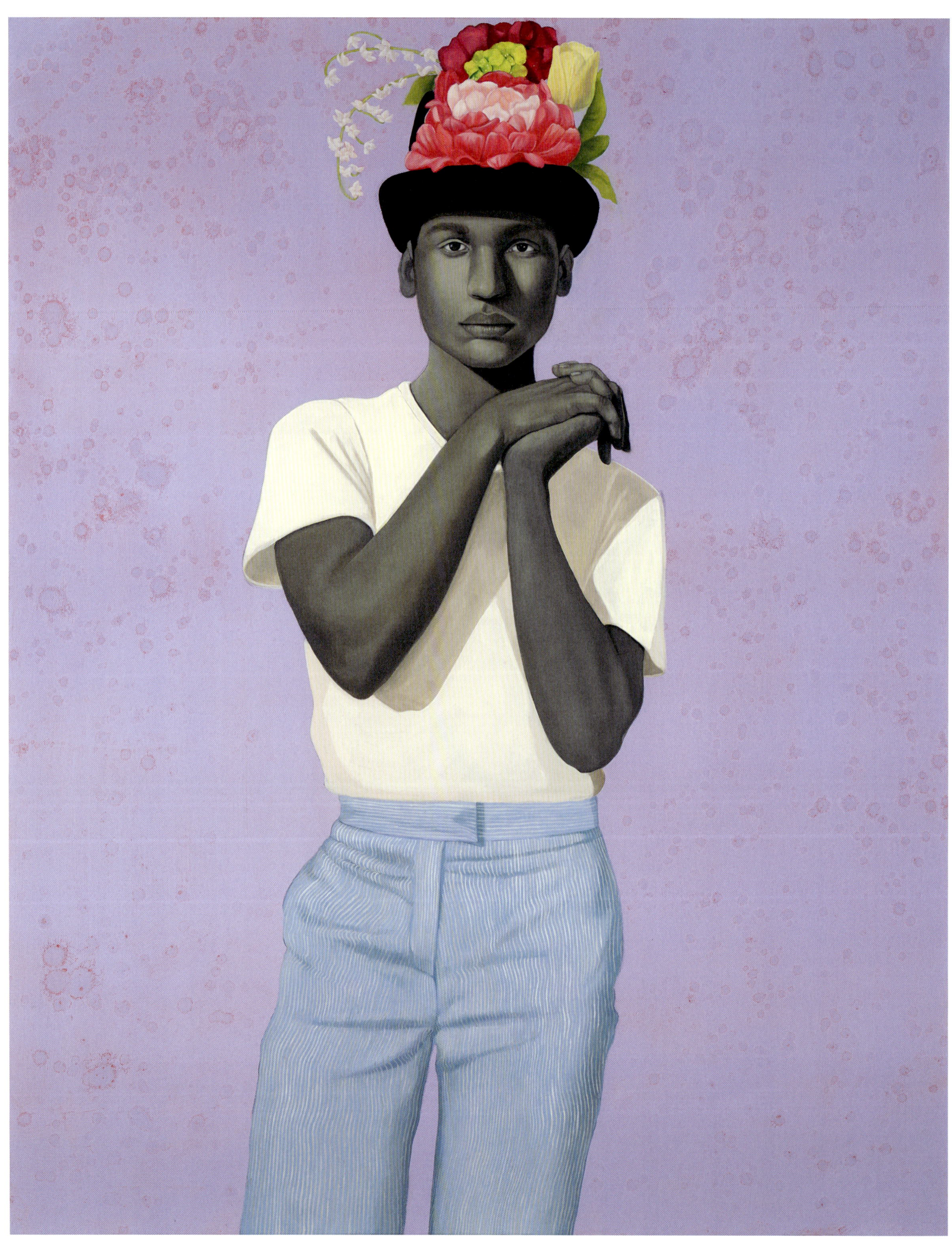

Try on dreams until I find the one that fits me. They all fit me, 2017
Oil on canvas, 54 × 43 in. (137.2 × 109.2 cm)

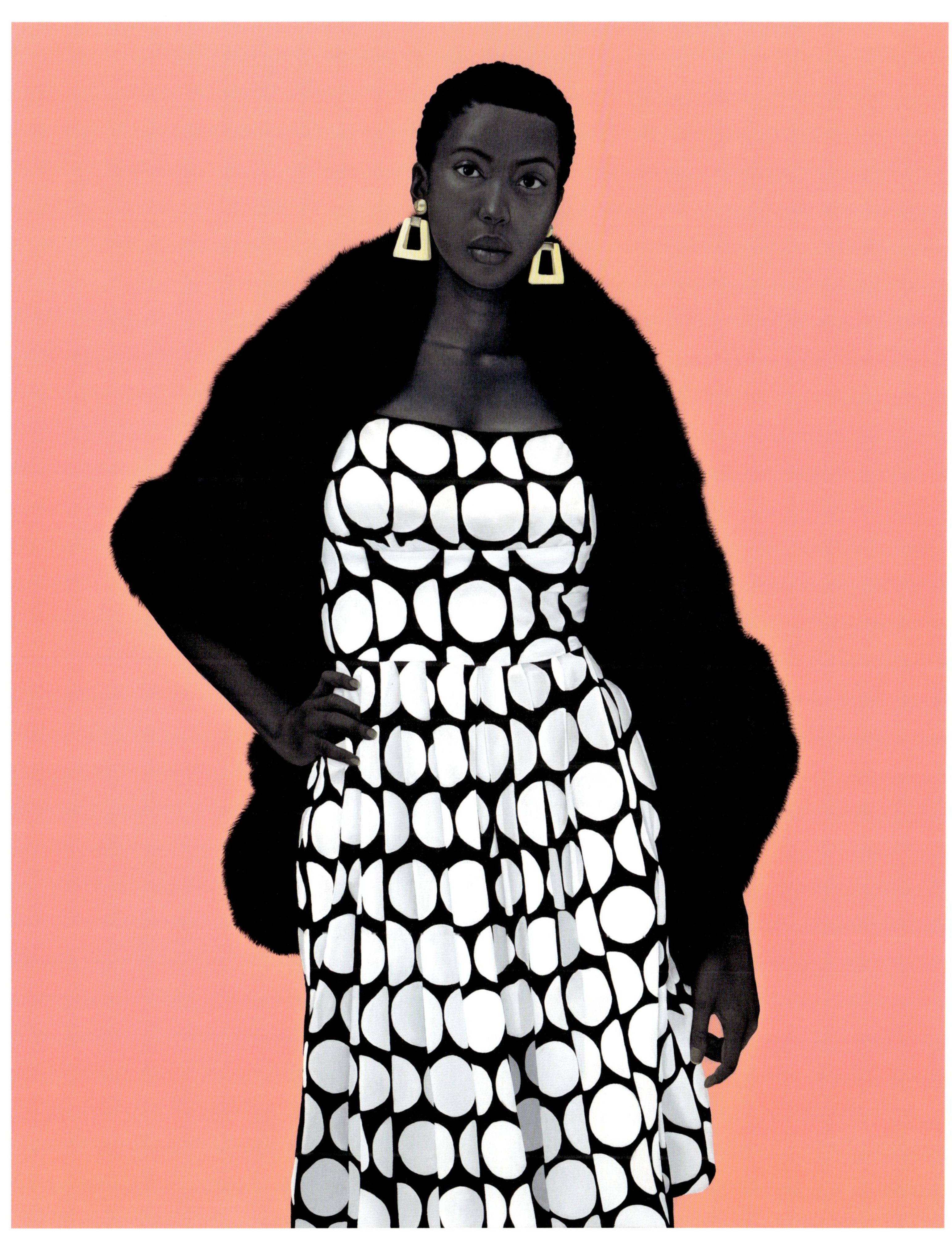

Mama Has Made the Bread (How Things Are Measured), 2018

Oil on canvas, 54 × 43 in. (137.2 × 109.2 cm)

Planes, Rockets, and the Spaces in Between, 2018
Oil on canvas, 100 × 67 in. (254 × 170.2 cm)

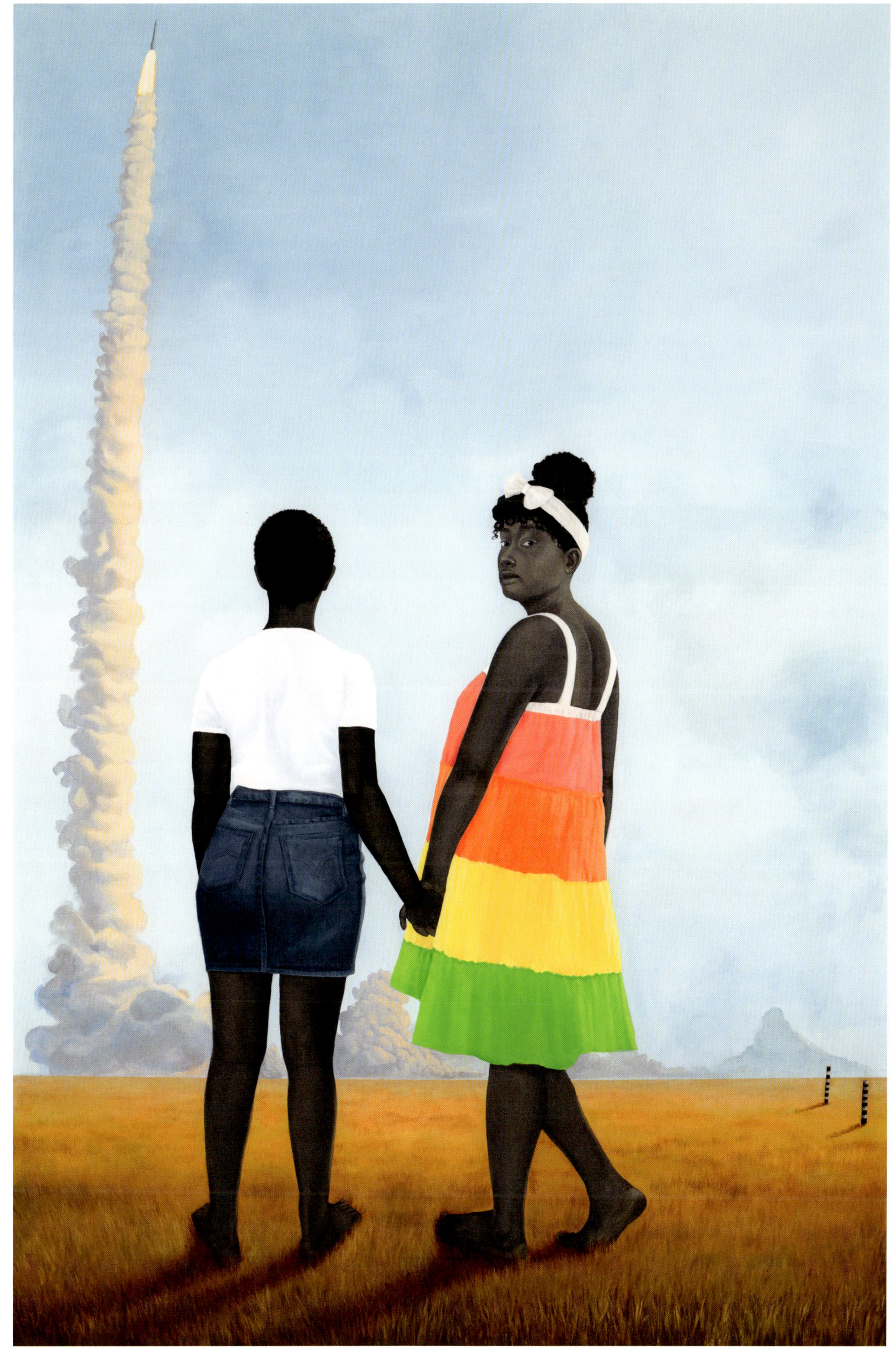

She Always Believed the Good about Those She Loved, 2018

Oil on canvas, 54 × 43 in. (137.2 × 109.2 cm)

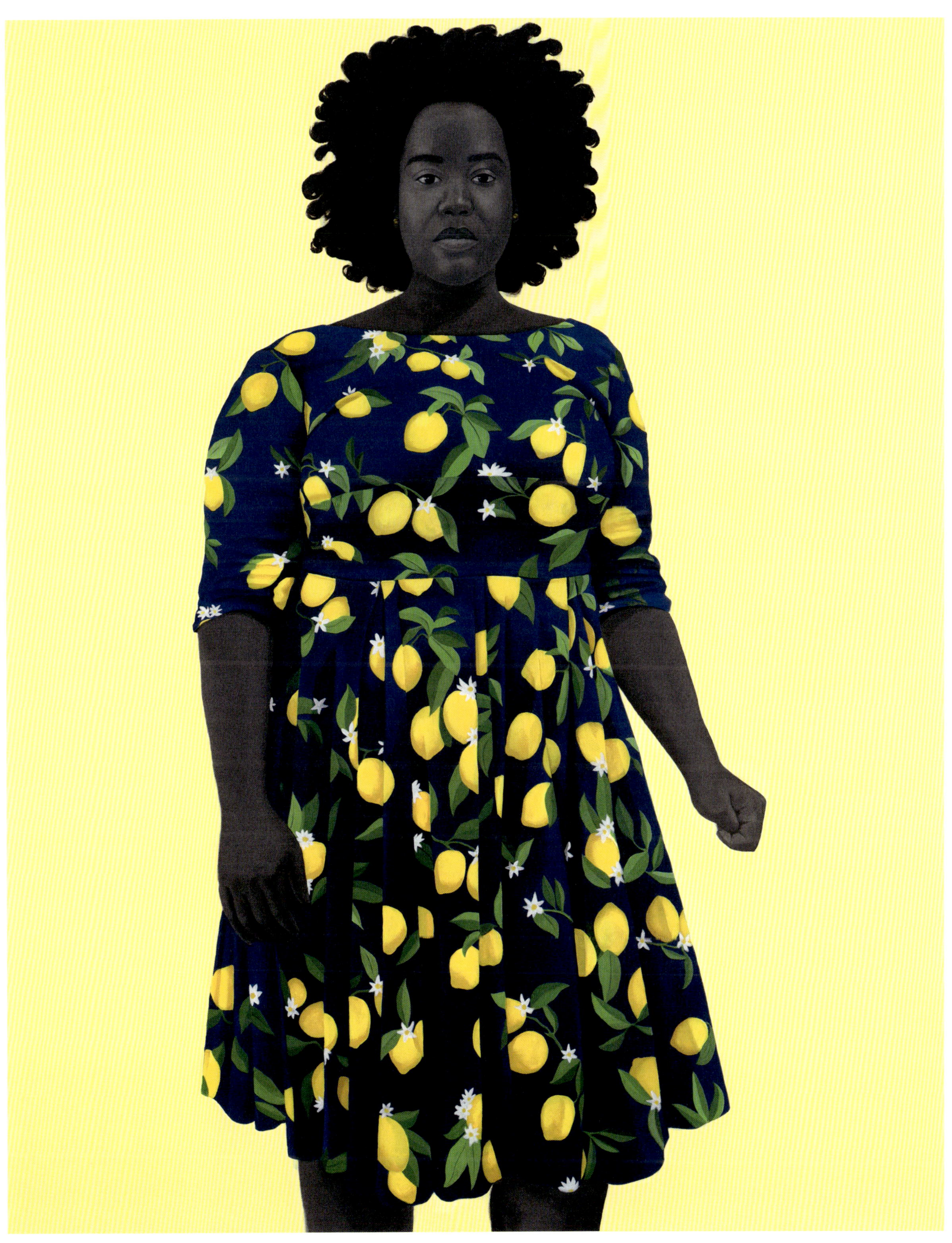

She had an inside and an outside now, and suddenly she knew how not to mix them, 2018
Oil on canvas, 54 × 43 in. (137.2 × 109.2 cm)

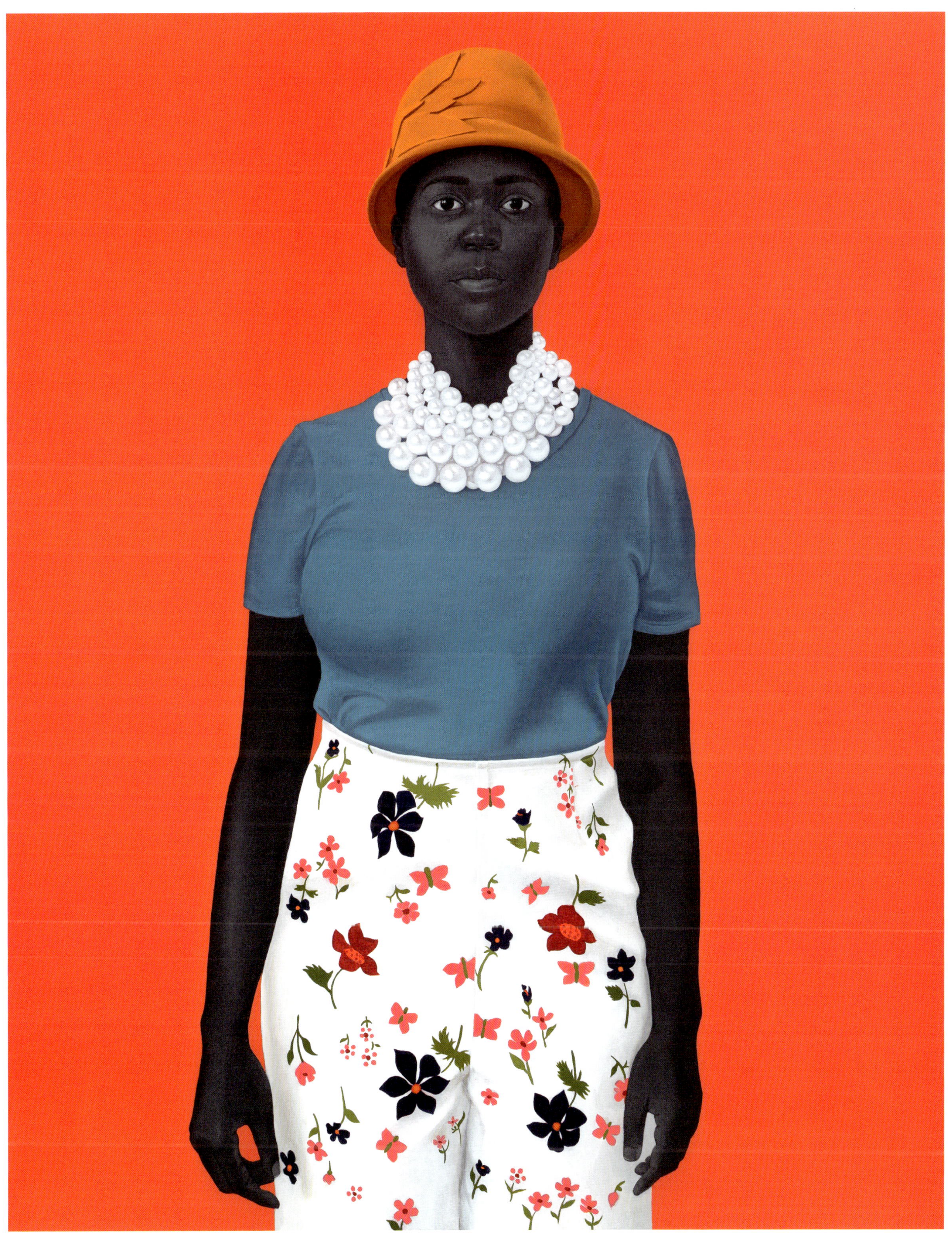

Michelle LaVaughn Robinson Obama, 2018

Oil on linen, 72⅛ × 60⅛ in. (183.2 × 152.7 cm)

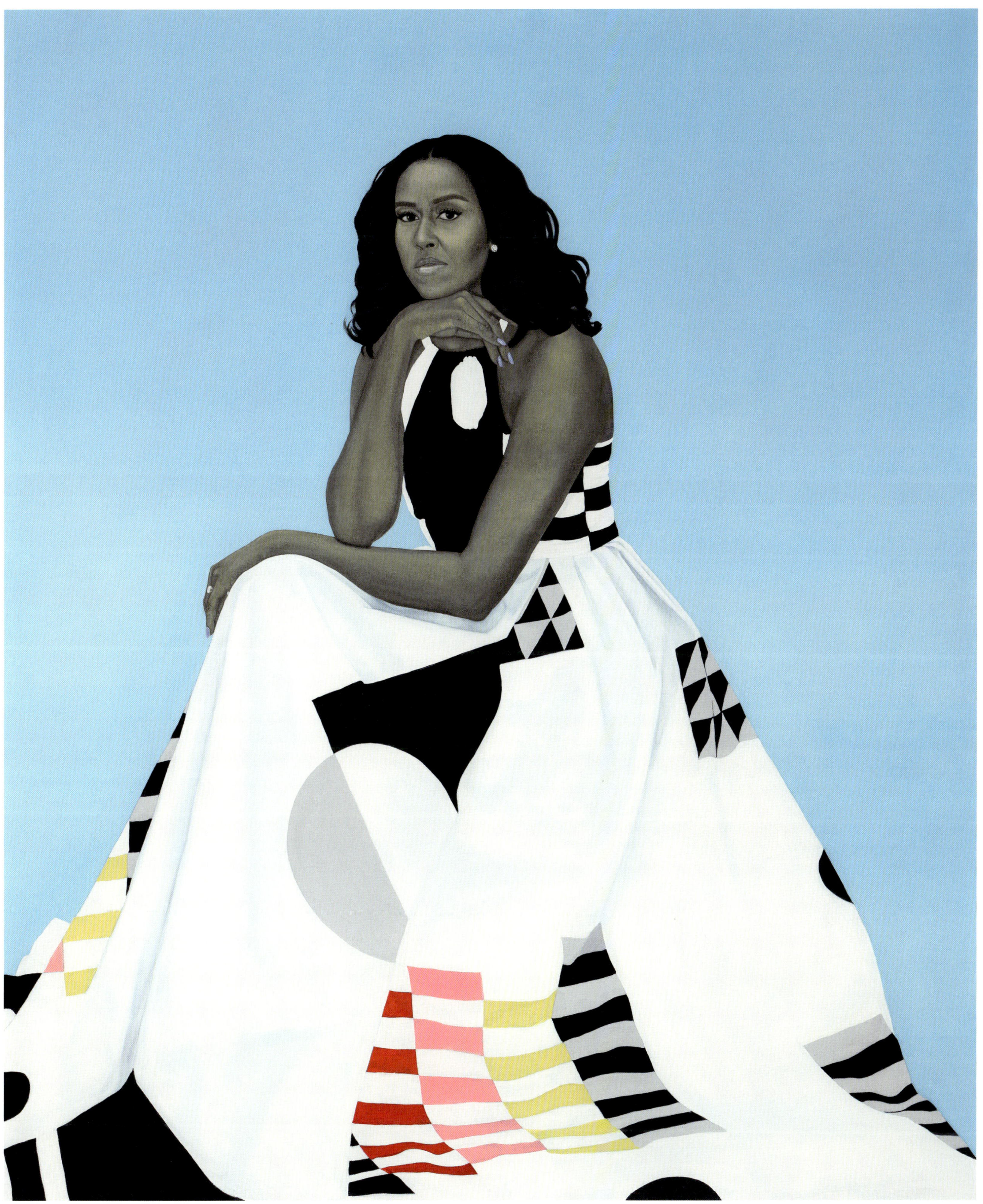

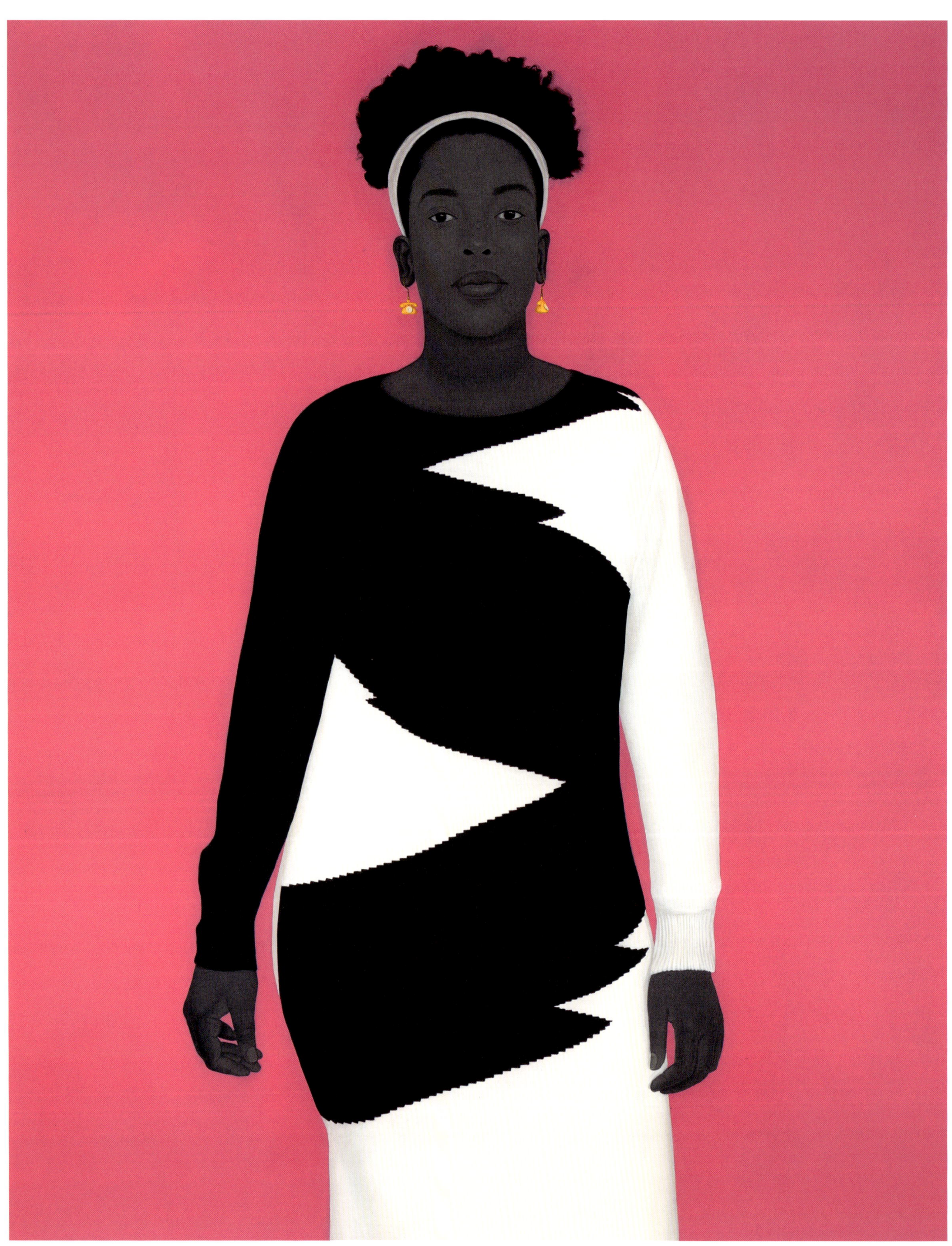

Sometimes the King Is a Woman, 2019
Oil on canvas, 54 × 43 in. (137.2 × 109.2 cm)

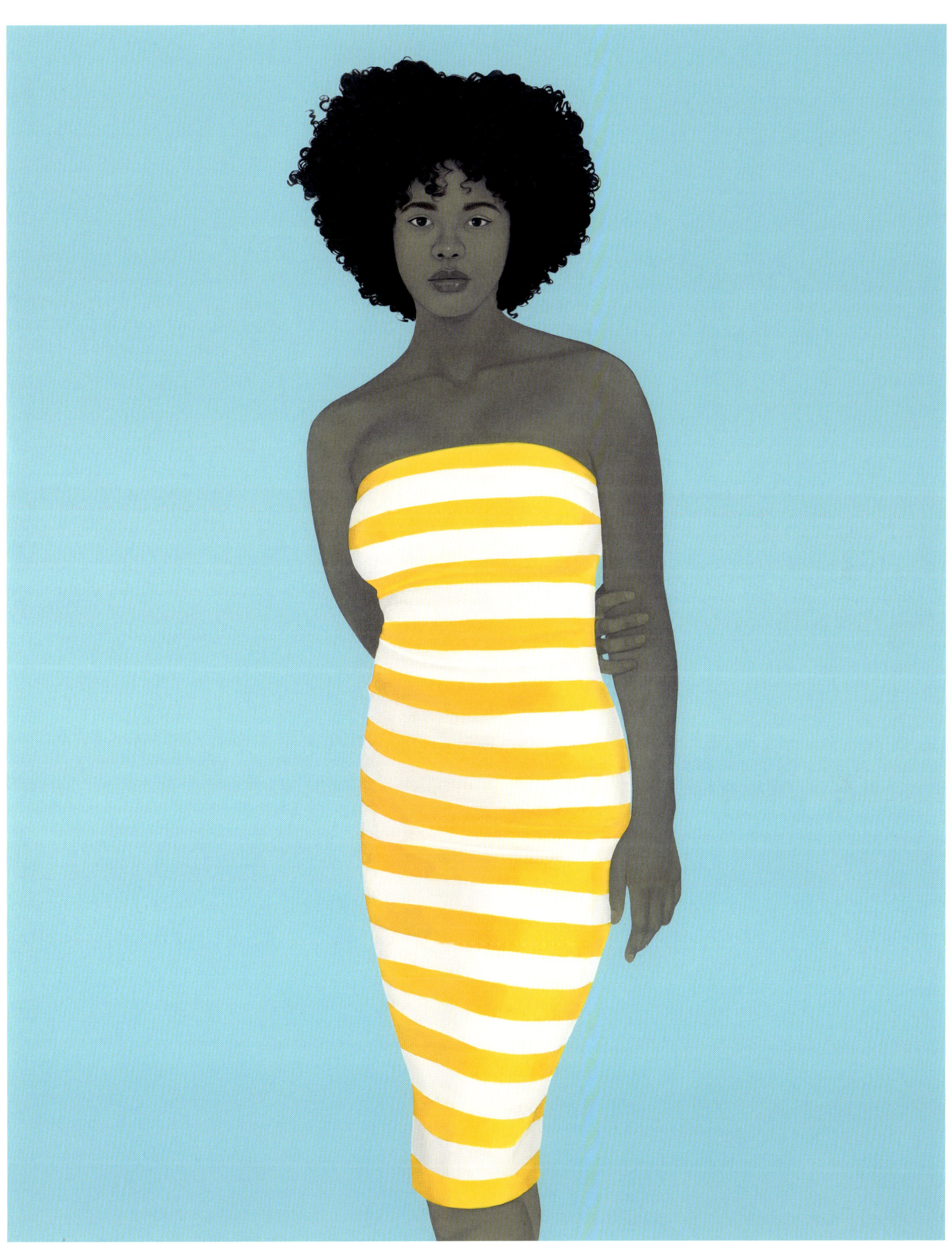

There Is No Charm Equal to Tenderness of Heart, 2019

Oil on canvas, 54 × 43 in. (137.2 × 109.2 cm)

If You Surrendered to the Air, You Could Ride It, 2019

Oil on linen, 130 × 108 in. (330.2 × 274.3 cm)

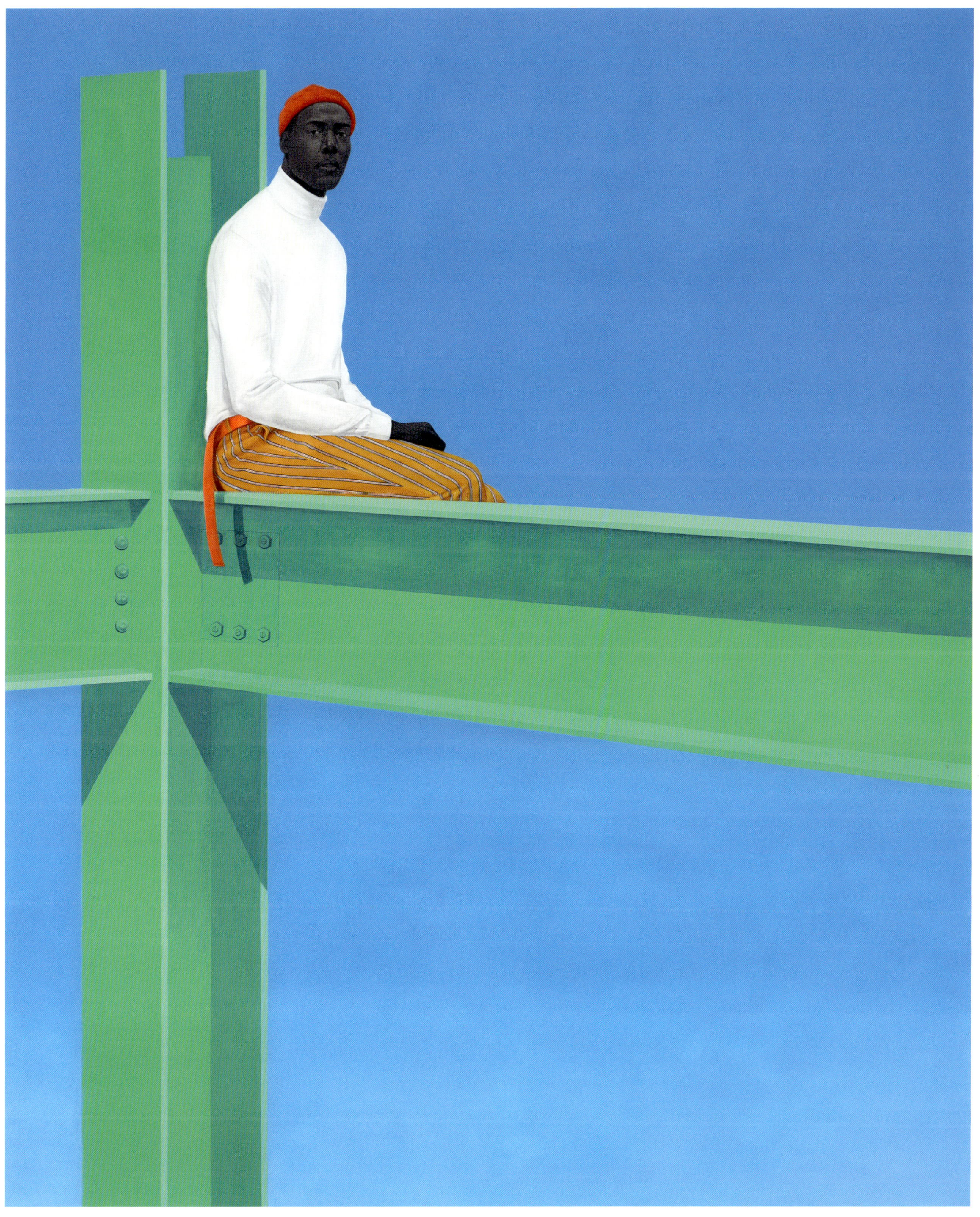

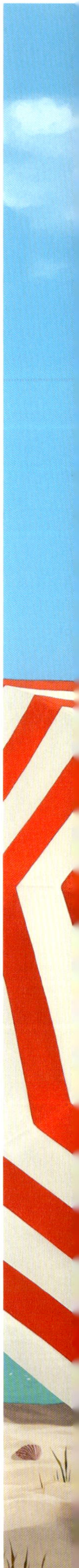

Precious Jewels by the Sea, 2019

Oil on linen, 120 × 108 in. (305 × 274.3 cm)

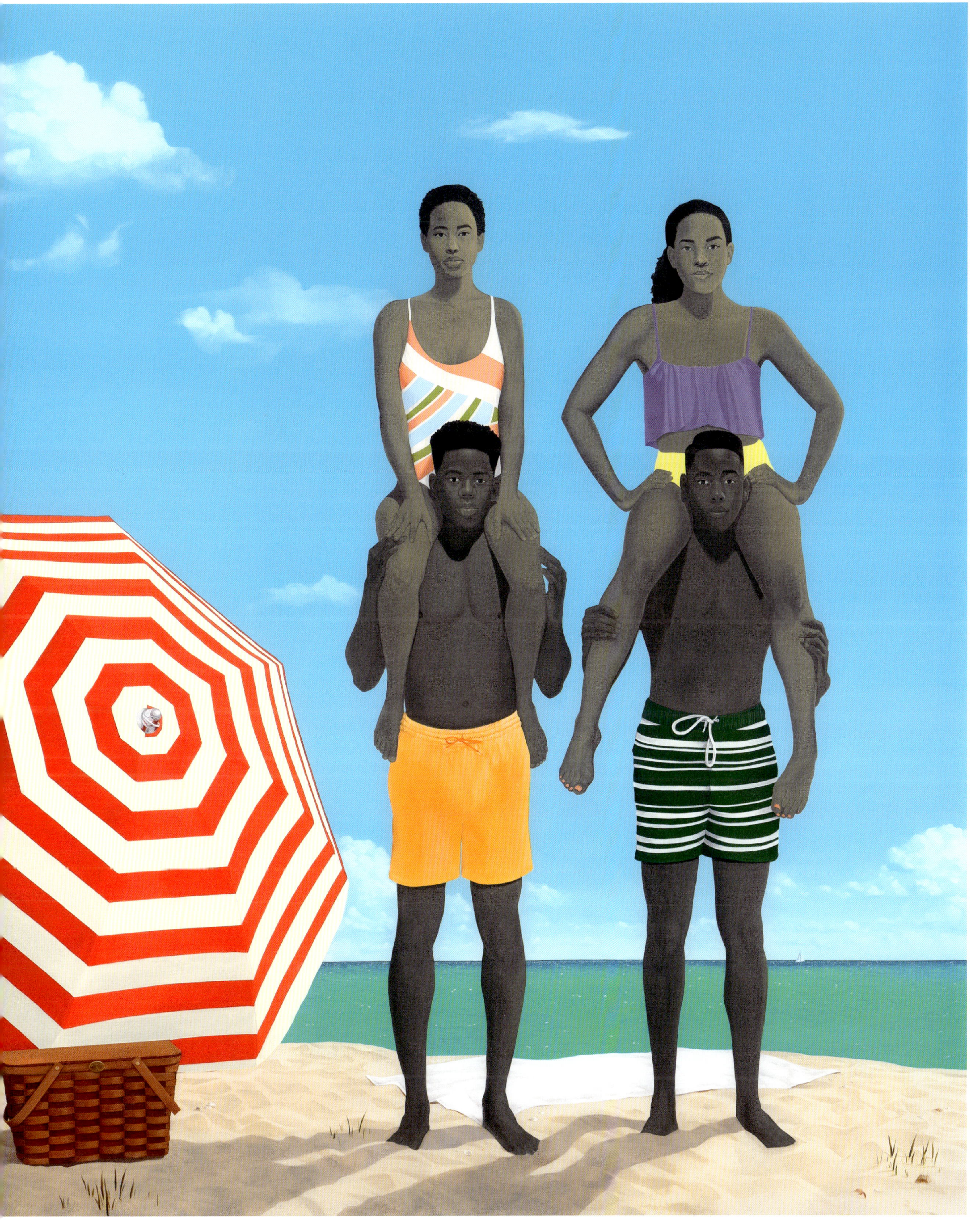

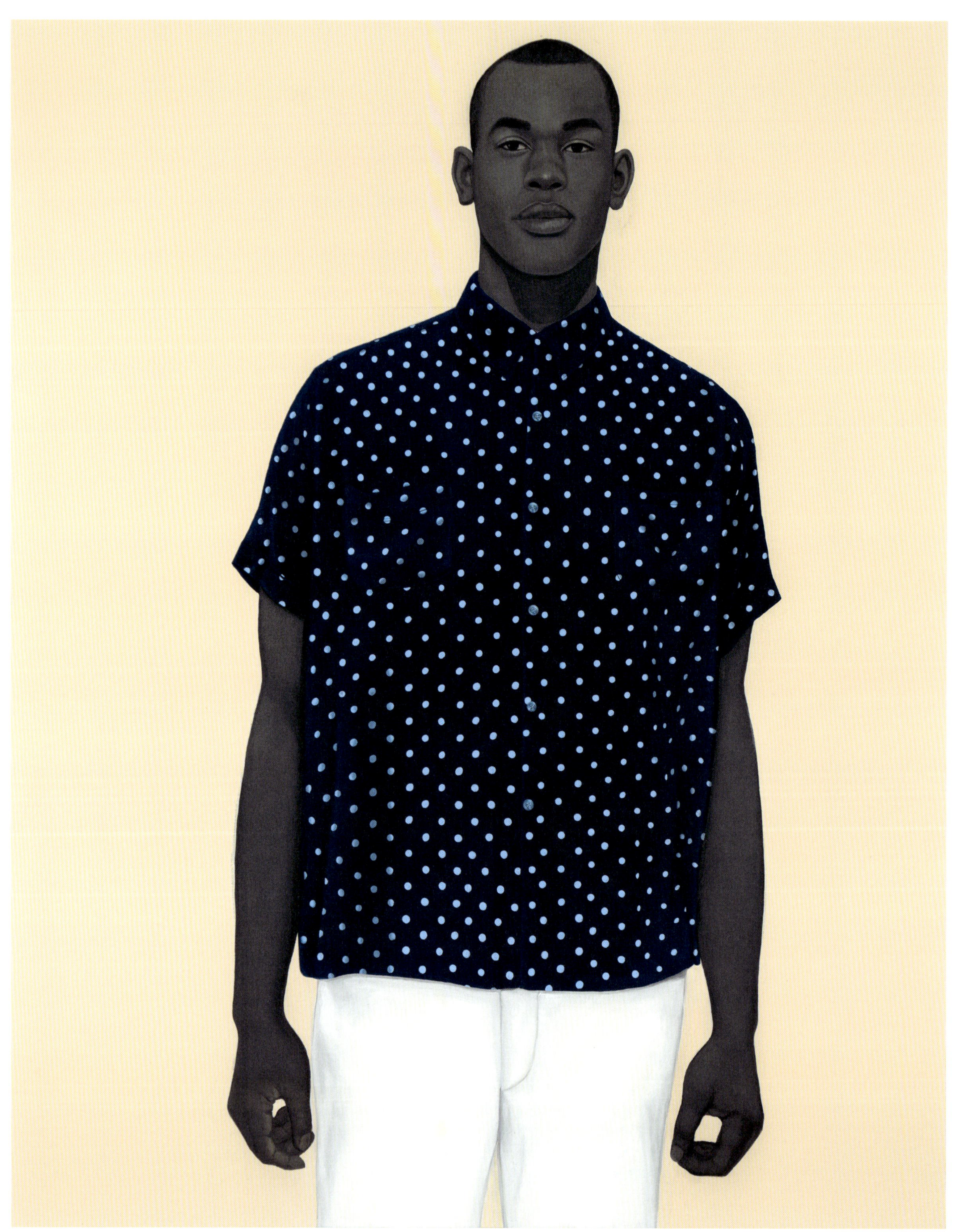

Handsome, 2019

Oil on canvas, 54 × 43 in. (137.2 × 109.2 cm)

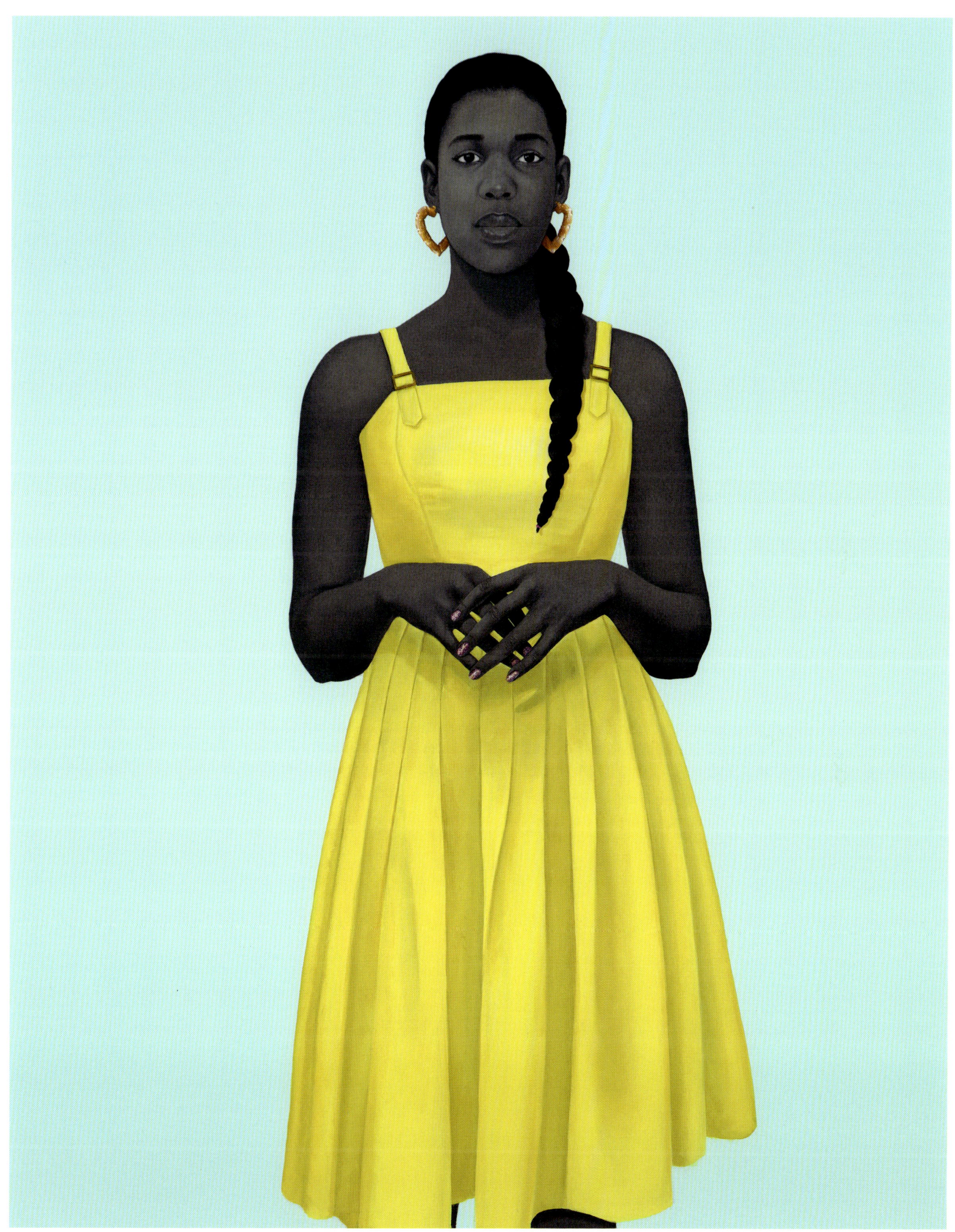

Untitled (Opal), 2019
Oil on linen, 54 × 43 in. (137.2 × 109.2 cm)

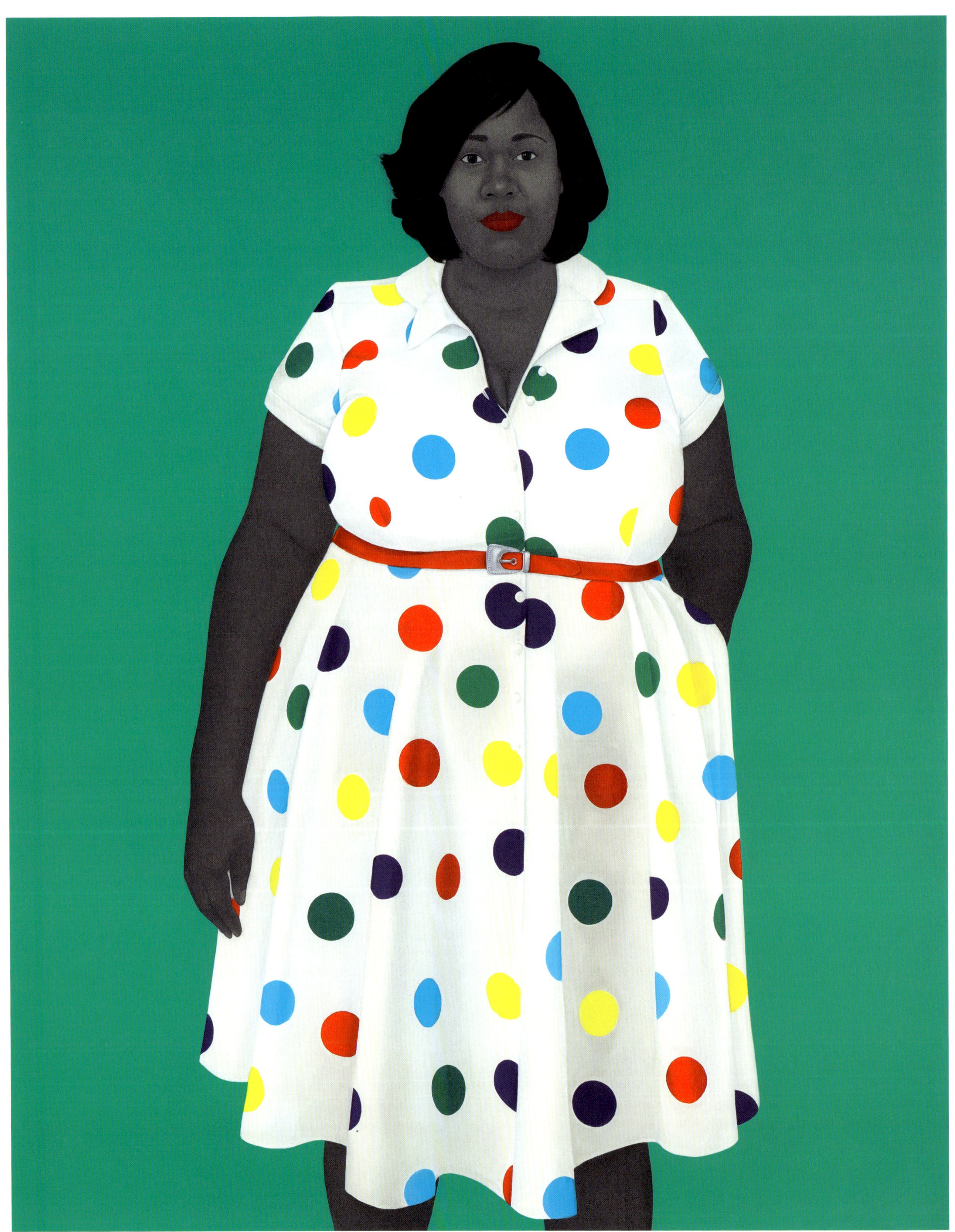

The Girl Next Door, 2019

Oil on canvas, 54 × 43 in. (137.2 × 109.2 cm)

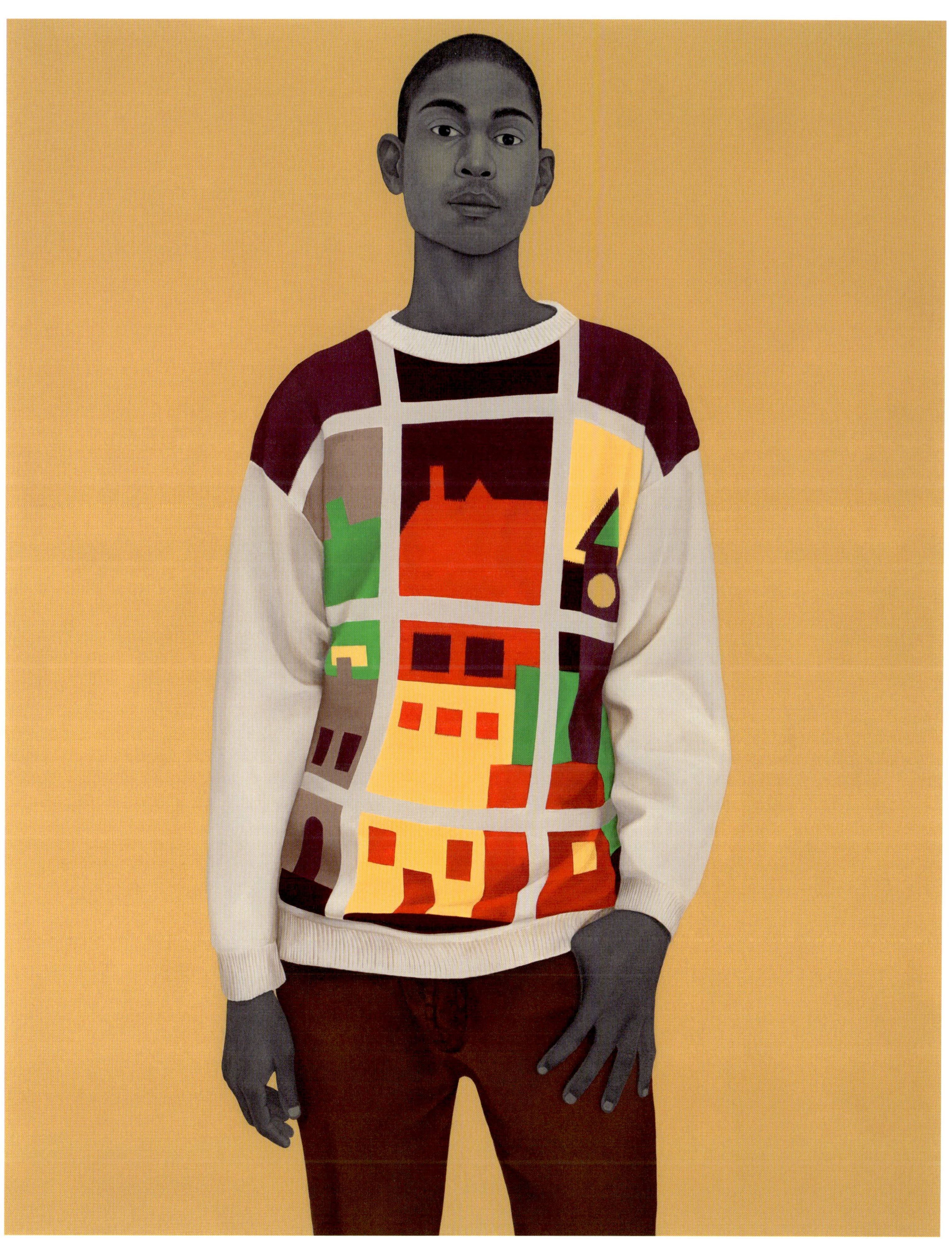

A Single Man in Possession of a Good Fortune, 2019
Oil on canvas, 54 × 43 in. (137.2 × 109.2 cm)

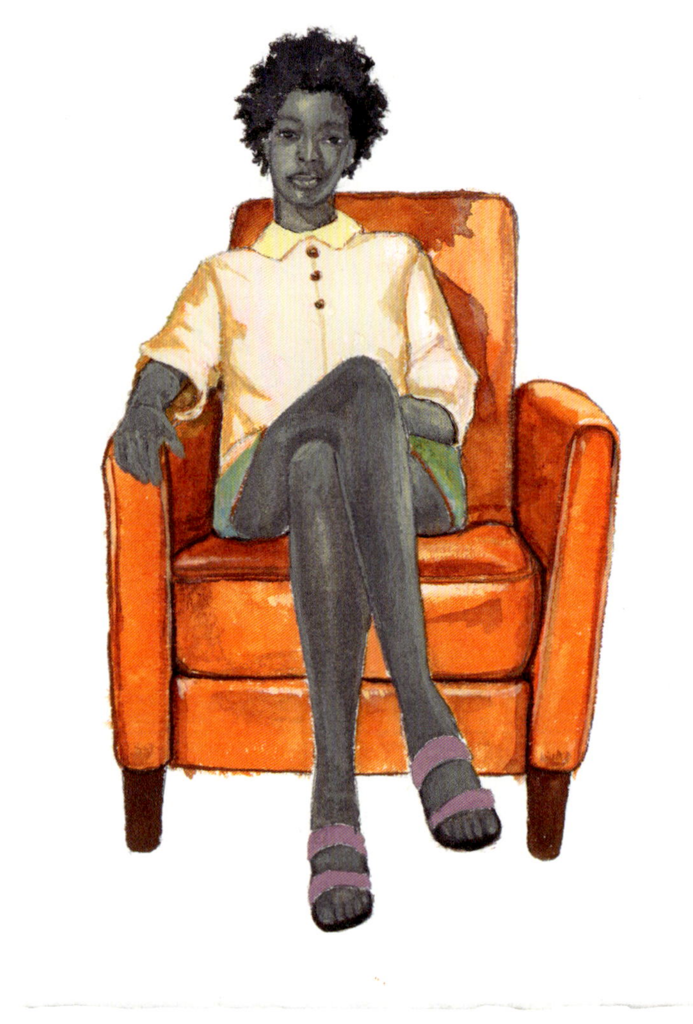

Untitled, 2020

Gouache on paper, 11 × 7½ in. (27.9 × 19.1 cm)

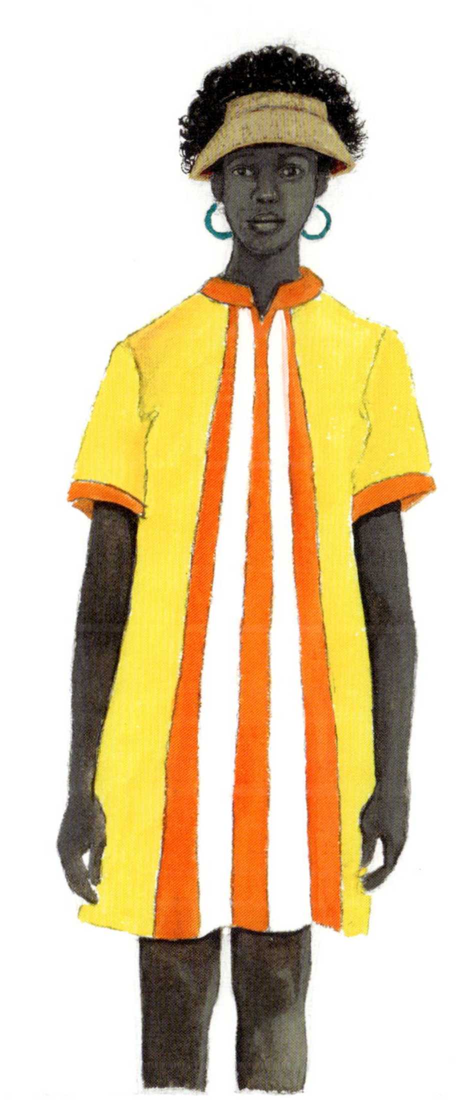

Untitled, 2020
Gouache on paper, 11 × 7½ in. (27.9 × 19.1 cm)

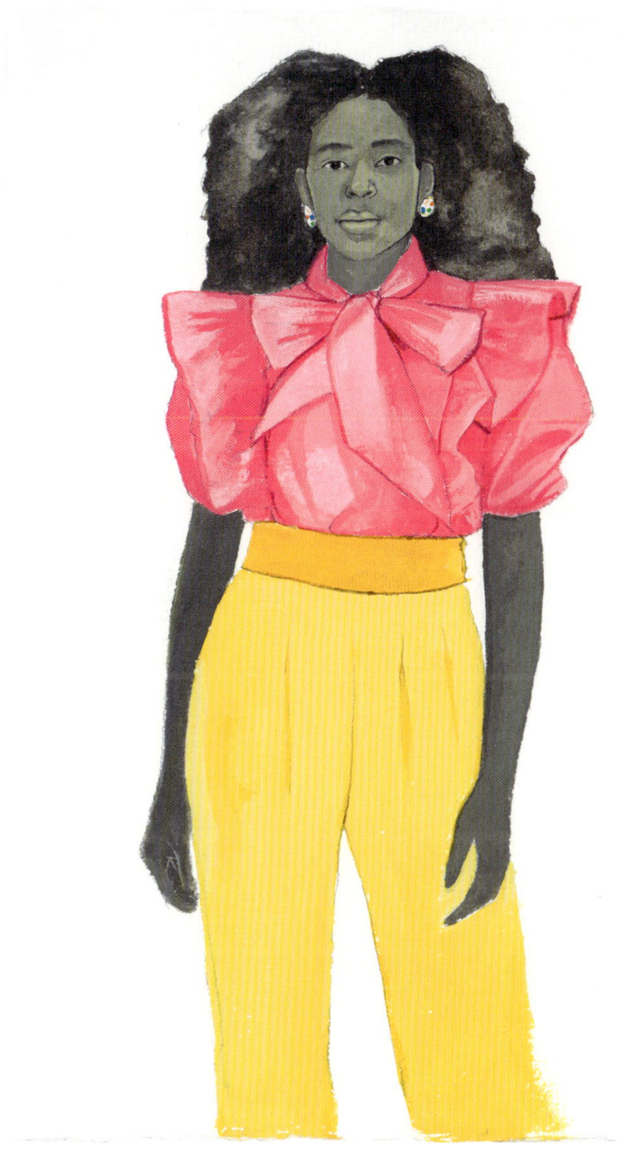

Untitled, 2020
Gouache on paper, 11 × 7½ in. (27.9 × 19.1 cm)

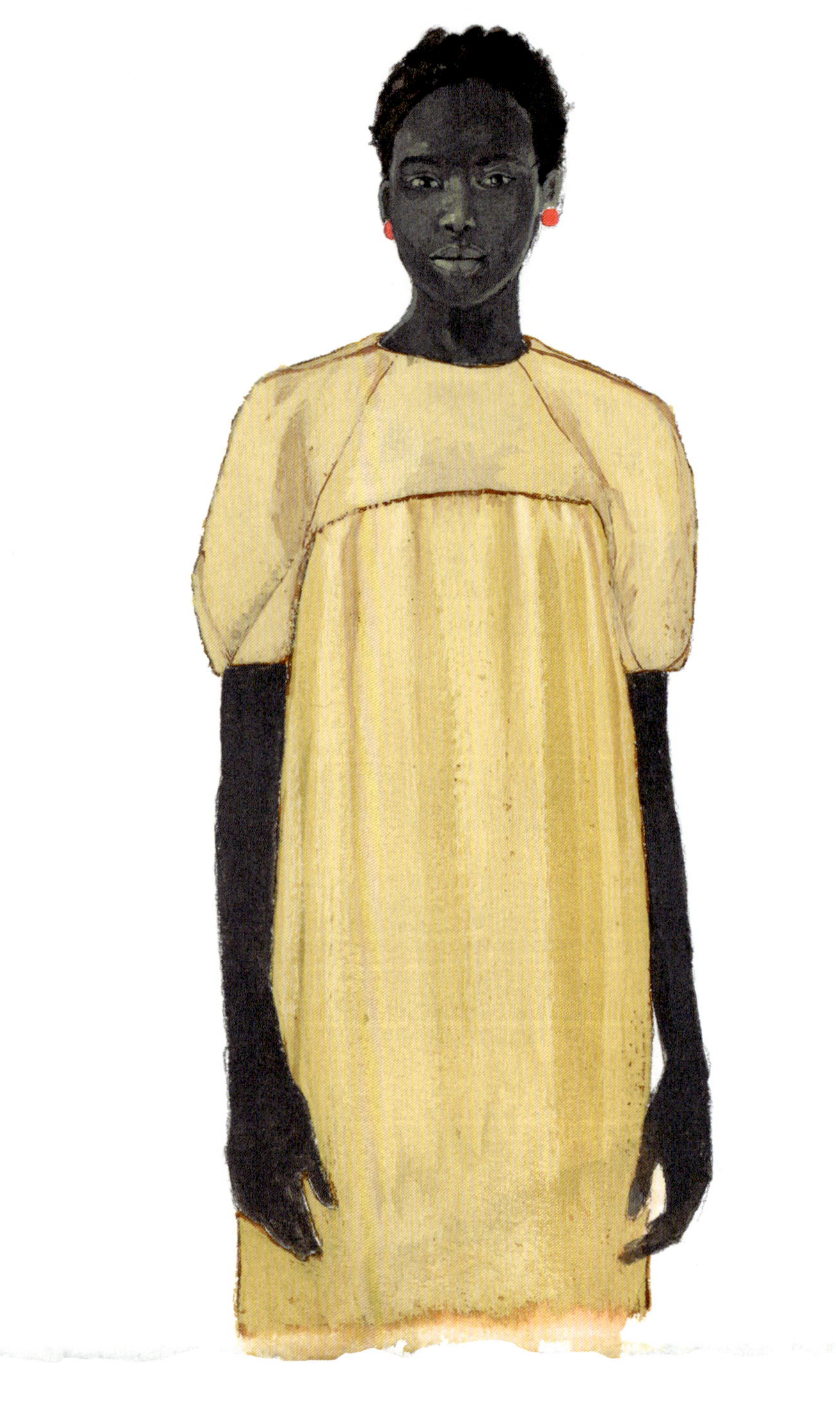

Untitled, 2020
Gouache on paper, 15 × 22 in. (38 × 55.9 cm)

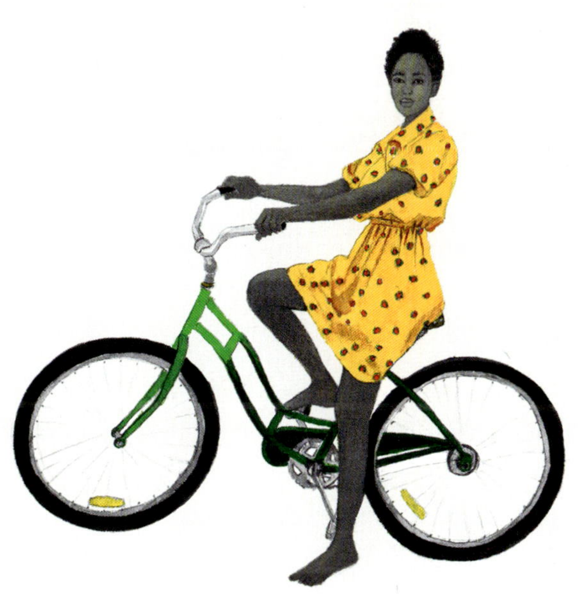

Untitled, 2020
Gouache on paper, 7½ × 11 in. (19.1 × 27.9 cm)

Breonna Taylor, 2020

Oil on linen, 54 × 43 in. (137.2 × 109.2 cm)

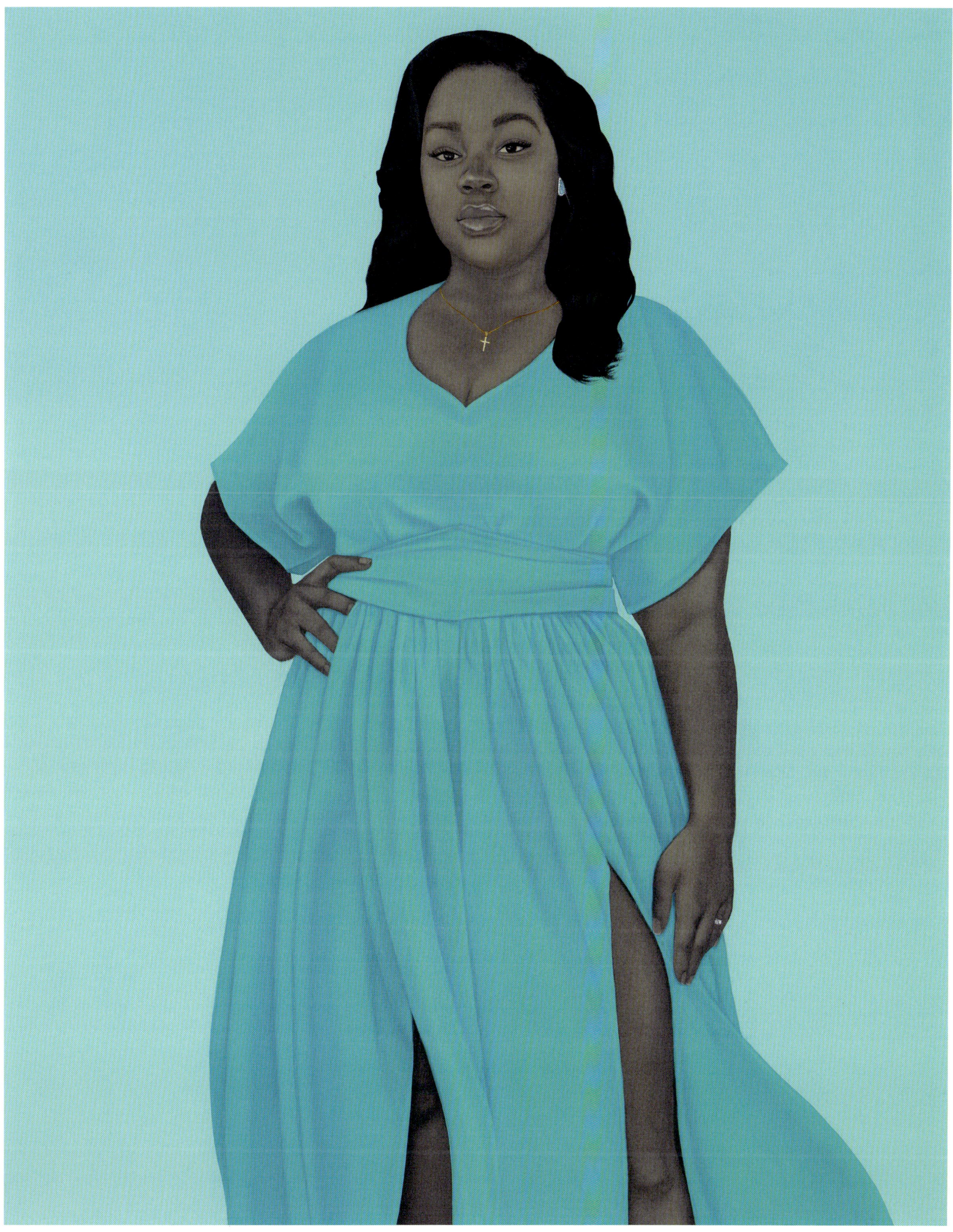

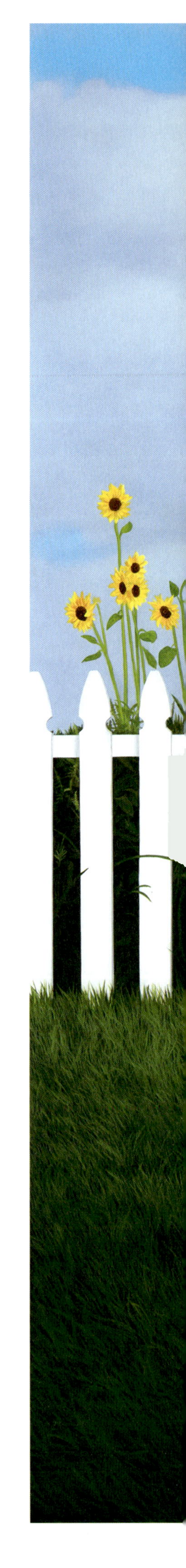

A Midsummer Afternoon Dream, 2021
Oil on canvas, 106 × 101 in. (269.2 × 256.5 cm)

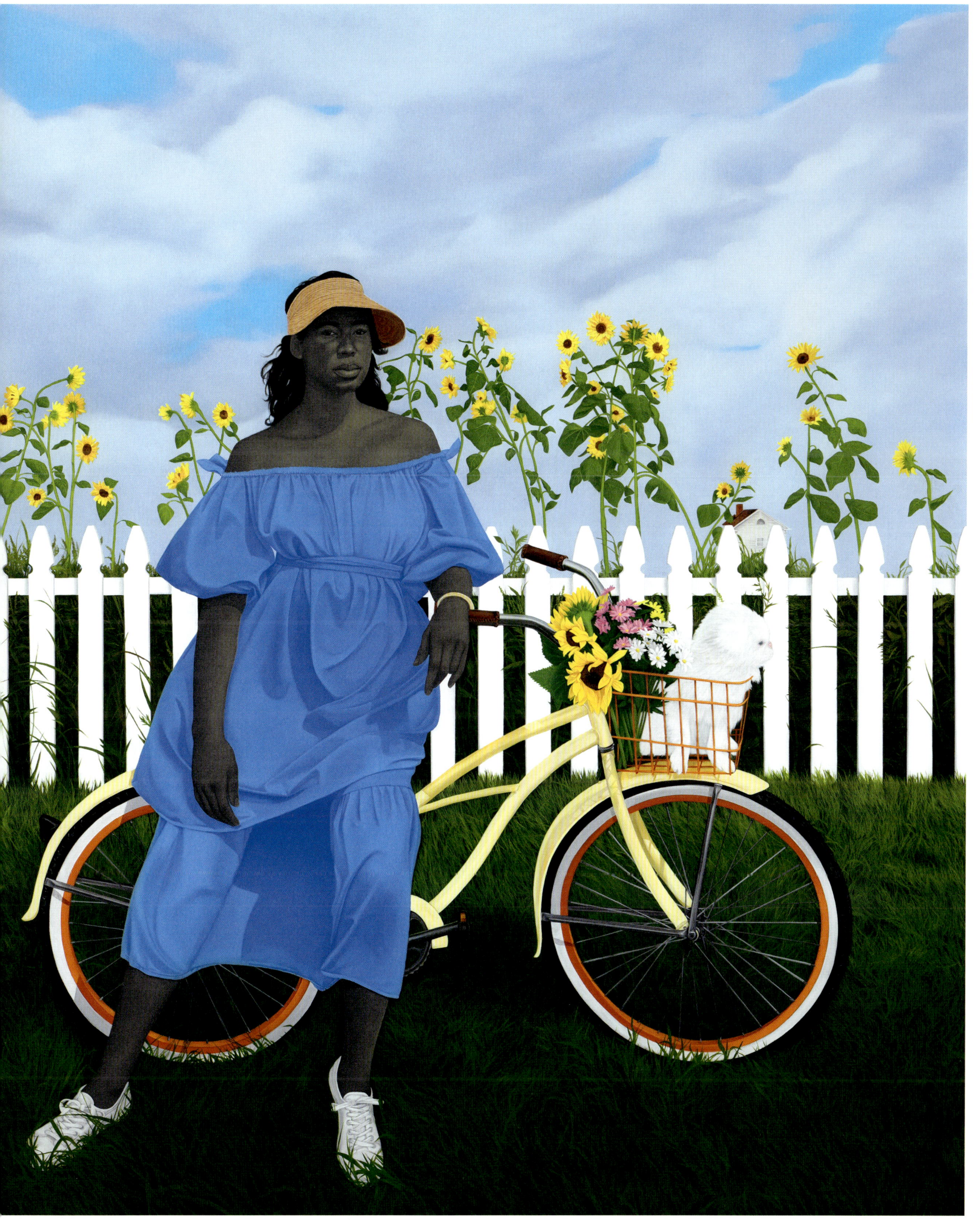

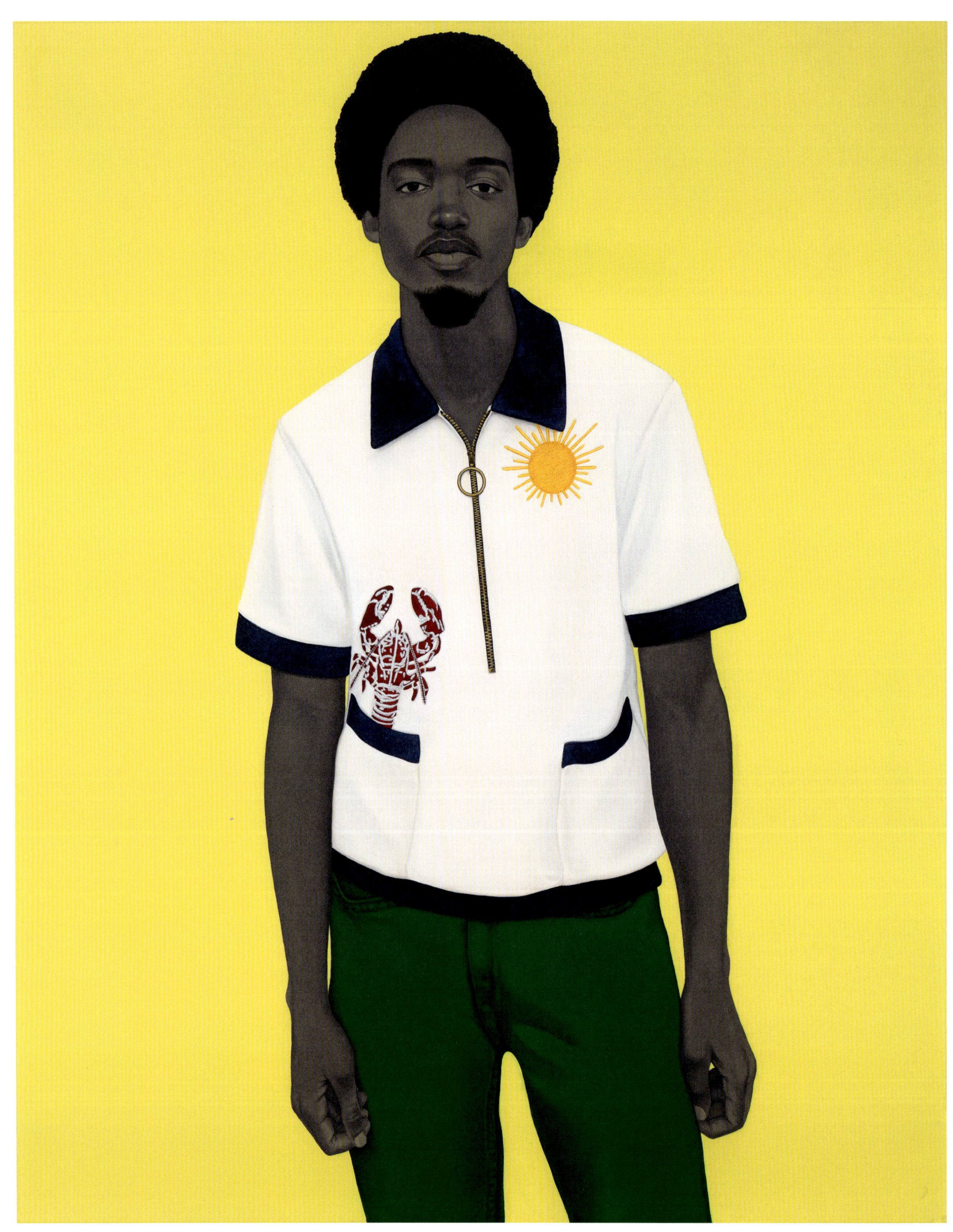

A Bucket Full of Treasures (Papa Gave Me Sunshine to Put in My Pocket), 2020
Oil on linen, 54 × 43 in. (137.2 × 109.2 cm)

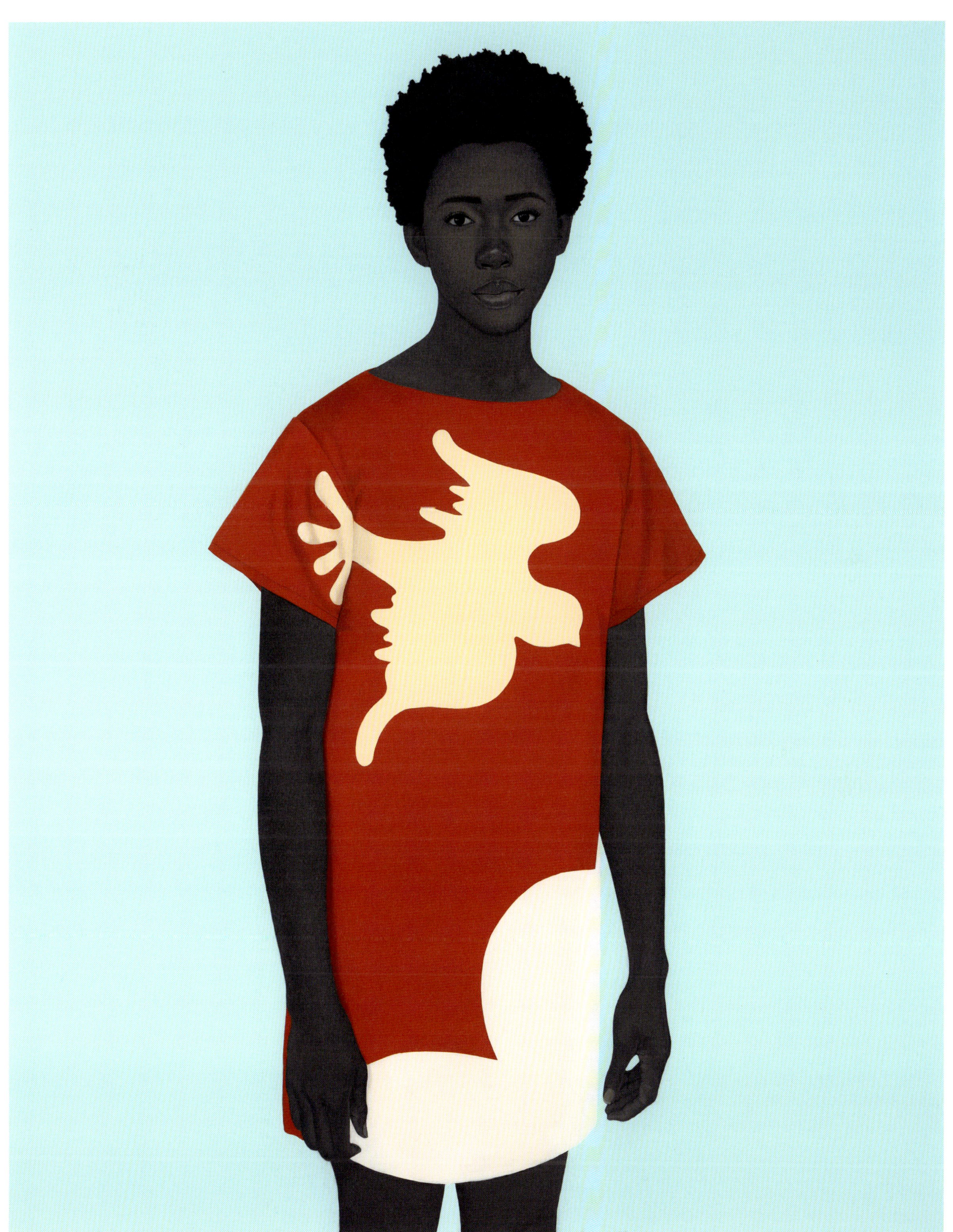

Hope Is the Thing with Feathers (The Little Bird), 2020
Oil on linen, 54 × 43 in. (137.2 × 109.2 cm)

As American as Apple Pie, 2021

Oil on canvas, 123 × 101 in. (312.4 × 256.5 cm)

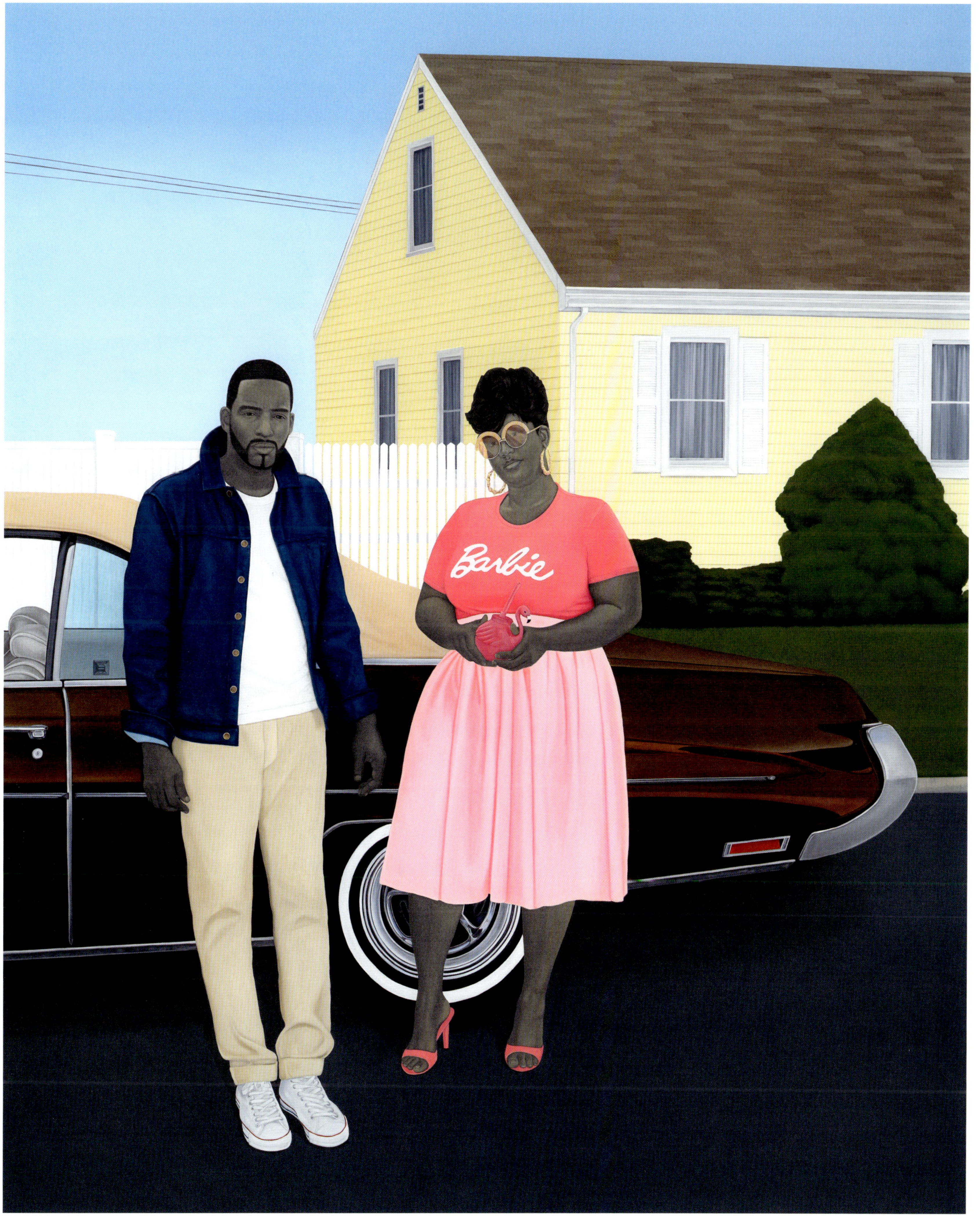
Barbie

For Love, and for Country, 2022
Oil on linen, 123¼ × 93⅛ in. (313 × 236.5 cm)

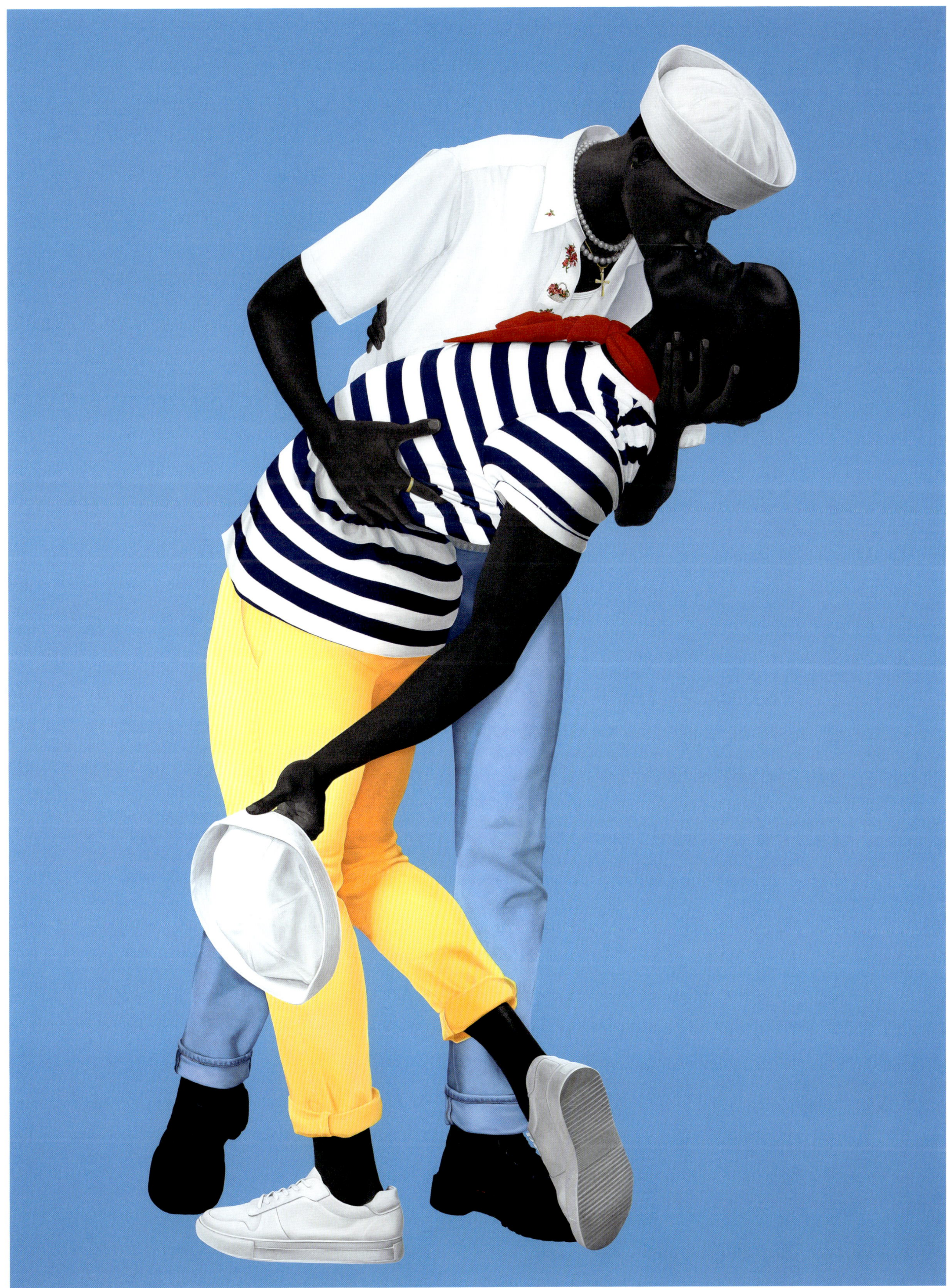

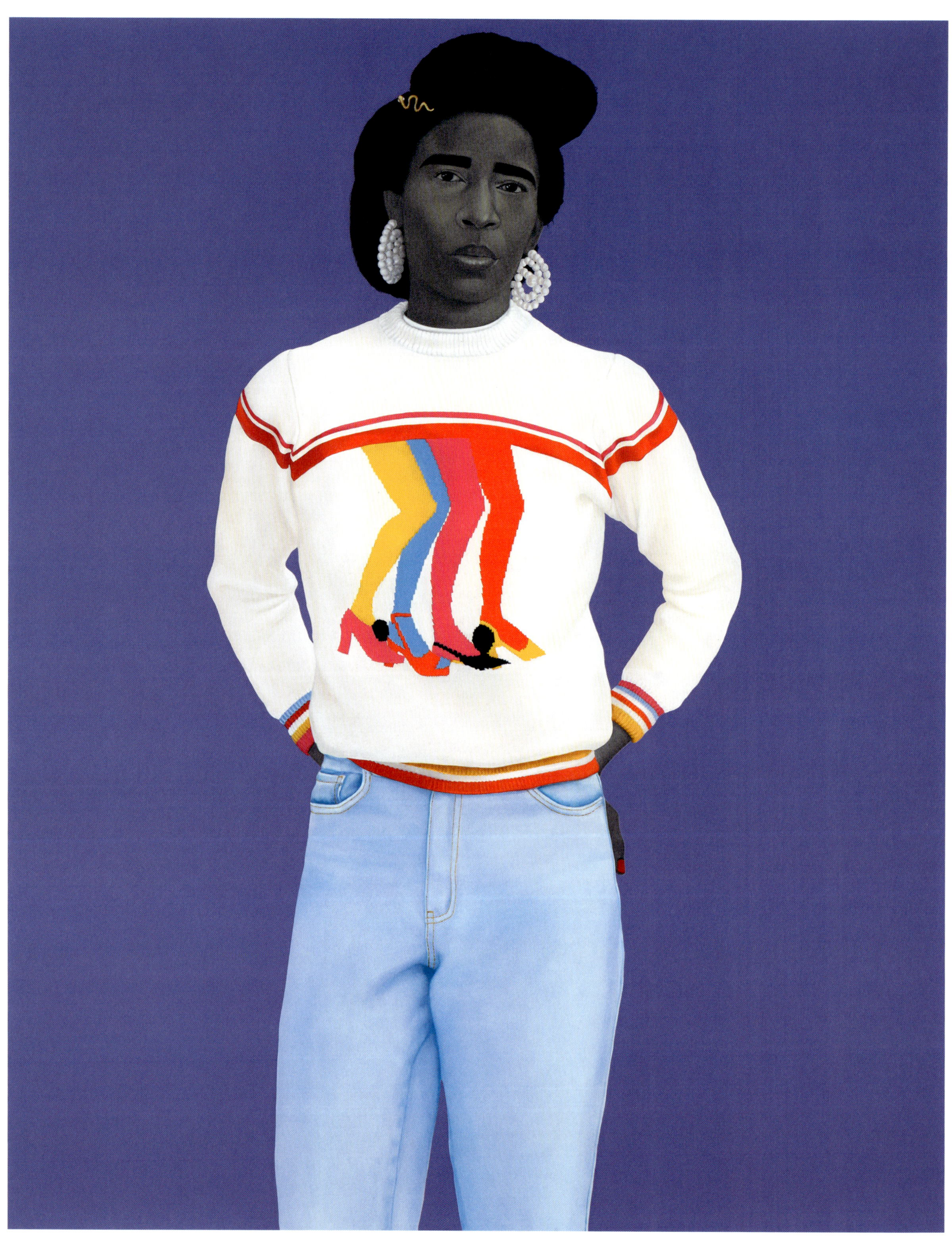

To Tell Her Story You Must Walk in Her Shoes, 2022
Oil on linen, 54 × 43 in. (137.2 × 109.2 cm)

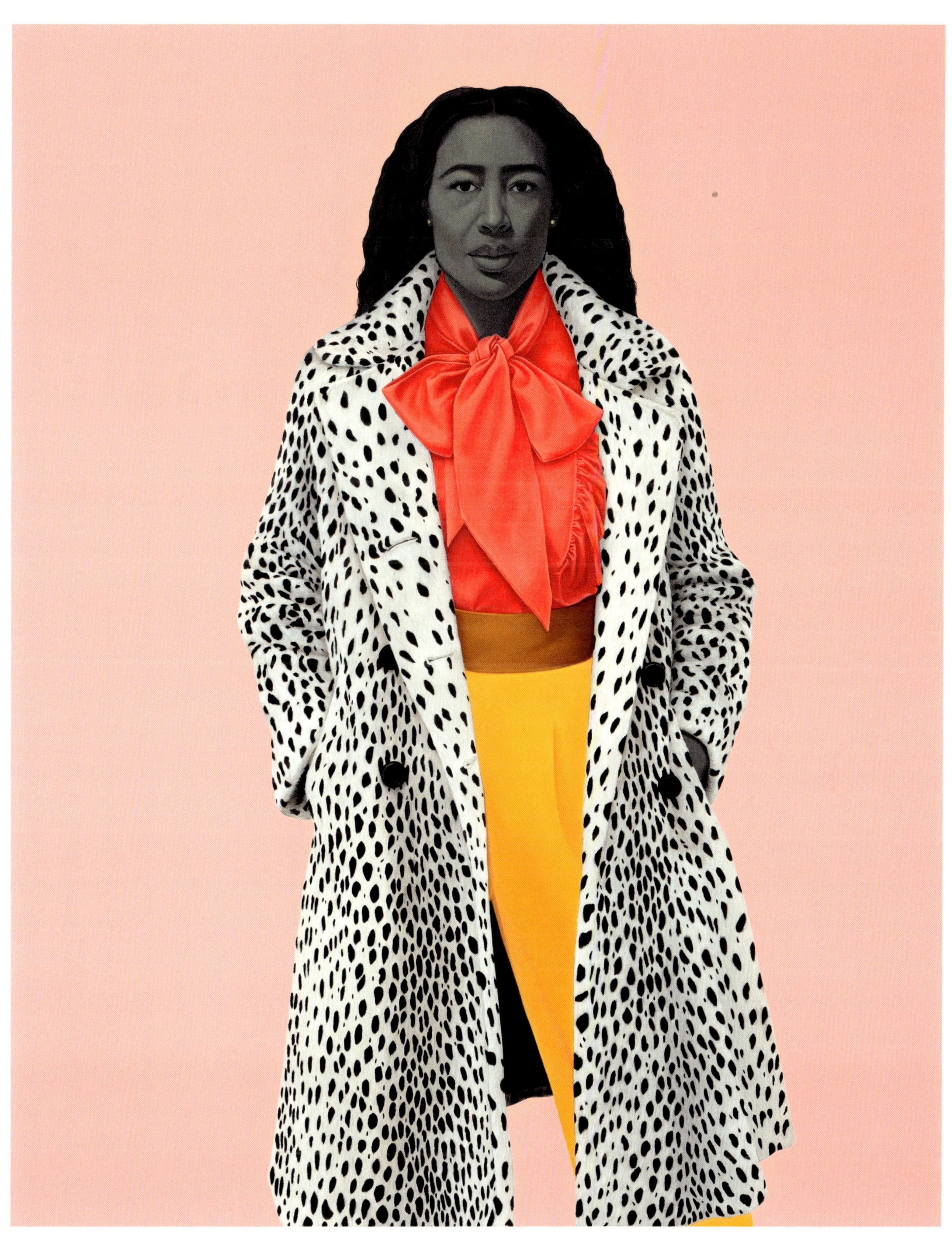

As Soft as She Is . . ., 2022
Oil on linen, 54 × 43 in. (137.2 × 109.2 cm)

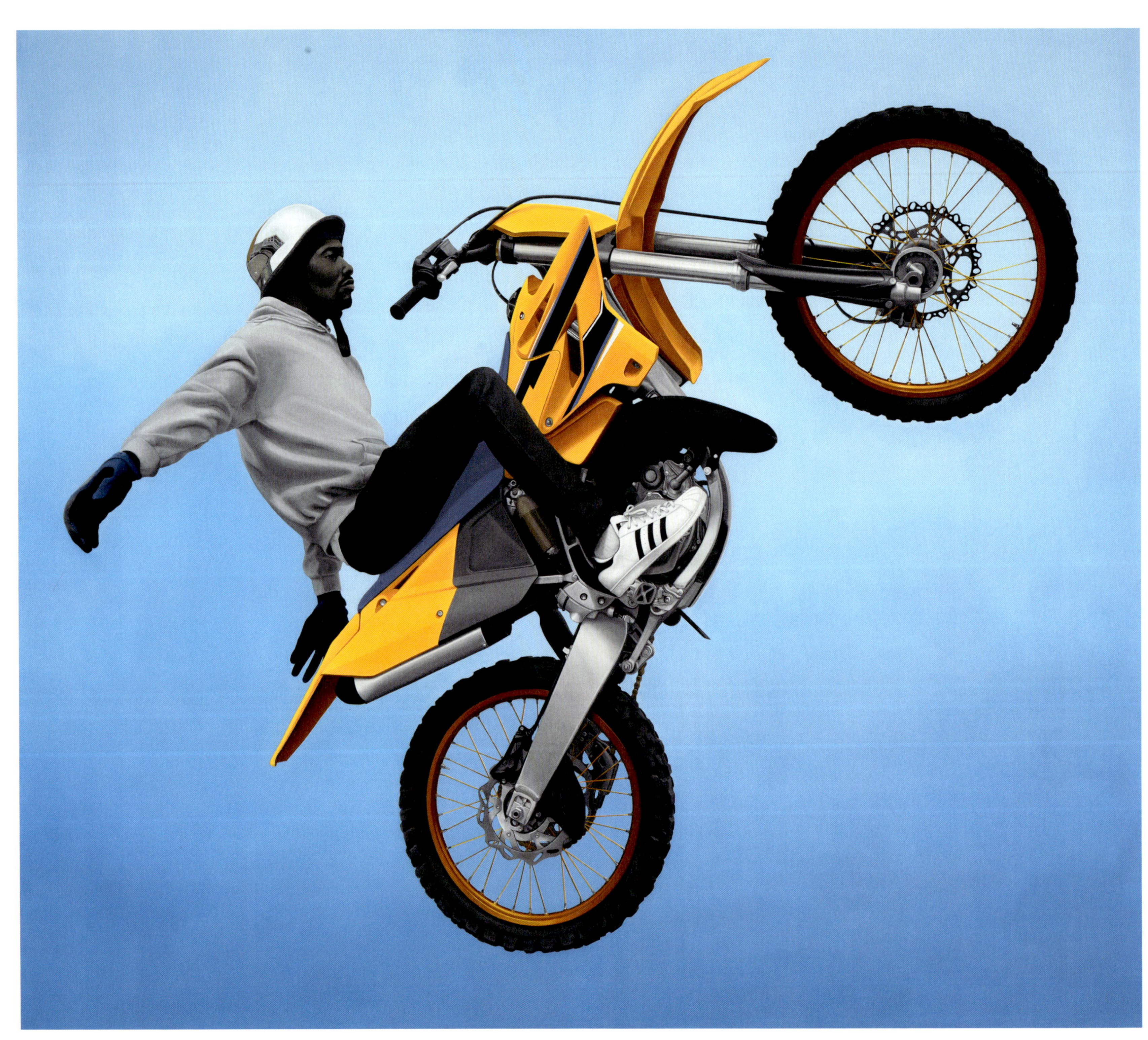

Deliverance, 2022
Oil on linen, two panels, overall: 108⅜ × 266½ in. (274.8 × 676.9 cm)

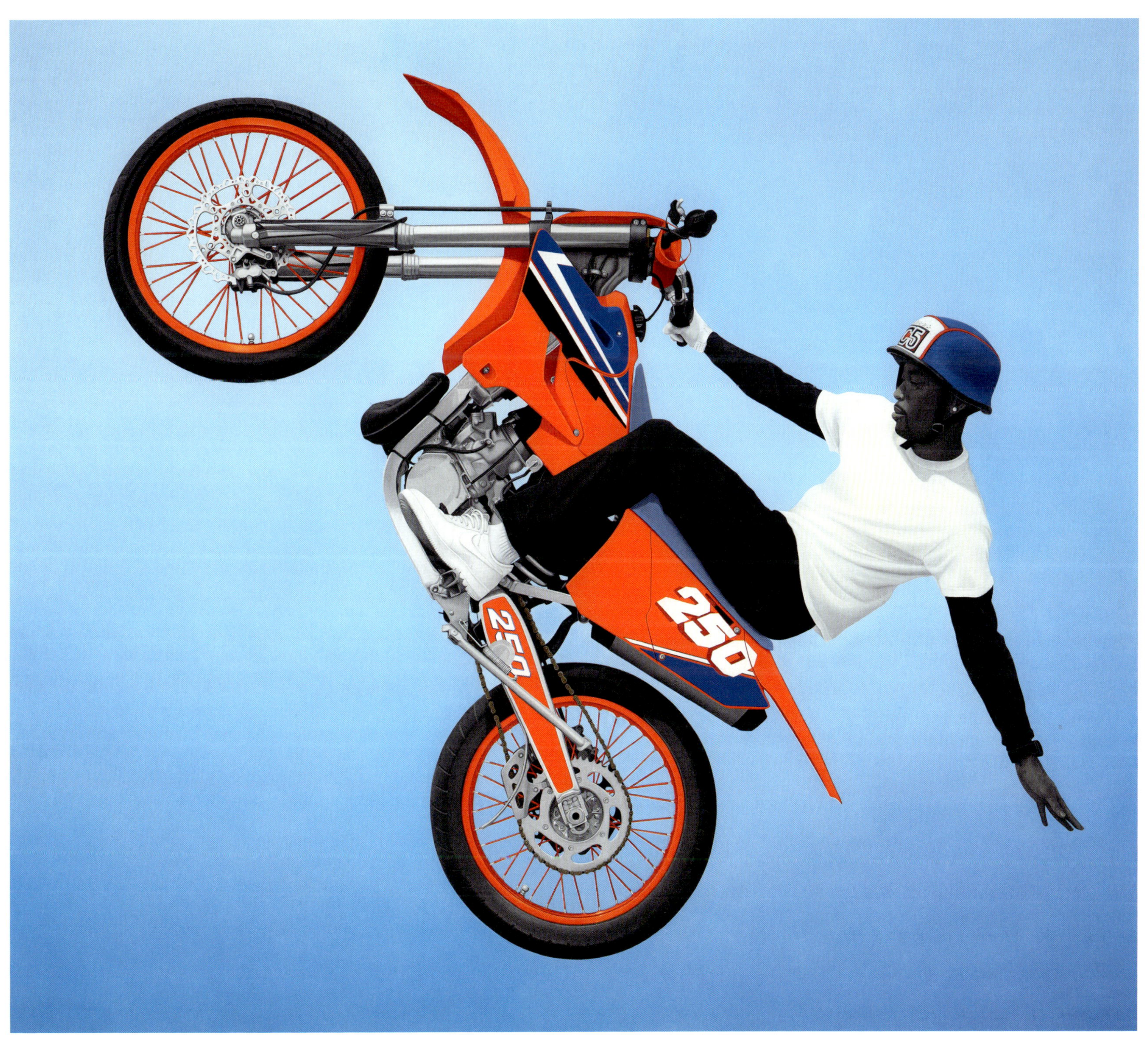
250
250

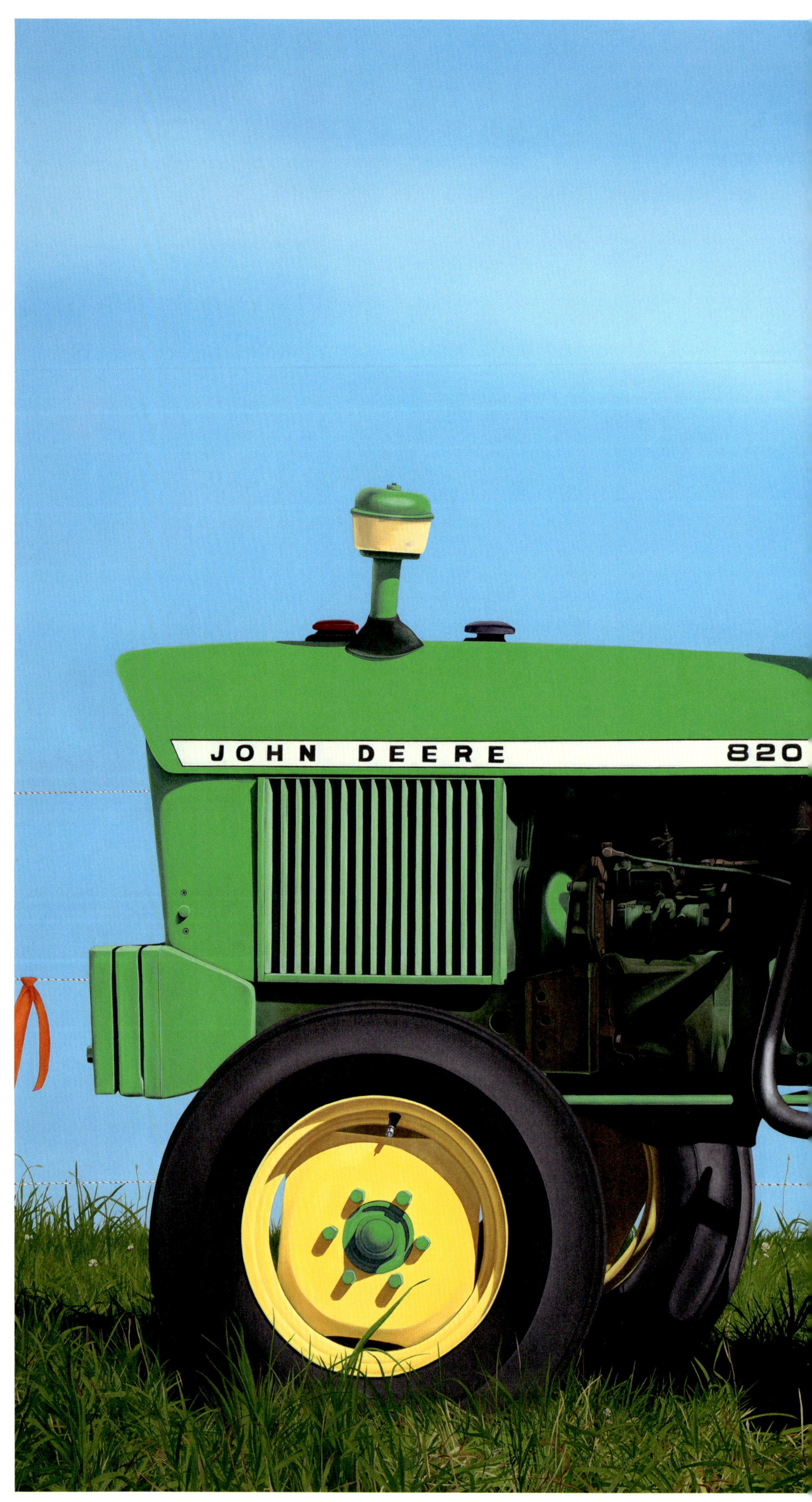

A God Blessed Land (Empire of Dirt), 2022
Oil on linen, 96⅛ × 130⅛ in. (244.3 × 331 cm)

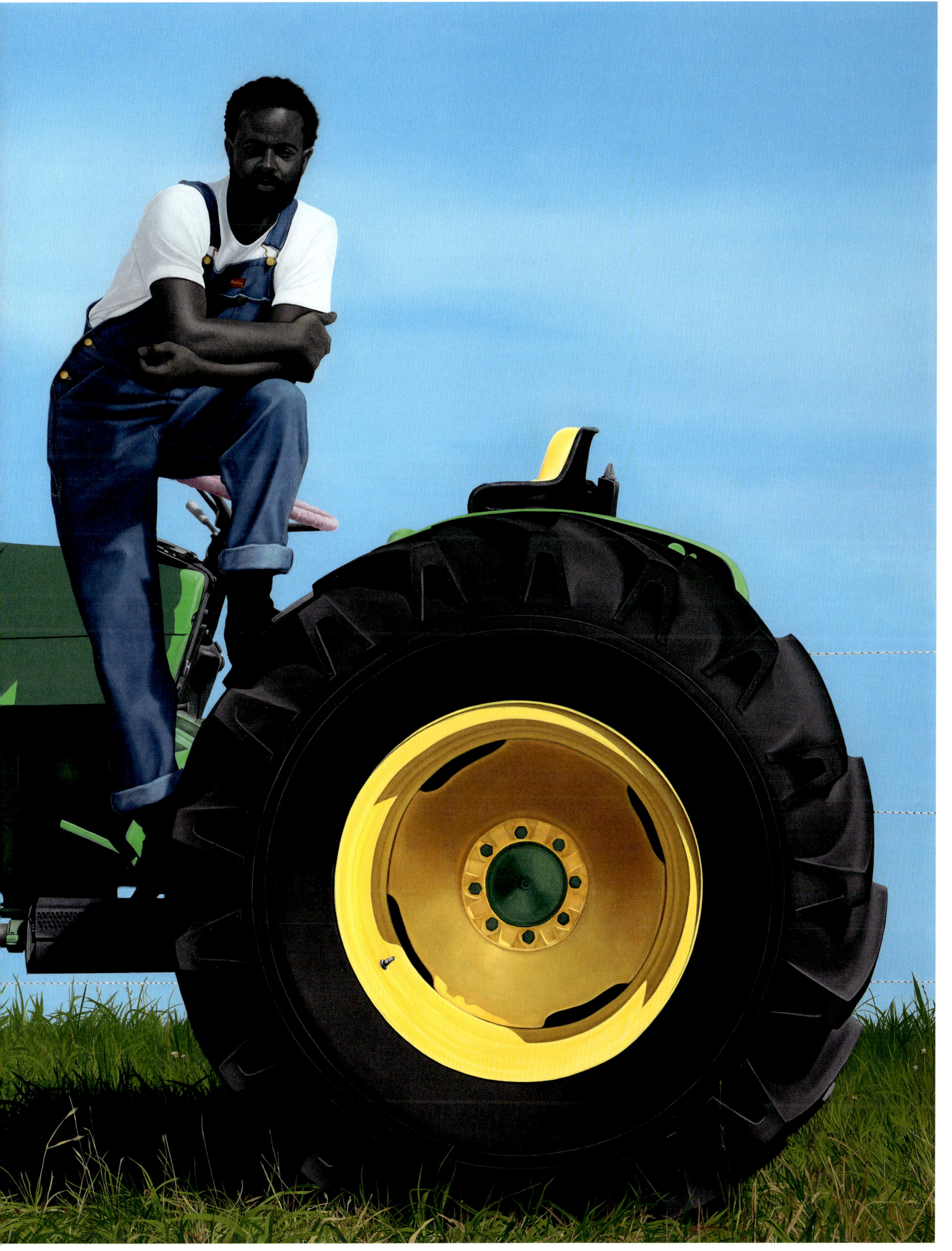

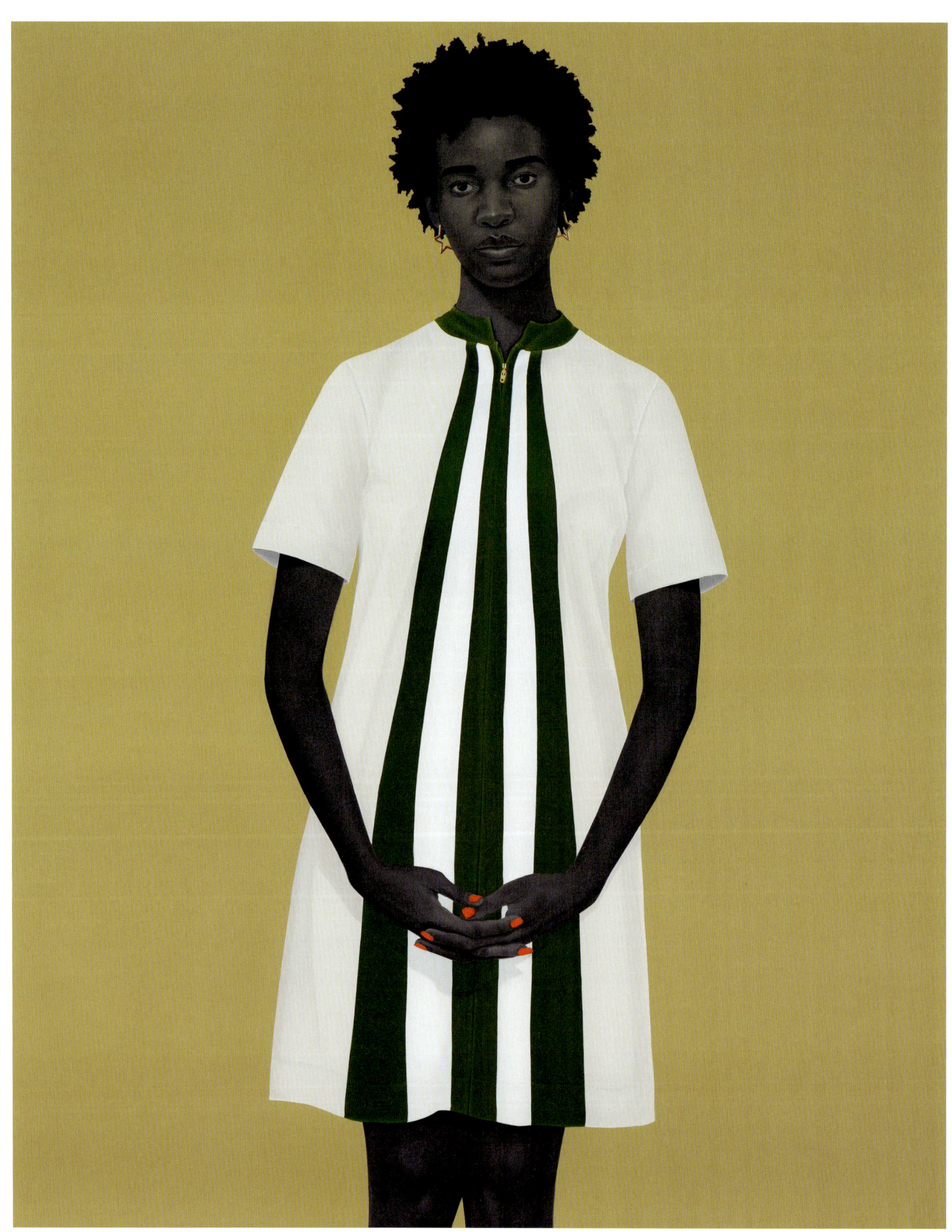

A Certain Kind of Happiness, 2022
Oil on linen, 54 × 43 in. (137.2 × 109.2 cm)

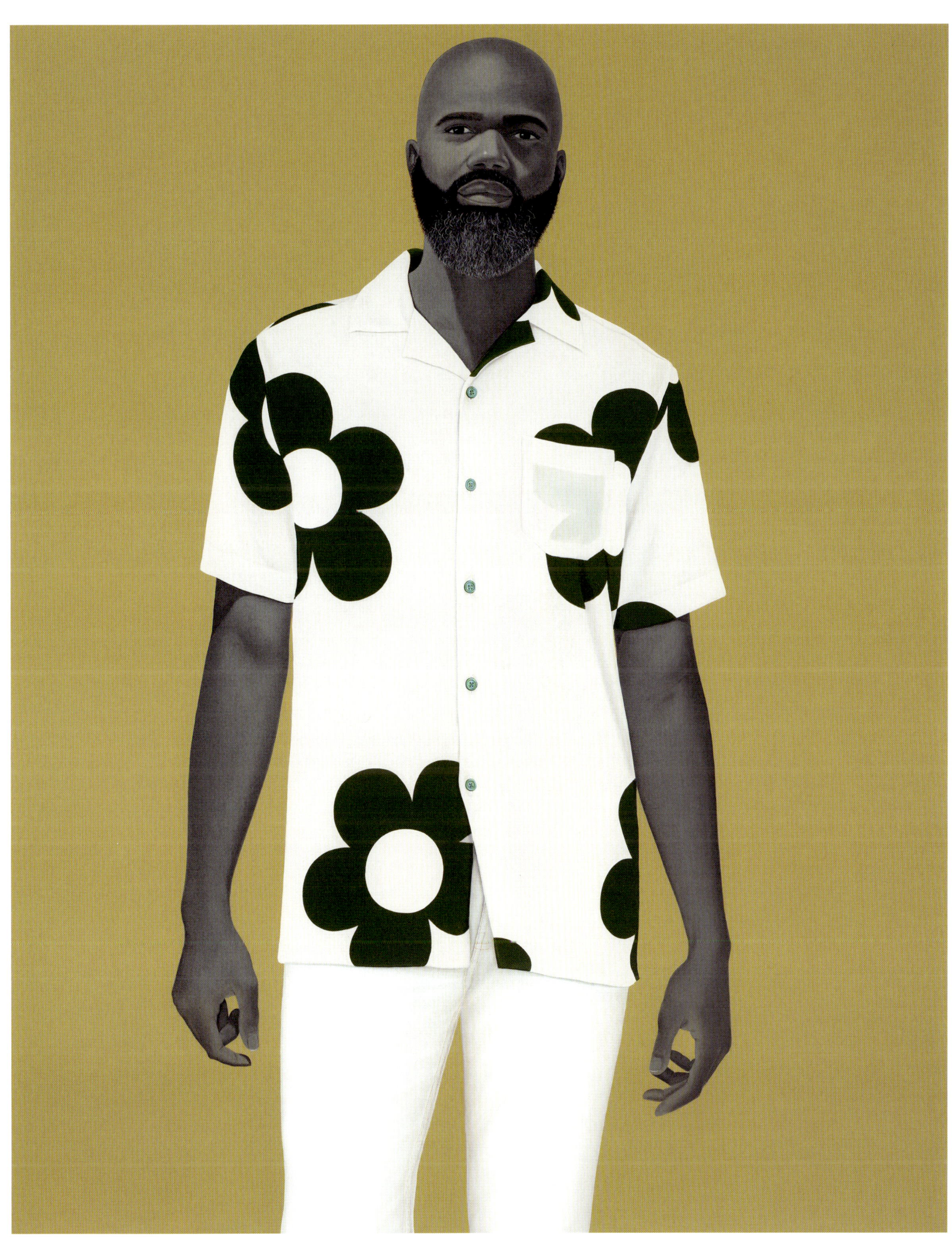

A Certain Kind of Happiness, 2022
Oil on linen, 54 × 43 in. (137.2 × 109.2 cm)

Kingdom, 2022

Oil on linen, $117\frac{1}{8} \times 92$ in. (297.5 × 233.7 cm)

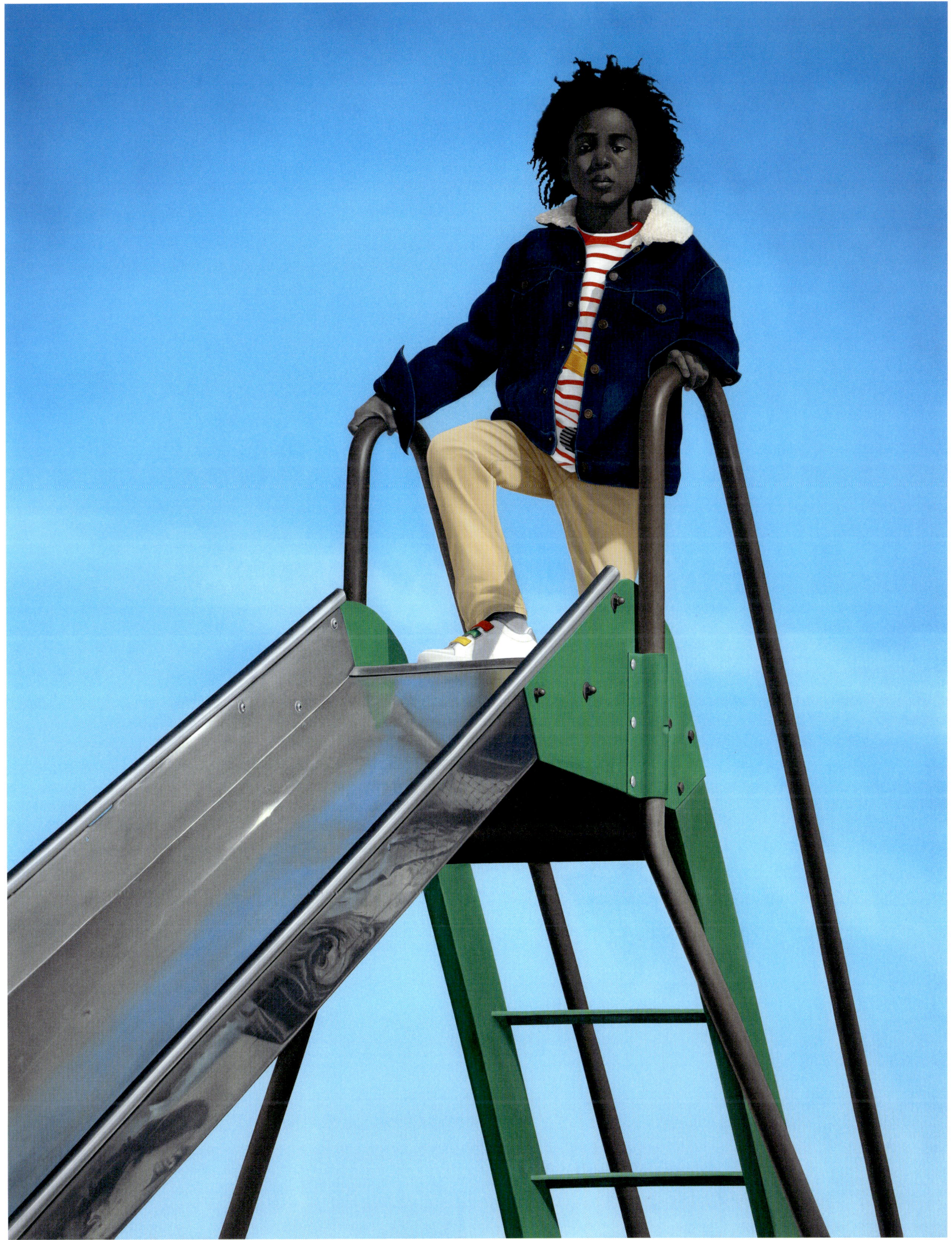

The Beauty of Change (A Beautiful Man), 2023

Oil on linen, 54 × 43 in. (137.2 × 109.2 cm)

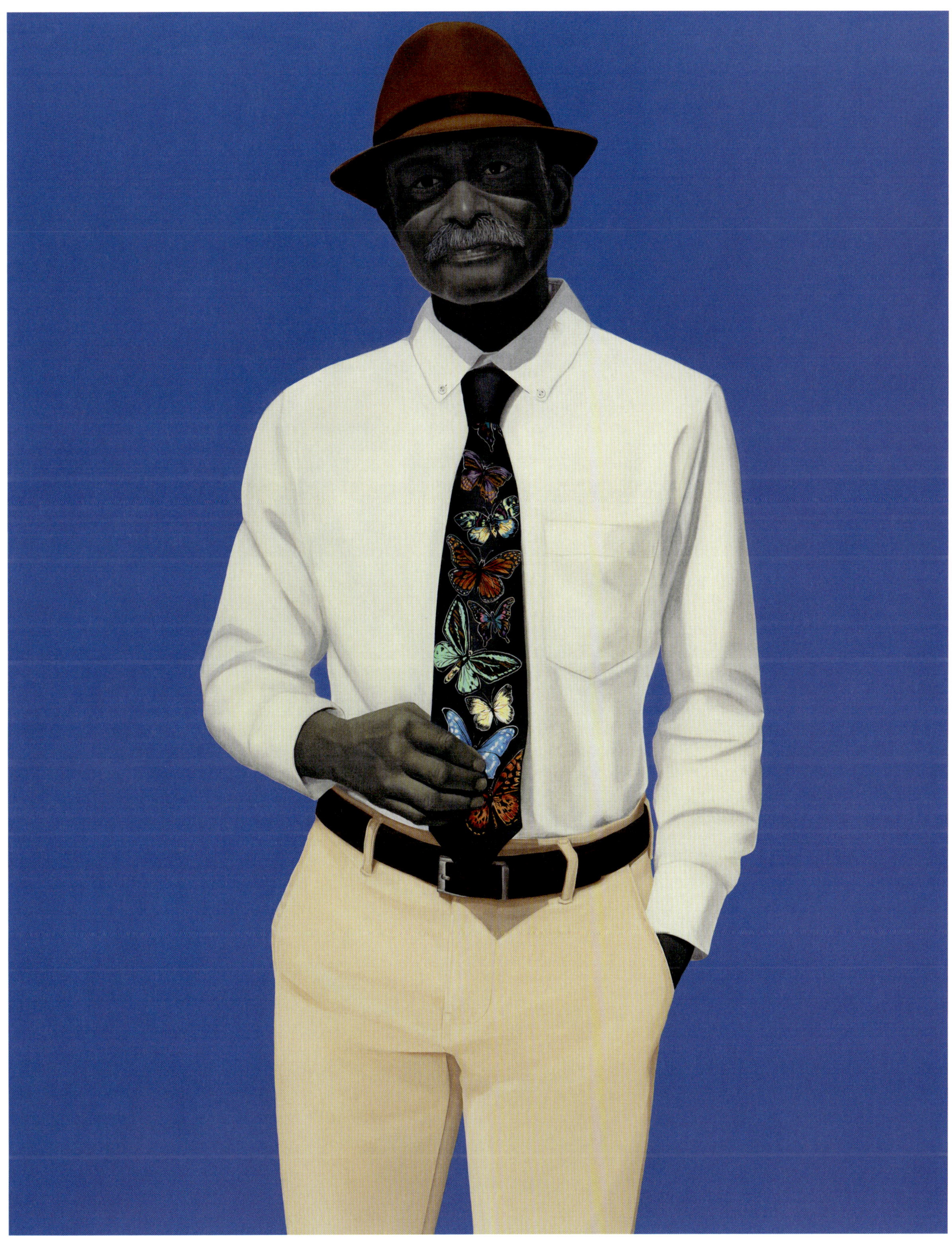

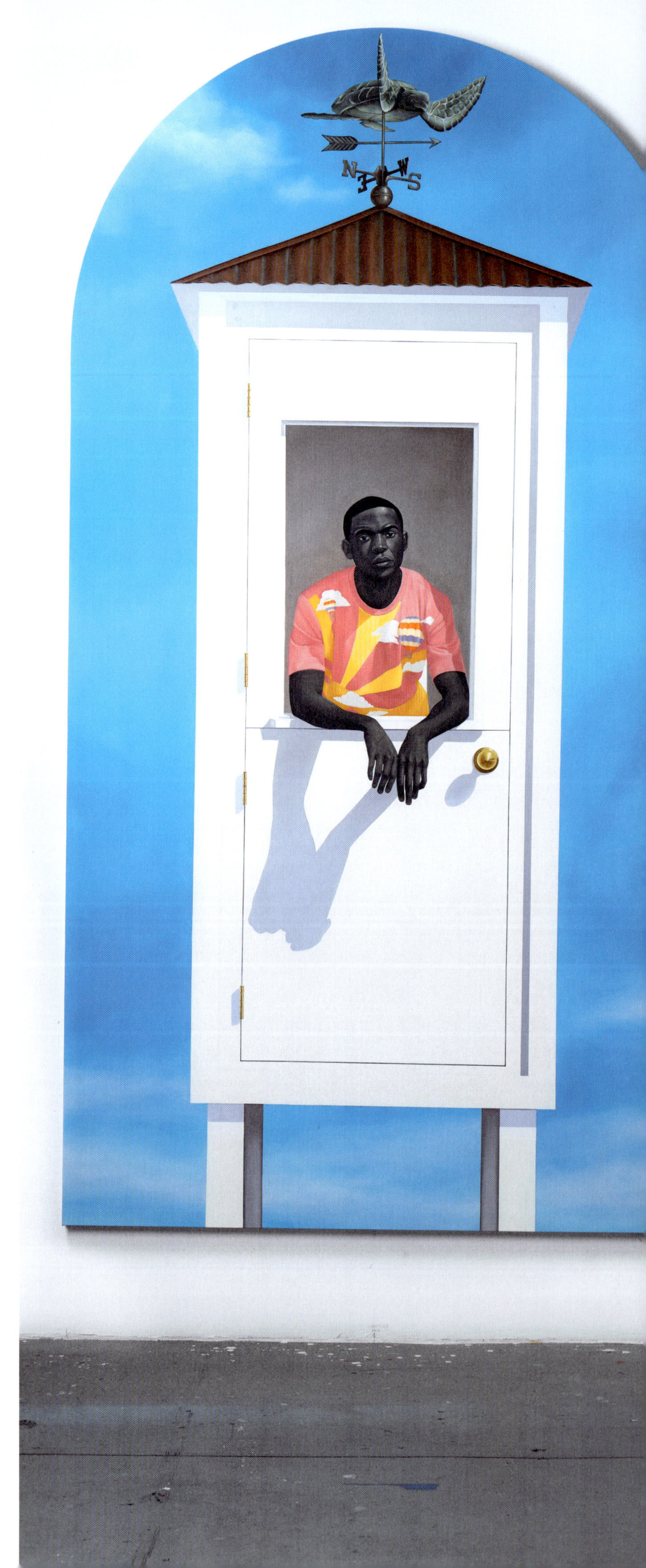

Amy Sherald and August in her studio with an in-progress view of *Ecclesia (The Meeting of Inheritance and Horizons)* in the background, 2024

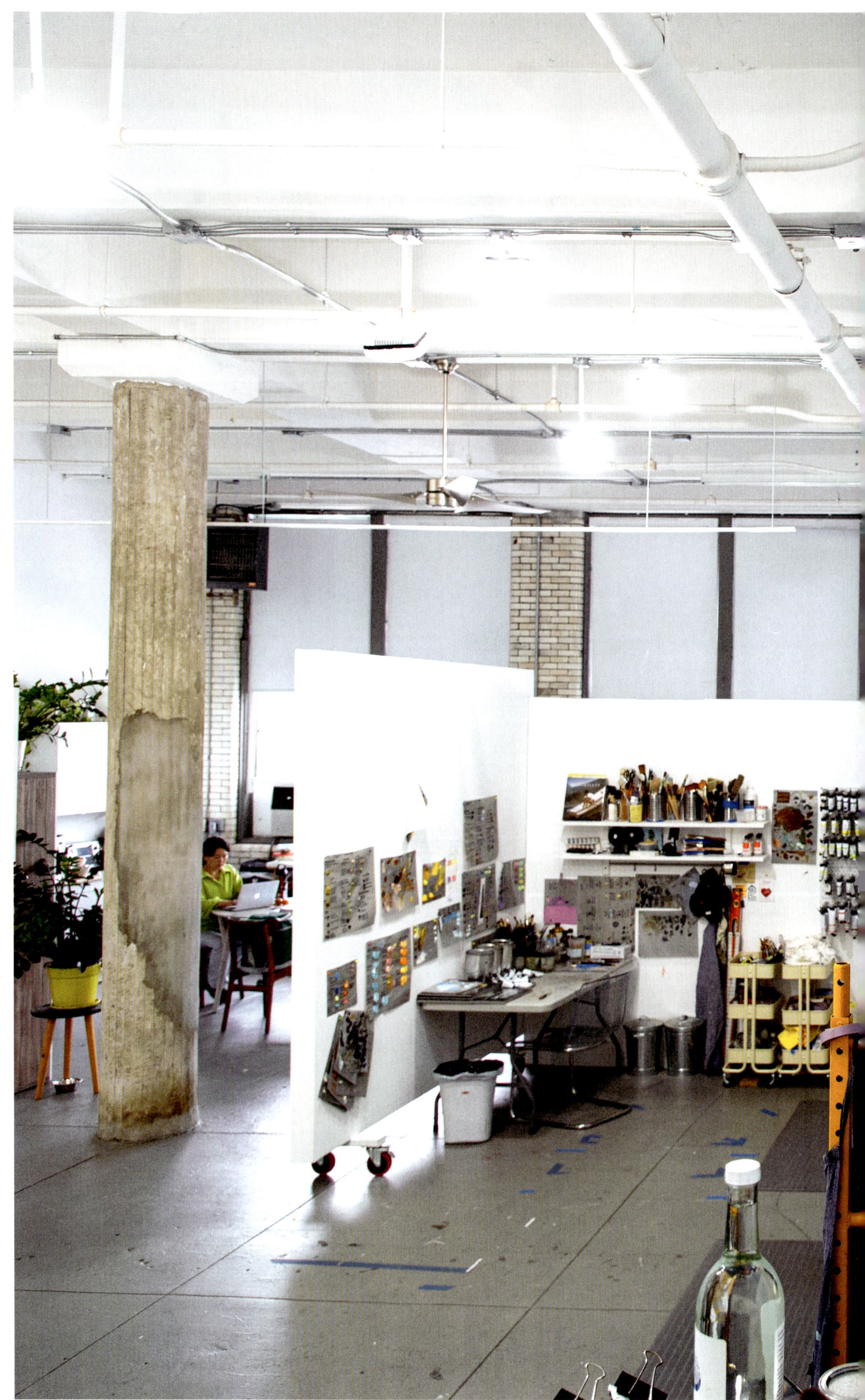

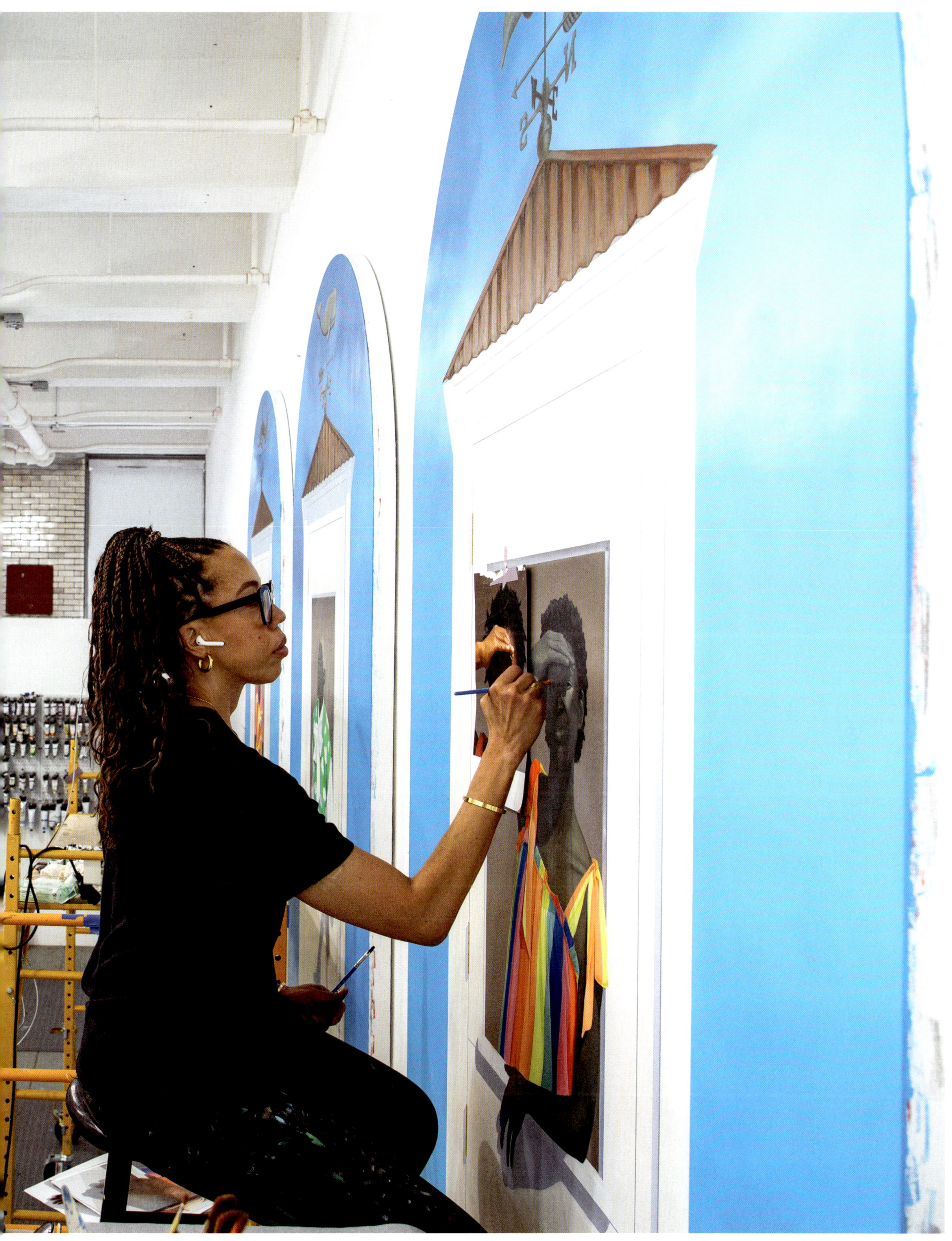

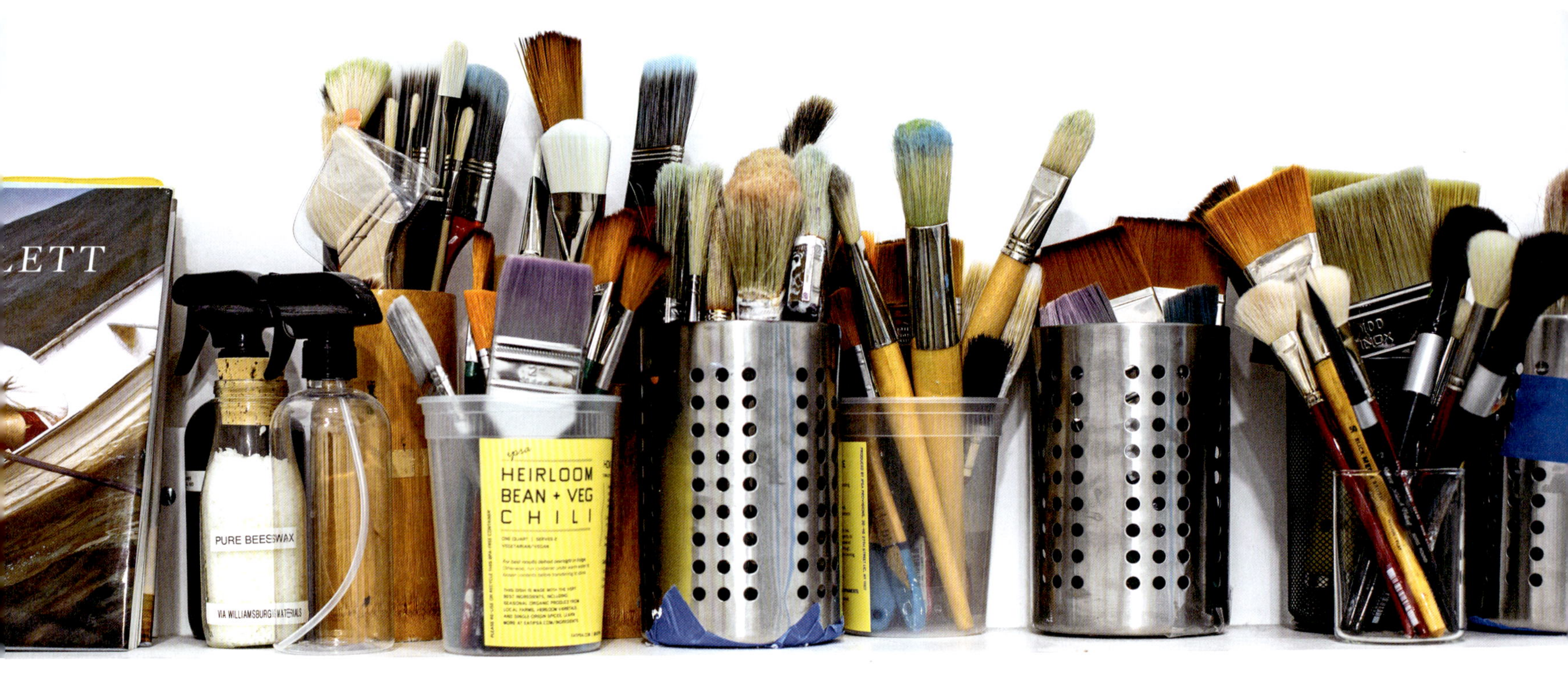
PURE BEESWAX
HEIRLOOM
BEAN + VEG
CHILI

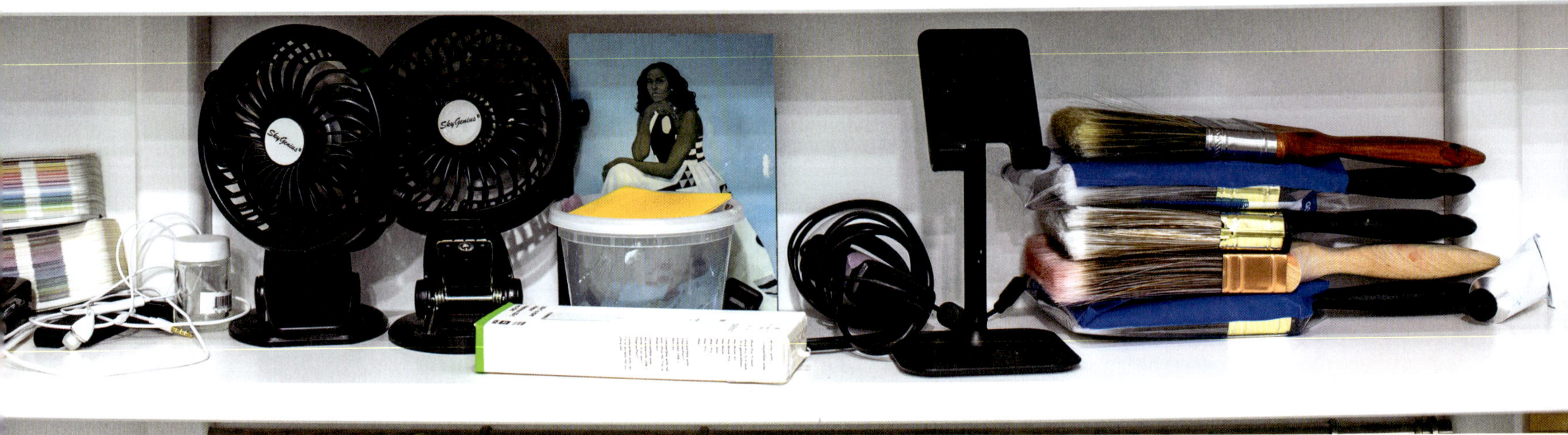

Index of Illustrated Works by Amy Sherald

This listing reflects the information available at the time of publication.

Hangman, 2007
Oil on canvas, 100 × 67 in. (254 × 170.2 cm)
Collection of Sheryll Cashin and Marque Chambliss
p. 51

Equilibrium, 2008
Oil on canvas, 100 × 67 in. (254 × 170.2 cm)
Art in Embassies Permanent Collection, US Embassy Dakar, Senegal
p. 55

The Fairest of the Not So Fair, 2008
Oil on canvas, 54 × 43 in. (137.2 × 109.2 cm)
Private collection
p. 52

Pony Boy, 2008
Oil on canvas, 54 × 43 in. (137.2 × 109.2 cm)
Collection of Vladimir Alexanyan family
p. 57

Puppetmaster, 2008
Oil on canvas, 72 × 51 in. (182.9 × 129.5 cm)
DC Commission on the Arts and Humanities
p. 53

Well Prepared and Maladjusted, 2008
Oil on canvas, 54 × 43 in. (137.2 × 109.2 cm)
Private collection
p. 56

The Rabbit in the Hat, 2009
Oil on canvas, 54 × 43 in. (137.2 × 109.2 cm)
Green Family Art Foundation, courtesy Adam Green Art Advisory
p. 58

They Call Me Redbone, but I'd Rather Be Strawberry Shortcake, 2009
Oil on canvas, 54 × 43 in. (137.2 × 109.2 cm)
National Museum of Women in the Arts, Washington, DC, gift of Steven Scott, Baltimore, in honor of the artist and the 25th anniversary of National Museum of Women in the Arts
p. 59

Guide Me No More, 2011
Oil on canvas, 54 × 43 in. (137.2 × 109.2 cm)
Collection of Mr. and Mrs. Bryant Gumbel
p. 61

It Made Sense . . . Mostly in Her Mind, 2011
Oil on canvas, 54 × 43 in. (137.2 × 109.2 cm)
Nancy and Sean Cotton Collection
p. 60

Grand Dame Queenie, 2012
Oil on canvas, 54 × 43 in. (137.2 × 109.2 cm)
Smithsonian National Museum of African American History and Culture, Washington, DC
p. 65

Welfare Queen, 2012
Oil on canvas, 54 × 43 in. (137.2 × 109.2 cm)
Nancy and Sean Cotton Collection
p. 63

Freeing herself was one thing, taking ownership of that freed self was another, 2013
Oil on canvas, 54 × 43 in. (137.2 × 109.2 cm)
Green Family Art Foundation, courtesy Adam Green Art Advisory
p. 71

The Boy with No Past, 2014
Oil on canvas, 54 × 43 in. (137.2 × 109.2 cm)
Private collection
p. 67

Fact was she knew more about them than she knew about herself, having never had the map to discover what she was like, 2014
Oil on canvas, 54 × 43 in. (137.2 × 109.2 cm)
Collection of Robert F. Smith
p. 70

Miss Everything (Unsuppressed Deliverance), 2014
Oil on canvas, 54 × 43 in. (137.2 × 109.2 cm)
Private collection
p. 69

The Bathers, 2015
Oil on canvas, 72⅛ × 67 in. (183.2 × 170.2 cm)
Private collection
pp. 74–75

Saint Woman, 2015
Oil on canvas, 54 × 43 in. (137.2 × 109.2 cm)
Private collection, courtesy Monique Meloche Gallery and Hauser & Wirth
p. 73

All Things Bright and Beautiful, 2016
Oil on canvas, 54 × 43 in. (137.2 × 109.2 cm)
Collection of Frances and Burton Reifler, Winston-Salem, North Carolina
p. 85

The Boy with the Big Fish, 2016
Oil on canvas, 54 × 43 in. (137.2 × 109.2 cm)
Private collection
p. 83

A Golden Afternoon, 2016
Oil on canvas, 54 × 43 in. (137.2 × 109.2 cm)
Private collection
p. 76

Innocent You, Innocent Me, 2016
Oil on canvas, 54 × 43 in. (137.2 × 109.2 cm)
Private collection
p. 78

Listen, you a wonder. You a city of a woman. You got a geography of your own, 2016
Oil on canvas, 54 × 43 in. (137.2 × 109.2 cm)
Collection of Rashid Johnson and Sheree Hovsepian
p. 84

The Make Believer (Monet's Garden), 2016
Oil on canvas, 54 × 43 in. (137.2 × 109.2 cm)
Private collection
p. 79

Mother and Child, 2016
Oil on canvas, 54 × 43 in. (137.2 × 109.2 cm)
The Blanchard Nesbitt Family
p. 77

Pilgrimage of the Chameleon, 2016
Oil on canvas, 72 × $51\frac{1}{8}$ in. (182.9 × 130 cm)
Private collection, Europe
p. 81

A Clear Unspoken Granted Magic, 2017
Oil on canvas, 54 × 43 in. (137.2 × 109.2 cm)
Private collection
p. 91

The Lesson of the Falling Leaves, 2017
Oil on canvas, 54 × 43 in. (137.2 × 109.2 cm)
The Museum of Contemporary Art, Los Angeles, purchase with funds provided by the Acquisition and Collection Committee
p. 87

Light Is Easy to Love, 2017
Oil on canvas, 54 × 43 in. (137.2 × 109.2 cm)
Nasher Museum of Art at Duke University, Durham, North Carolina, gift of Jennifer McCracken New (T '90, L '94) and Jason G. New (L '94), in honor of Sarah Schroth
p. 90

Try on dreams until I find the one that fits me. They all fit me, 2017
Oil on canvas, 54 × 43 in. (137.2 × 109.2 cm)
Kemper Museum of Contemporary Art, Kansas City, Missouri, museum purchase made possible by a gift from the Bebe and Crosby Kemper Foundation
p. 92

What's different about Alice is that she has the most incisive way of telling the truth, 2017
Oil on canvas, 54 × 43 in. (137.2 × 109.2 cm)
The Columbus Museum, Georgia
p. 86

What's precious inside of him does not care to be known by the mind in ways that diminish its presence (All American), 2017
Oil on canvas, 54 × 43 in. (137.2 × 109.2 cm)
Private collection, courtesy Monique Meloche Gallery
p. 89

Mama Has Made the Bread (How Things Are Measured), 2018
Oil on canvas, 54 × 43 in. (137.2 × 109.2 cm)
Private collection
p. 93

Michelle LaVaughn Robinson Obama, 2018
Oil on linen, 72⅛ × 60⅛ in. (183.2 × 152.7 cm)
National Portrait Gallery, Smithsonian Institution, Washington, DC, gift of Kate Capshaw and Steven Spielberg; Judith Kern and Kent Whealy; Tommie L. Pegues and Donald A. Capoccia; Clarence, DeLoise, and Brenda Gaines; Jonathan and Nancy Lee Kemper; The Stoneridge Fund of Amy and Marc Meadows; Robert E. Meyerhoff and Rheda Becker; Catherine and Michael Podell; Mark and Cindy Aron; Lyndon J. Barrois and Janine Sherman Barrois; The Honorable John and Louise Bryson; Paul and Rose Carter; Bob and Jane Clark; Lisa R. Davis; Shirley Ross Davis and Family; Alan and Lois Fern; Conrad and Constance Hipkins; Sharon and John Hoffman; Audrey M. Irmas; John Legend and Chrissy Teigen; Eileen Harris Norton; Helen Hilton Raiser; Philip and Elizabeth Ryan; Roselyne Chroman Swig; Josef Vascovitz and Lisa Goodman; Eileen Baird; Dennis and Joyce Black Family Charitable Foundation; Shelley Brazier; Aryn Drake-Lee; Andy and Teri Goodman; Randi Charno Levine and Jeffrey E. Levine; Fred M. Levin and Nancy Livingston, The Shenson Foundation; Monique Meloche Gallery, Chicago; Arthur Lewis and Hau Nguyen; Sara and John Schram; Alyssa Taubman and Robert Rothman
p. 101

Planes, Rockets, and the Spaces in Between, 2018
Oil on canvas, 100 × 67 in. (254 × 170.2 cm)
Baltimore Museum of Art, purchase with exchange funds from the Pearlstone Family Fund and partial gift of The Andy Warhol Foundation for the Visual Arts, Inc.
p. 95

She Always Believed the Good about Those She Loved, 2018
Oil on canvas, 54 × 43 in. (137.2 × 109.2 cm)
Private collection, courtesy Monique Meloche Gallery
p. 97

She had an inside and an outside now, and suddenly she knew how not to mix them, 2018
Oil on canvas, 54 × 43 in. (137.2 × 109.2 cm)
Bill and Christy Gautreaux Collection, Kansas City, Missouri
p. 99

The Girl Next Door, 2019
Oil on canvas, 54 × 43 in. (137.2 × 109.2 cm)
Private collection
p. 110

Handsome, 2019
Oil on canvas, 54 × 43 in. (137.2 × 109.2 cm)
Collection of Anderson Cooper
p. 108

If You Surrendered to the Air, You Could Ride It, 2019
Oil on linen, 130 × 108 in. (330.2 × 274.3 cm)
Whitney Museum of American Art, New York, purchase, with funds from the Painting and Sculpture Committee, Sascha S. Bauer, Jack Cayre, Nancy Carrington Crown, Nancy Poses, Laura Rapp, and Elizabeth Redleaf
p. 105

Precious Jewels by the Sea, 2019
Oil on linen, 120 × 108 in. (305 × 274.3 cm)
Crystal Bridges Museum of American Art, Bentonville, Arkansas
pp. 106–7

A Single Man in Possession of a Good Fortune, 2019
Oil on canvas, 54 × 43 in. (137.2 × 109.2 cm)
Private collection
p. 111

Sometimes the King Is a Woman, 2019
Oil on canvas, 54 × 43 in. (137.2 × 109.2 cm)
Marieluise Hessel Collection, Center for Curatorial Studies, Bard College, Annandale-on-Hudson, New York
p. 102

There Is No Charm Equal to Tenderness of Heart, 2019
Oil on canvas, 54 × 43 in. (137.2 × 109.2 cm)
Private collection
p. 103

Untitled (Opal), 2019
Oil on linen, 54 × 43 in. (137.2 × 109.2 cm)
Collection of Robert F. Smith
p. 109

Breonna Taylor, 2020
Oil on linen, 54 × 43 in. (137.2 × 109.2 cm)
The Speed Art Museum, Louisville, Kentucky, purchase made possible by a grant from the Ford Foundation; and the Smithsonian National Museum of African American History and Culture, Washington, DC, purchase made possible by a gift from Kate Capshaw and Steven Spielberg/The Hearthland Foundation
p. 117

A Bucket Full of Treasures (Papa Gave Me Sunshine to Put in My Pocket), 2020
Oil on linen, 54 × 43 in. (137.2 × 109.2 cm)
Private collection
p. 120

Hope Is the Thing with Feathers (The Little Bird), 2020
Oil on linen, 54 × 43 in. (137.2 × 109.2 cm)
Collection of the artist, courtesy Hauser & Wirth
p. 121

Untitled, 2020
Gouache on paper, 11 × 7½ in. (27.9 × 19.1 cm)
Courtesy the artist and Hauser & Wirth
p. 112

Untitled, 2020
Gouache on paper, 11 × 7½ in. (27.9 × 19.1 cm)
Courtesy the artist and Hauser & Wirth
p. 113

Untitled, 2020
Gouache on paper, 11 × 7½ in. (27.9 × 19.1 cm)
Private collection
p. 113

Untitled, 2020
Gouache on paper, 15 × 22 in. (38 × 55.9 cm)
Private collection
p. 114

Untitled, 2020
Gouache on paper, 7½ × 11 in. (19.1 × 27.9 cm)
Courtesy the artist and Hauser & Wirth
p. 115

As American as Apple Pie, 2021
Oil on canvas, 123 × 101 in. (312.4 × 256.5 cm)
Long Museum, Shanghai
p. 123

A Midsummer Afternoon Dream, 2021
Oil on canvas, 106 × 101 in. (269.2 × 256.5 cm)
Private collection
pp. 118–19

As Soft as She Is . . ., 2022
Oil on linen, 54 × 43 in. (137.2 × 109.2 cm)
Tate, purchased with funds provided by the Tymure Collection
p. 127

A Certain Kind of Happiness, 2022
Oil on linen, 54 × 43 in. (137.2 × 109.2 cm)
Collection of the artist, courtesy Hauser & Wirth
p. 132

A Certain Kind of Happiness, 2022
Oil on linen, 54 × 43 in. (137.2 × 109.2 cm)
The Art Institute of Chicago, purchased with funds provided by the Dean Collection
p. 133

Deliverance, 2022
Oil on linen, two panels, overall: 108⅜ × 266½ in. (274.8 × 676.9 cm)
The Dean Collection, courtesy Swizz Beatz and Alicia Keys
pp. 128–29

For Love, and for Country, 2022
Oil on linen, 123¼ × 93⅛ in. (313 × 236.5 cm)
San Francisco Museum of Modern Art, purchase, by exchange, through a gift of Helen and Charles Schwab
p. 125

A God Blessed Land (Empire of Dirt), 2022
Oil on linen, 96⅛ × 130⅛ in. (244.3 × 331 cm)
Tymure Collection
pp. 130–31

Kingdom, 2022
Oil on linen, 117⅛ × 92 in. (297.5 × 233.7 cm)
The Broad Art Foundation
p. 135

To Tell Her Story You Must Walk in Her Shoes, 2022
Oil on linen, 54 × 43 in. (137.2 × 109.2 cm)
Private collection
p. 126

The Beauty of Change (A Beautiful Man), 2023
Oil on linen, 54 × 43 in. (137.2 × 109.2 cm)
Joslyn Art Museum, Omaha, Nebraska, gift of The Sherwood Foundation
p. 137

Acknowledgments

It has been a pleasure and an honor to delve deeply into the bold, brilliant, and moving paintings of Amy Sherald, whose approach to art and life has changed the face of American painting over the past two decades. I am immensely grateful to Christopher Bedford, SFMOMA's Helen and Charles Schwab Director, for suggesting that we undertake this project, one that grew naturally out of his long and unwavering support of Sherald's work.

I deeply appreciate the many museums that join SFMOMA as lenders to this exhibition, allowing their paintings to leave their own walls and travel for an extended period. I give my thanks to these institutions' current and former staff members who have assisted with loans: Asma Naeem, Jessica Bell Brown, and Jaimee Shim of the Baltimore Museum of Art; Joanne Heyler, Ed Schad, and Alexandra Moran of The Broad Art Foundation; Marianne Richter and Aimee Brooks of The Columbus Museum; Rod Bigelow and Miquel Geller of Crystal Bridges Museum of American Art; Jessica May, Erin Dziedzic, and Molly McVey of the Kemper Museum of Contemporary Art; Kevin Young, Michele Moresi Gates, and Drew Talley of the National Museum of African American History and Culture, Smithsonian Institution; Susan Fisher Sterling, Kathryn Wat, and Neda Amouzadeh of the National Museum of Women in the Arts; Kim Sajet, Rhea L. Combs, Marisa Olivas, and Dominique Lopes DelGiudice of the National Portrait Gallery, Smithsonian Institution; Raphaela Platow, Tyler Blackwell, Kim Spence, and Hannah McAulay of the Speed Art Museum; Karin Hindsbo and Shaz Hussain of the Tate; and Scott Rothkopf, Rujeko Hockley, and Jennie Goldstein of the Whitney Museum of American Art.

I am also grateful to the many private collectors who agreed to make their treasured paintings available for this project: Vladimir Alexanyan and family; the Blanchard Nesbitt Family; Sheryll Cashin and Marque Chambliss; Anderson Cooper; Nancy and Sean Cotton; Bill and Christy Gautreaux; Green Family Art Foundation and Adam Green Art Advisory; Mr. and Mrs. Bryant Gumbel; Rashid Johnson and Sheree Hovsepian; Monique Meloche and Evan Boris, Monique Meloche Gallery; Frances and Burton Reifler; Robert F. Smith; Tymure Collection; and the generous lenders who prefer to remain anonymous.

For critical assistance locating works of art and facilitating loans, I thank Robert Manley and Karen Garka-Prince of Phillips and Lauren Barach of the Seattle Art Museum. I also offer warm thanks for aid with loans to Jonathan Boos, Carla Caputo, Laura Dameme, Jean Marie Damico, Rob Davis, Rebecca Fine, Joëlle Griesmaier, Shaelyn Hanes, Maria Sullivan Hemphill, Marisa Kayyem, Nicole Moffatt, Sandra Newman, Megan Noh, Mary Kate O'Hare, Bailey Summers, and Nancy Whyte.

I am thrilled that following the presentation at SFMOMA, versions of this exhibition will travel to the Whitney Museum and the National Portrait Gallery, both of which have been outstanding institutional partners. I am grateful to Whitney director Scott Rothkopf for his early commitment to this project, and to Rujeko Hockley and David Lisbon for their exceptional dedication to realizing it in New York. The exhibition will then travel to Washington, DC, to the site of two major milestones of Sherald's career—being awarded the grand prize in the 2016 Outwin Boochever Portrait Competition, and the 2018 unveiling of her official portrait of Michelle Obama. For their enthusiastic partnership, I thank National Portrait Gallery director Kim Sajet, as well as Rhea L. Combs and Marlene Harrison.

An exhibition as ambitious as this requires the dedicated backing of museum leadership and the extended efforts of numerous team members. I give my heartfelt thanks to Janet Bishop, Thomas Weisel Family Chief Curator, for her decades of mentorship, friendship, and support of this and every project I have undertaken as a curator at SFMOMA. For their diligence in realizing this exhibition, I offer my sincere thanks to current and former colleagues across SFMOMA: Jillian Aubrey, David Funk, Angelo Harrison, and Angie Wilson, Exhibitions and Program Management, under the leadership of Dee Minnite; Bosco Hernández, Fernanda Carlovich, Michael Torchia, Meghan Berckes, and Amy Yu Gray, Design Studio; Naheed Simjee, Director's Office; Michelle Barger and Jennifer Hickey, Conservation; Maren Jones and Jennifer Hing, Registration; Clare Jacobson, Publications; Rico Solinas and his exceptional Installations team; Brandon Larson, Brian Weinstein, and the Fabrication team; David Senior, Abby Bridge, and Erin Parker, Library and Archives; Erica Gangsei and Kevin Carr, Interpretive Media; Tomoko Kanamitsu, Public Engagement; Gamynne Guillotte, Chief Education and Public Engagement Officer; Alison Bowman, Kellee Dawkins, Jacqueline Rais, Kerry Swenson, Daniel Johnson, Misty Youmans, and Suzy Varadi, Philanthropy, under the leadership of Samantha Leo; Layna White, Marla Misunas, Sriba Kwadjovie Quintana, and Don Ross, Collections; Sheila Shin, Clara Hatcher Baruth, Clare Bradley, Alexandra Nguy, and Cristina Chan, Marketing and Communications; Nicole Meshack, Brianna Jilson, Ric Weaver, and their Visitor Experience team; Julie Charles and her Teacher & Family Programs team; Anna Tang and Nahshon Clark, Finance; Courtney Costello, Garzo Garcia, Walter Logue, and Tim Tengonciang, Operations; and Tobey Martin, Museum Store. I especially thank current and former members of the Painting and Sculpture Department Auriel Garza, Jenny Dally, and Adrianne Ramsey for their research and organizational contributions.

This superb book was produced by SFMOMA's stellar Publications Department under the expert direction of managing editor Amanda Glesmann, with early assistance from Jessica Sevey. As this is the artist's first museum publication, it was critical to present her multifaceted body of work from a variety of perspectives. I am honored that the book includes compelling new essays by Elizabeth Alexander, Dario Calmese, Rhea L. Combs, and Deborah Willis. Miko McGinty is responsible for its elegant and inspired design, which beautifully aligns with the feeling and message of the paintings. Elizabeth Levy guided the complex project through its rapid development and production. Cecile Shellman provided invaluable guidance for select essays in this volume with regard to issues of race and identity. Deirdre O'Dwyer brought a keen editorial eye to the texts. Jennifer Boynton and Beth Turk were exceptionally attentive reviewers and proofreaders. Pauline Lopez provided essential assistance with sourcing and licensing illustrations. All of the images in the book greatly benefited from the expert color work of Tony Manzella and his team at Echelon Color, Los Angeles. I am delighted that this catalogue is co-published by Yale University Press and extend my thanks to Katherine Boller, Nicholas Geller, and their colleagues for their enthusiastic support and partnership.

One of the most gratifying aspects of working on this exhibition has been getting to know the extraordinary community around Sherald, from her fellow artists to friends and longtime followers and collectors. I am especially indebted to Dr. Leslie King Hammond for the meaningful conversations we had as I was thinking through my approach to writing about Sherald's impact on painting and her navigation of her position as a Black artist in the field of American art. I extend my deep appreciation to friends, teachers, and advocates of Sherald's who took the time to share invaluable insights: Jordan Casteel, Alonzo Davis, Arturo Lindsay, Dominique Naja, Cara Ober, Valeska Populoh, Amy Raehse, Calida Rawles, Lowery Stokes Sims, and Darren Walker. Their warmth, conversations, unparalleled perceptions, and personal memories have informed the exhibition and publication in myriad ways. At Hauser & Wirth, I would like to recognize Marc Payot, Madeline Warren, and Johanna Rietveld for their dedicated support of the artist and exceptional response to the many demands of this project. This exhibition and book could not have been realized without Nancy Hollinghurst's steadfast work with Amy in her studio, or without Rina Kim's supreme efficiency and good spirit in fielding institutional requests too numerous to count.

My deep appreciation goes to all my friends and family for the many ways they bolstered me throughout this project, especially Corey Keller, Diana Markley, and Elizabeth Friedman. Special thanks are due to Merry Roberts for providing research assistance at a critical juncture. As always, Keith, Merry, Ellie, and Jackson Roberts are the center of everything and have kept me afloat through planning, research, writing, and installation.

From our first fleeting conversation in 2018 to the realization of the exhibition in 2024, I have found working with Amy Sherald to be a great pleasure and a singular experience. For graciously answering my endless questions, spending so much precious studio time talking with me about paintings in every phase of execution, and trusting me to tell the story of her extraordinary work through this exhibition and book, I extend to her my profound respect and deepest thanks.

—Sarah Roberts

Getting to this moment has been no small feat. I have many people to acknowledge for their contributions large and small—all of them, in summation, equally important.

I thank my family and parents, especially my mother, who pushed me to be anything but an artist. She was the perfect mother for me; resistance can be one's greatest motivator. To my chosen family, thank you for your commitment and loyalty. Your feedback and encouragement have been instrumental, and you are deeply a part of my work and all that I do. You have kept me inspired, on course, and sustained in ways I never knew I needed as this plot called life has unfolded.

My deepest gratitude goes to my organ donor, Kristin Smith. Without our paths crossing, none of this would have been possible.

To all those I met along the way who played critical roles in my journey of becoming, thank you. I am grateful to Geri Davis, who was my first art teacher, and to Dr. Arturo Lindsay, who took me under his wing when I was a young painting student at Spelman College. Jeffrey Kent's gift of free studio space in Baltimore gave me a place to work after I finished graduate school at the Maryland Institute College of Art. Dr. Adlai Pappy generously offered me shelter at a pivotal moment, enabling me to quit my waitressing job and focus on painting.

Chasing deadline after deadline for this project often took me away from my dogs August, George, and Weezie. To everyone who helped look after them, thank you. I could not have done this without you.

I extend special thanks to Dr. Leslie King Hammond, Darrell Walker, Mark Bradford, Rashid Johnson, Dawoud Bey, Thelma Golden, Darren Walker, Dorothy Moss, Kate Capshaw, Steven Spielberg, Michelle Obama, Calida Rawles, Deborah Roberts, Jordan Casteel, Shadra Strickland, Dana Reifler, Maori Karmael Holmes, Shauna Bain-Smith, Valeska Populoh, and Kojo Griffin for their support, counsel, and friendship.

To anyone whose name I may have forgotten, because you know I'm forgetful, this line is for you.

To my studio team, past and present, and my Hauser & Wirth family, thank you for all of your hard work, dedication, and passion.

To everyone who played a part in making this exhibition and book possible—including the powers of this magical universe we live in—thank you. It has been a dream to see this project come to life.

—Amy Sherald ♥

IMAGE CREDITS

All artworks by Amy Sherald © Amy Sherald, courtesy the artist and Hauser & Wirth. Photography credits are provided below. Copyright for the other artworks reproduced in this book is held by the artists and/or their representatives as noted here.

Listings are identified by page number.

Cover, 2, 4, 7, 9: Joseph Hyde. 10: bpk Bildagentur / Art Resource, New York. 13: artwork © Lorna Simpson, courtesy the artist and Hauser & Wirth. 15: image courtesy Bo Bartlett, Miles McEnery Gallery, New York, and The Bo Bartlett Center, Columbus, GA. 16: image courtesy Nerdrum Museum, Norway. 19: © 2003 Columbia Pictures Industries, Inc. All Rights Reserved. Courtesy Columbia Pictures. 20: artwork © 2024 C. Herscovici / Artists Rights Society (ARS), New York; image courtesy Banque d'Images, ADAGP / Art Resource, New York. 24: artwork © The Estate of Alice Neel, courtesy The Estate of Alice Neel and David Zwirner. 28: image courtesy Amy Sherald. 30 (top): image courtesy Amy Sherald. 30 (bottom): image courtesy Condé Nast. 32: Kelvin Bulluck. 40 (left and right): Collection of the Smithsonian National Museum of African American History and Culture, © Smithsonian National Museum of African American History and Culture, Washington, DC.

PLATES
51, 53: Kelvin Bulluck for SFMOMA. 52: Ryan Stevenson. 55: image courtesy Michael Bowles, Art in Embassies Permanent Collection, US Embassy Dakar, Senegal. 56: Kevin Allen for SFMOMA. 57: Glen Cheriton for SFMOMA. 58: Christina Hussey @christinahussey. 59: Ryan Stevenson. 60, 63: image courtesy Lowy Fine Art Services, New York, Digital Photography Department. 61: Oriol Tarridas for SFMOMA. 65: image courtesy Smithsonian National Museum of African American History and Culture, Washington, DC. 67, 138–40, 142–43, 144: Kelvin Bulluck. 69: Jon Etter. 70–71, 73–79, 81, 83–87, 89–93, 95, 97, 99, 101–3, 105–11, 117–21, 123, 125–33, 135: Joseph Hyde. 112–15, 137: Thomas Barratt.

Published on the occasion of *Amy Sherald: American Sublime*, an exhibition organized by the San Francisco Museum of Modern Art.

Lead support for *Amy Sherald: American Sublime* is provided by the Mimi and Peter Haas Fund and Diana Nelson and John Atwater.

Major support is provided by Sir Deryck and Lady Va Maughan, Katie and Matt Paige, and Shelagh Rohlen in memory of Tom Rohlen.

Significant support is provided by Maria Manetti Shrem and Jan Shrem, Jessica Moment, Deborah and Kenneth Novack, and Sonja Hoel Perkins and Jonathan Perkins.

Meaningful support is provided by Alka and Ravin Agrawal, Dolly and George Chammas, Jessica and Matt Farron, Maryellen and Frank Herringer, Alison Pincus, Komal Shah and Gaurav Garg, Gary Steele and Steven Rice, and Barbara and Stephan Vermut.

San Francisco Museum of Modern Art
151 Third Street
San Francisco, CA 94103
sfmoma.org

Published in association with

Yale University Press
302 Temple Street
PO Box 209040
New Haven, CT 06520-9040
yalebooks.com

Library of Congress Control Number:
2024940501

ISBN: 978-0-300-27938-2

10 9 8 7 6 5 4 3

Authorized Representative in the EU: Easy Access System Europe, Mustamäe tee 50, 10621 Tallinn, Estonia, gpsr.requests@easproject.com

This book was produced by the Publications Department at the San Francisco Museum of Modern Art (Kari Dahlgren, director of publications; Amanda Glesmann, managing editor; Clare Jacobson, editor; Jessica Sevey, assistant editor).

Project Editor: Amanda Glesmann
Designer: Miko McGinty, Miko McGinty Inc.
Editors: Deirdre O'Dwyer with Jennifer Boynton
Editorial project management: Elizabeth Levy
Typesetter: Tina Henderson, Miko McGinty Inc.
Proofreader: Beth Turk
Image permissions: Pauline Lopez, Lopez Media Clearances

Color separations by Echelon, Los Angeles
Printed in Italy by Verona Libri
Set in Empirica
Printed on GardaMatt Ultra 150gsm

Cover: *A God Blessed Land (Empire of Dirt)* (detail, pp. 130–31).
2: *Saint Woman* (detail, p. 73). 4: *If You Surrendered to the Air, You Could Ride It* (detail, p. 105). 7: *She had an inside and an outside now, and suddenly she knew how not to mix them* (detail, p. 99). 9: *What's precious inside of him does not care to be known by the mind in ways that diminish its presence (All American)* (detail, p. 89). 32: Bookcase at Amy Sherald's studio, 2024. 142–43, 144: Views of Amy Sherald's studio, 2024.